Healthy
JEWISH
COOKING

Healthy JEWISH COOKING

Steven Raichlen

PHOTOGRAPHY BY GREG SCHNEIDER
STYLING BY JAKE KLEIN

VIKING

VIKING
Published by the Penguin Group
Penguin Putnam Inc., 375 Hudson Street,
New York, New York 10014, U.S.A.
Penguin Books Ltd, 27 Wrights Lane, London W8 5TZ, England
Penguin Books Australia Ltd, Ringwood, Victoria, Australia
Penguin Books Canada Ltd, 10 Alcorn Avenue,
Toronto, Ontario, Canada M4V 3B2
Penguin Books (N. Z.) Ltd, 182–190 Wairau Road,
Auckland 10, New Zealand

Penguin Books Ltd, Registered Offices:
Harmondsworth, Middlesex, England

LIBRARY OF CONGRESS CATALOGING-IN-PUBLICATION DATA

Raichlen, Steven.
Healthy Jewish cooking / Steven Raichlen ; photography by Greg Schneider ; styling by Jake Klein.
p.   cm.
ISBN 0-670-89312-9
1. Cookery, Jewish.   2. Low-fat diet—Recipes.   I. Title.
TX724.R34   2000
641.5′676—dc21   00-038149

This book is printed on acid-free paper.

∞

Printed in China
Set in Goudy

The older I get, the more I come to appreciate the monumental importance of family. I've been shaped by family more than I can ever say—by my parents, grandparents, great-grandparents, aunts, uncles, and cousins—many of whom have passed on, but who live on in my heart and memory. Their love nourished me as much as their cooking. I truly believe that what good lies within me comes from them.

This book is dedicated in loving memory to:

Bertha "Bubbe Birdy" Fribush
Jenny "Bubbe" Marks
Grammie Ethel Raichlen
Grandfather Samuel "Dear" Raichlen
Grandpa Jack Goldman
Great-aunt Lily Modiano
Uncle Sylvan Farber
Uncle Morty Rabineau
Uncle Henry Aronson
Aunt Vivian "Vi" Rabineau
Aunt Rena Aronson
Uncle Irving Goldstein
Aunt Minne Jacobs
Uncle Sammy Marks
Uncle Will Marks
Uncle Frank Marks
Mamie and Harry Millison
Carl Millison
Father-in-law, Phil Seldin
My mother, the ballet dancer, Frances Raichlen

ACKNOWLEDGMENTS

The most enjoyable part of writing any book is thanking the people who helped make it possible. This one involved a legion of culinary experts and support staff. The author would like to offer special thanks to:

For photography and prop styling:

Greg Schneider for his spectacular photographs
Jake Klein for photo styling and recipe testing
Maria Jose "Chichi" Mari for photographic assistance
Cherna Shovers from The Carefully Chosen Gallery on Miami Beach for props
Barton Weiss of Barton G. Design Ltd. for fabrics and surfaces
Eugenia Schneider (Greg's mom) for props
Lidia Guterman (Greg's aunt) for props
David Ramchal and Bobby Ramnath at LIB Color Labs
Jeff Piccoli from the Eastman Kodak Co.
Monica, Samson, Bradley, and Kayley Schneider for photographic inspiration

For their Jewish culinary expertise:

Sonya and Robin Azoulay
Janice and Michael Freeman
Esther Korman
Hannah Kuperstock
Edda Servi Machlin
Rabbi Gil Marks

Connie Nahmad
Irene Roth
Franya Rubinek
Leeor Sabbah
Esther Salzburg
Marion Schenker
Regina Spiegel

For editorial support at Viking:

Sarah Baker, editor
Lucia Watson, editorial assistant
Dawn Drzal, editor emeritus
Jaye Zimet, design director
Beth Greenfeld, copy editor
Clare Ferraro, publisher

For keeping the home fires burning:

Barbara Raichlen, super wife
Miriam Seldin, super mother-in-law
Jake Klein, Mark and Betsy Billings, super kids
Donna Morton de Souza, nutritionist
Elida Proenza, recipe tester
Heather Short, editorial assistant

Special family members:

Annette Farber, Linda Millison, Rosa and Sheldon Miller, the late Lily Modiano.
And my dear friend Shirley Drevich

CONTENTS

INTRODUCTION

❧❧❖❧❧

Indulge me in a few memories.

It's Friday night. I'm eight years old. We're dining at the home of my grandparents. Just as I'll do virtually every Sabbath for the first seventeen years of my life. Grammie and "Dear" aren't particularly religious—there are no long prayers, no synagogue after dinner, although my grandmother makes a point of lighting the Sabbath candles in brass candlesticks she received for her wedding. Like many reformed Jews of the 1950s, we lived our Judaism through our food.

There was chopped liver of ethereal lightness that my grandmother made in an old hand-cranked meat grinder. There was chicken soup the color of pale gold, lavished with crunchy mandelech (soup "nuts") and meaty marrow bones. When my great-grandmother Grandma Fribush was still alive, we'd have freshly baked pirogi, oniony meat turnovers that shattered into a million tasty shards when you took a bite. Dinner was brisket or prime rib served with a casserole made from frozen green beans and cream of mushroom soup. And dessert, well, all week long we looked forward to Grammie Ethel's cookies and my great-grandmother's yeasty, flaky, sugary, cocoa-stuffed chocolate roll.

Another memory. I'm thirteen years old. It's the first night of Passover and we're headed to the home of my Aunt Rena. I'm too nervous to think about food: as the youngest male (and the only grandson on both sides of my family), I will have to ask the four questions. There'll be thirty people crammed at the

L-shaped table that stretches from the dining room into the living room. I go over the words again—"Ma nishtanah halailah hazeh . . ." Whether I'm more afraid that I'll forget my Hebrew or that my voice will crack, I can't say.

While I worry, my great-aunts, Annette Farber and Rena Aronson, have been toiling all day in a kitchen that most modern cooks would find hopelessly spartan. Huge pots simmer away on the stove: one brimming with fragrant broth enriched with capons and flanken (beef ribs), another filled with knaidlach (matzo balls) the size of baseballs, and golden tsimmis (that Eastern European stew of carrots, sweet potatoes, and prunes). An army of lettuce-lined plates waits on an old Formica table, ready to receive shimmering ovals of gefilte fish and dollops of fiery red horseradish. There are capons, briskets, and kugels, jockeyed from oven to table and back to keep them warm for serving. Come dessert, fruit compotes glisten in cut-crystal serving bowls and my Aunt Annette swats greedy fingers away from platters of handmade strudel. My aunts never seem to break a sweat preparing this Rabelaisian feast.

A final memory, this one at the home of my Aunt Rosa and Uncle Sheldon Miller in Silver Spring, Maryland. My prayer performance anxiety gives way to a different sort of nervousness as we arrive at the Millers. Rosa is the Sephardic Jew in the family. As a youngster, I was a finicky eater (that's putting it mildly) and Rosa is forever serving weird foods: filo dough and feta cheese, chickpeas and strange vegetables. Her food is always alarmingly assertively flavored. What's worse, unless I clean my plate, I know I won't get any of the one Aunt Rosa specialty I eat without hesitation: homemade baklava.

I didn't realize at the time that there was anything special about my childhood diet. That the homey Jewish cooking I grew up on would lay the groundwork for my career as a food writer. That my very sense of Jewishness would be bound up in the foods I ate as a child.

Looking back on it, I grew up at an extraordinary time in the history of American Jewry. Both of my great-grandmothers—Grandma Fribush and Bubbe Marks—were born in Eastern Europe, the former in Latvia, the latter in Lithuania. I was lucky enough to have both great-grandmothers until I was in my twenties. All four of my grandparents were first-generation Americans and at least one, my grandfather "Dear," loved to regale us with tales of what it was like to grow up in an immigrant household in the early years of this century.

When my great-grandmothers still cooked (and they did well into their eighties), they would take the streetcar to Lexington Market in downtown Baltimore (I grew up in the Baltimore suburb of Pikesville), buy capons or turkeys with the feathers still on, and pluck them at home, just as they did in the Old Country. No one knew from convenience foods—everything was made from scratch.

Our holiday dinners were multigenerational affairs, involving twenty, thirty, forty people. How we all squeezed into what today would be considered highly modest homes baffles me still. Yes, they were crowded and noisy. Yes, you got your cheeks pinched and slobbered on by relatives you barely knew. But in today's fragmented society, where family members seldom live in the same city, I look back on these huge, extended-family dinners as something indescribably precious. It makes me sad that their age has passed.

The food was remarkable, too. Remarkable for its plate-burying bounty, its soulful flavors, its connection with the past. I grew up in a family that made its own gefilte fish and horseradish, its own matzo balls and strudels. Much of our food was enjoyed by Ashkenazi Jews across America, but we Raichlens also had specialties that were unique to our family. Sauerkraut soup, for example, was a Raichlen family favorite for Thanksgiving. (You'll read why on page 32.) Another delicacy were zibulnikas, the green onion and cottage cheese buns my grandfather remembered eating when he came home from elementary school.

Not everyone in my family was a great cook, not by a long shot. My mother hated cooking and did so as seldom as possible. (I'm probably the nation's only food writer who grew up on TV dinners!) My Grammie Ethel made the world's best cookies, but you needed a chain saw to cut her pot roast. My Grammie Sarah had a profound distrust of meat that was served anything less than overcooked to shoe-leather toughness, but she made salmon croquettes that I still long for to this day. My Aunt Vi was too busy as a Washington, D.C., fund-raiser to be much of a cook, but her cabbage borscht was legendary.

The master cook in our family was my great-aunt Annette Farber. At the age of ninety-two, Aunt Annette is the last survivor of my first-generation American relatives and she's certainly earned the right not to cook now. I was lucky enough to spend a few days in the kitchen with her fifteen years ago, when she still did cook and she taught me how to make many family favorites. In the following pages, you'll experience her extraordinary matzo balls, gefilte fish, horseradish sauce, gedemfted chicken, compote, and strudel. The great cook on my mother's side of the family was my great-great aunt, Lily Modiano, a Sephardic Jew from Salonika, Greece. Lily had a master's touch with the foods of the Mediterranean. It wouldn't be stretching the truth much to say that she was to Greek Sephardic cooking what Alain Ducasse is to French.

Some books are written out of intellectual curiosity. This one was written for love. Love for the family members—grandparents, great-grandparents, aunts and uncles; many of whom unfortunately have passed away—who fed me with generosity, nurtured me with affection, and taught me the importance of family.

Love for a religious heritage that stretches back for more than five thousand years.

Times have changed, not only in what we eat, but also how we eat it. The great cooks of my childhood—who came of age during the Depression—were more interested in filling plates than in the health consequences of their dinners. No one knew from cholesterol, calorie counting, fat grams, saturated fats, or antioxidants. Food was made to be enjoyed, not taken as medicine. The fact that most of my relatives lived into their nineties makes me wonder if they didn't have more wisdom in their ignorance than we do in our obsession with nutrition!

Few of us today can imagine sitting down to the egg- and chicken-fat-laden Jewish dishes of yesteryear. Even if we could survive the onslaught of saturated fats and cholesterol, we would find many of these dishes too heavy for our liking.

Which brings us, in a roundabout way, to the subject of this book, *Healthy Jewish Cooking*. No, it's not an oxymoron! (The typical response when I would mention I was writing this book.) This reaction was fine by me, because I love a challenge. In the past year, I've discovered that Jewish cooking can be stripped of much of its fat and still remain delicious. In fact, I've come to prefer many of my low-fat versions to the dishes I grew up on.

As in my other health-oriented cookbooks, I've launched a three-pronged attack on the fat in traditional Jewish cooking.

First, I've tried to focus on dishes that are naturally low in fat. This isn't quite as difficult as it may seem, as many of the dishes of the Sephardic world—especially of Israel and the Near East—are based on beans, grains, vegetables, salads, and olive oil and are intrinsically low in fat. Even in the Ashkenazi tradition, you can find lean braised meats, low-fat soups, and luscious fruit desserts, like compote. The trick is ferreting them out amid the butter- and schmaltz-laden fare most of us grew up on.

The second approach has been to lighten up traditional Jewish recipes, using the techniques I've evolved over a decade of high-flavor, low-fat cooking. Using egg substitute or egg whites in place of whole eggs in kugels, for example. Or chicken broth in place of schmaltz in dips, spreads, and casseroles. By increasing the proportion of vegetables to meats, I've been able to keep the traditional flavor profile of many dishes, while greatly reducing the fat. A technique called bake-frying has enabled me to re-create kreplach, knishes, and borekas that adhere to the health principles of modern eating. Below you'll find a list of these tips in the "Ten Commandments of Healthy Jewish Cooking."

The third approach has been to create dishes that are Jewish in feel, but that your grandmother probably never heard of. Consider my "amazing low-fat chopped liver," for example, a pâté made from roasted mushrooms, with just a little chicken liver for flavor.

Here, then, are more than 175 recipes for great-looking, great-tasting, entirely hamish Jewish food that will satisfy your soul without clogging your arteries.

TEN COMMANDMENTS OF HEALTHY JEWISH COOKING

❧❀❧

Since this is a book on healthy Jewish cooking, it seems only appropriate to include a set of Ten Commandments. Follow these simple tips and your food will taste great and authentic and be good for you to boot.

1. THINK FLAVOR, NOT FAT

In the days of my grandparents, Jewish cooks achieved flavor through a generous use of animal fats: schmaltz, butter, margarine, cream, and egg yolks. The healthy Jewish cook uses fresh herbs, whole spices, roasted vegetables, and intensely flavored condiments, like vinegar, citrus juice, and tamarind, to add excitement to food without fat.

2. WHEN YOU DO USE FATS, CHOOSE FLAVORFUL FATS AND USE THEM STRATEGICALLY

You'll note that my cooking is low-fat, not no-fat. I believe that a little bit of fat adds a richness you simply can't achieve without fat. Virtue alone won't keep people on a healthy diet; you have to satisfy taste. When I do use fat, I try to choose a fat that has a flavor dividend, like extra-virgin olive oil or schmaltz. (For the surprisingly healthy nutritional breakdown of chicken fat, see page 192.) I lightly spray pastries with oil prior to "bake-frying" to give them a crisp crust. I even use a little butter from time to time to add richness to a cookie dough or bread. Whatever fat I use, I try to place it strategically (usually on the surface of the food), so it's the first thing you taste. This surface application of fat tricks your tastebuds into thinking there's fat found throughout the dish.

3. ROAST YOUR WAY TO AROMA

One of my favorite high-flavor, low-fat cooking techniques is roasting foods in a hot oven. Roasting and broiling intensify the sweetness of many vegetables (see pickled peppers on page 142), while bringing out an earthy richness in others. (Roasted mushrooms are the secret ingredient in the amazing low-fat chopped liver—page 15.) Likewise, by roasting nuts and bread crumbs, you bolster their flavor, so that less goes a longer way.

4. SAUTÉ IN A NONSTICK FRYING PAN

The nonstick frying pan (and its analogue, the nonstick baking sheet) have revolutionized the art of low-fat cooking. Sautéing gives foods a crisp crust and moist, tender interior. The nonstick surface allows you to sauté with a fraction of the fat you'd have used in the old days.

5. FRY IN YOUR OVEN

Deep-frying is popular among both Ashkenazi and Sephardic Jews—think of the popularity of kreplach, latkes, and borekas. Finger foods can be cooked in a hot oven using a technique I call bake-frying. To bake-fry, you lightly spray a pastry with oil and bake it on a nonstick baking sheet in a hot oven. When I make latkes or falafel, I preheat a generously oiled baking sheet in the oven, then bake-fry on it. The result? Crackling crisp "fritters" with a fraction of the traditional fat.

6. FIRE UP YOUR GRILL

Israelis don't need to be told twice to fire up the grill. Neither do Jews from North Africa, the Middle and Near East, and, of course, North America. Grilling is the ultimate high-flavor, low-fat cooking method, caramelizing the proteins in fish and meat and the sugars in vegetables, imparting a signature smoke flavor that adds a whole new dimension to many traditional Jewish dishes. Many Sephardic fish dishes that are traditionally deep-fried taste even better—and are a whole lot better for you—grilled. (See the grilled salmon with charmoula on page 75.) Until you've had baba ganoosh made with grilled eggplant (page 19), you haven't fully lived!

7. REPLACE WHOLE EGGS WITH EGG WHITES AND EGG SUBSTITUTES

As in many religions, the egg has deep symbolic significance in Judaism. Eggs are used to leaven cakes, set kugels, and hold matzo balls together, and are enjoyed in innumerable variations in omelettes, frittatas, and scrambles in both the Ashkenazi and Sephardic tradition. Egg yolks are loaded with fat and cholesterol, of course, but in most dishes the whites will do the leavening or setting equally well. Egg whites are the main ingredient in so-called "egg substitutes"—a horrid name for a natural product that's a great help to the low-fat cook. We often use egg substitute in our cooking at home: it saves having to figure out what to do with all the leftover egg yolks. You can certainly substitute 2 egg whites (or, for that matter, 1 whole egg) for ¼ cup of egg substitute.

Note: While whole eggs, whites, and egg substitutes generally are interchangeable in this book, some dishes just taste better made with a few whole eggs. In those recipes, the whole eggs (plus whites) are called for first, with the egg substitute as an alternative. Other recipes will taste the same no matter what sort of egg you use. In these recipes the egg substitute is called for first (with whole eggs and whites as an alternative). Often, I'll add one or two whole eggs to the egg substitute to provide a little extra richness. You should, too, if your fat budget allows it.

8. USE LOW-FAT DAIRY PRODUCTS

The advent of low- and no-fat dairy products in the early 1990s has revolutionized Jewish low-fat cooking. Some of these products are terrific—others, awful. In general, low-fat and no-fat sour creams and cottage cheeses are excellent. Reduced-fat cream cheese is a great help, but other low- and no-fat cheeses tend to be rubbery and awful. The new Fat Free Half & Half by Land O' Lakes is a fine product, but cook it briefly or it will separate into a gummy mess. Most of the recipes in this book that call for dairy products will give you the option of low fat or no fat. Obviously, low fat gives you a better flavor than no fat, so use it if your fat budget allows. But fine results can be obtained with the no-fat dairy alternative.

9. BENEFIT FROM BROTH

Broths and stocks are the soul of Jewish cooking and Jews make the very best. But soup is only a starting point: broth can be added in place of oil in salad dressings and sauces, in place of butter or cream in mashed potatoes and casseroles, and in place of schmaltz in many vegetable dishes and dips. Take the time to make the broths on pages 189, 190, and 191. They'll make your whole house smell nice. Moreover, they're ecologically sound. You can save vegetable trimmings and meat scraps in a bag in the freezer and make a batch of broth when you have enough. Store your broths in 1- and 2-cup containers in the freezer, so you always have a premeasured batch on hand.

10. EAT YOUR VEGETABLES AND EAT LESS MEAT

You don't need to be an expert on the food pyramid or the Mediterranean diet to know that the key to a healthy diet is to eat lots of grains, beans, fruits, and vegetables, and more modest amounts of meats. For healthier eating, increase the proportion of plant foods to animal foods in a dish. Use meat as a flavoring or condiment, not as the main attraction on the plate.

Above all, have fun. Jewish cooking is about family, love, and abundance. Cook with all three and your life will be rich beyond measure.

A NOTE ABOUT SPECIAL INGREDIENTS

The Jewish larder—particularly the Ashkenazi larder—is very basic. Most of the ingredients called for in this book are readily available at your local supermarket. Here are descriptions of some of the more esoteric items.

BULGHUR: Cracked wheat. Bulghur is a staple of Israeli/Middle East cooking and is the main ingredient in such dishes as tabouleh and kibbe. Available at Middle Eastern markets and most supermarkets, it comes in varying sizes.

COUSCOUS: Enjoyed by the Jews of North Africa, couscous is sometimes described as a grain. Actually, it's a type of pasta. (The dough is pushed through a sieve to create tiny, grainlike pellets.) Most Americans use the instant couscous sold in supermarkets: just add boiling water or broth, soak for a few minutes, and voilà, you have couscous. For a real treat, buy couscous at a Middle Eastern market and steam it from scratch, following the instructions on the package. Israeli couscous is much larger than conventional couscous (the balls will remind you a little of tapioca). See page 131 for cooking instructions.

FARFEL/MATZO FARFEL: Tiny bits of toasted egg noodle. Used in soups and side dishes.

OLIVE OIL: The butter and schmaltz of the Sephardic Jews. I always cook with extra-virgin olive oil (the grade with the richest flavor and lowest acidity). For sautéing, I use a good, moderately priced extra-virgin olive oil, like Colavita. If I'm drizzling a dish with olive oil for flavor, I use the best oil money can buy. Olive oil has great health benefits, boosting levels of HDL (high-density lipoproteins—the "good" cholesterol), while reducing levels of LDL (low-density lipoproteins—the "bad" cholesterol).

PAPRIKA: Generally associated with Hungarian-Jewish cooking, but in fact paprika is used worldwide in both Ashkenazi and Sephardic kitchens. Paprika comes both sweet (mild) and hot. The latter is more "warm" than hot—especially for a nation as enamored with hot chilies as we are. Hungarians make the best paprika, so try to use an imported brand. Two good brands are Szegd and Budapest's Best.

PARSLEY: A popular herb in both Sephardic and Ashkenazi kitchens. The traditional parsley is flat-leaf, sometimes called Italian parsley in this country. It has a more complex flavor than regular parsley.

PEPPER: Black pepper. I'm so used to writing "freshly ground black pepper" in my recipes that it took me a moment to realize that the great cooks in my family—my grandmother, my aunts Rosa and Annette—knew nothing from freshly ground pepper. So I suppose, to be authentic, you would use canned pre-ground black pepper. But I like the electrifying zing of freshly ground, so I call for it throughout the book.

SALT: Not surprisingly, kosher salt is my seasoning of choice for these recipes. Kosher salt (like all things kosher) is exceptionally pure. The coarse crystals dissolve slowly, giving you pleasing little salty bursts of flavor in salads and casseroles. Besides, the coarse grains feel great between your fingers when you take a pinch.

SUMAC: A tart, purplish berry grown in the Middle and Near East. Sumac powder is sprinkled on salads and grilled meats and seafood, the way fresh lemon might be squeezed over these foods in the West. Sold at Middle and Near Eastern markets.

WONTON and CHINESE RAVIOLI WRAPPERS: These are, perhaps, the most unexpected ingredients in this book, but I find them invaluable for making kreplach, pastechi, empanadas, and other Jewish hors d'oeuvres. Besides, the Jewish affinity for Chinese food in North America is well documented. Who else fills the Chinese restaurants on Christmas Day?! The California-based exotic food purveyor Frieda's distributes kosher wonton and ravioli wrappers, which are widely available. For a source near you, call 800-421-9477 or go to www.friedas.com.

A QUICK GUIDE TO THE KASHRUT

Encyclopedic commentaries, indeed, whole books have been written on the kashrut (the laws governing keeping kosher). It's beyond the scope of this book to offer more than a few broad observations.

When I was growing up, I was taught that the goal of the kashrut was purity and compassion. You didn't eat "unclean" animals, such as pigs and scavenger shellfish. You killed animals as quickly and as painlessly as possible for eating, not sport. And you didn't combine meat and dairy products in the same meal for fear you should commit the moral outrage of boiling a lamb or calf in its own mother's milk.

Another purpose of the kashrut may have been to strengthen Jewish communities by keeping Jews away from non-Jews. When you eat different foods than your neighbors do, you're less likely to intermarry. Perhaps this is one of the reasons, Jews have kept their cultural and religious identity intact for five thousand years, despite being scattered all over the world.

Our Reconstructionist rabbi, Rami Shapiro (of Temple Beth Or in Miami), adds a third goal of the kashrut. He maintains that compassion extends to social justice. Rami believes that using fertilizers that harm the environment, nonbiodegradable packaging, foods harvested by exploited or oppressed laborers,

also violates the kashrut. It's an interesting notion and a compelling example of how Judaism continually updates its traditions to the concerns of contemporary life.

Quickly, then, here are the major regulations of the kashrut:

Eat meats only from "clean" animals (like cows, sheep, chickens, etc.). "Clean" animals chew their cud and have split or cloven hooves: they include beef, veal, lamb, and goat, but not pork. Poultry is kosher. Koshered meat has been slaughtered according to certain rules and has been treated (often by salting) to remove as much blood as possible. Kosher meat can be found at a Jewish butcher or supermarket in a Jewish neighborhood.

Eat only fish that has scales and fins. Avoid all shellfish.

Don't mix meats and dairy products. Meat-based meals are called "fleischig"; dairy-based meals "milchig." Jews who keep kosher have separate sets of plates for each. Beware of hidden meat products, like gelatin (which is made from animal bones). Gelatin-based desserts cannot be served at a fleischig meal.

Don't eat bread or any products made with flour or leavening during Passover.

Healthy
JEWISH
COOKING

Appetizers

✣ Spiced Chickpeas ✣

Spiced, toasted chickpeas are a popular snack in our home—a good source of protein for the non-meat-eaters of the family and a great munchie to have with cocktails. Yemenite Jews call them jhalla *and serve them with glasses of* arak *(anise-flavored liquor) at parties. Traditionally, the chickpeas would be roasted in a dry skillet over an open fire outdoors. We opt for the convenience of roasting the peas on a baking sheet in the oven.* **Note:** *The oil is optional. Using it will give you slightly crunchier chickpeas, but perfectly tasty results can be obtained without it.*

PREPARATION TIME: 5 MINUTES   COOKING TIME: 25 TO 35 MINUTES

1 (15-ounce) can chickpeas, drained, rinsed well with cold water, drained again, and blotted dry
1 tablespoon olive oil (optional)
½ teaspoon ground cumin
½ teaspoon ground turmeric

½ teaspoon hot or sweet paprika
¼ to ½ teaspoon ground black pepper
Salt to taste (canned chickpeas are quite salty to begin with, so go easy on the salt)

1. Preheat the oven to 400 degrees.
2. In a bowl, toss the chickpeas with the oil (if using) and spices. Spread them on a nonstick baking sheet and bake until golden brown and crisp, 25 to 34 minutes.

Serves 4 (1¼ cups)

109 CALORIES PER SERVING; 5 G PROTEIN; 1 G FAT; .0 G SATURATED FAT; 15 G CARBOHYDRATE; 300 MG SODIUM; 0 MG CHOLESTEROL

Quick bake-fried kreplach.

⚸ Bake-Fried Falafel ⚸
(Chickpea "Fritters")

These crusty chickpea fritters—redolent with garlic and cumin—are Israel's national fast food, served at countless shops and street stalls from Acre to Elat. The simple fritter becomes a whole meal when piled in a pita bread with pickled vegetables, diced tomatoes, shredded lettuce or cabbage, and tahini sauce. Normally, the deep-frying would preclude inclusion in a low-fat cookbook, so I decided to try bake-frying the fritters in the oven. For extra tenderness, I used canned, not the traditional raw and soaked, chickpeas. I think you'll be pleasantly surprised by the results.

PREPARATION TIME: 20 MINUTES (PLUS 2 HOURS FOR SOAKING THE BULGHUR)   COOKING TIME: 15 MINUTES

¼ cup fine bulghur
1 (15-ounce) can chickpeas, drained, rinsed, and drained
¼ medium onion, cut into 1-inch pieces
3 cloves garlic, cut in half
¼ cup egg substitute or 2 egg whites
2 tablespoons chopped parsley (preferably flat-leaf)
2 tablespoons chopped cilantro
½ teaspoon salt, or to taste

1½ teaspoons ground coriander
1 teaspoon ground cumin
½ teaspoon black pepper
¼ to ½ teaspoon cayenne pepper (optional)
½ teaspoon baking powder
2 tablespoons matzo meal or bread crumbs, or as needed
Spray olive oil

1. Place the bulghur in a bowl with 1 cup cold water. Soak for 2 hours.

2. Drain the bulghur in a strainer, then squeeze it between your fingers to wring out the water.

3. Place the chickpeas in a food processor with the bulghur, onion, and garlic and grind until smooth. Work in the egg substitute, parsley, cilantro, salt, spices, and baking powder and puree until smooth. Add enough matzo meal to obtain a thick puree. Correct the seasoning, adding salt or cayenne to taste.

4. Meanwhile, generously spray a nonstick baking sheet with oil. Place it in the oven on the lowest rack and preheat the oven to 450 degrees.

5. Using 2 spoons, transfer mounds of falafel mixture to the hot baking sheet to form 2-inch ovals, smoothing the tops with the back of a wet fork. Generously spray the tops of the falafels with oil.

6. Bake the falafels until crusty and golden brown, 6 to 8 minutes per side, turning with a spatula. For an appetizer, serve the falafels with bowls of zehug (page 151) and/or tahini sauce (page 149). To eat the falafel sandwich-style, place 2 or 3 falafels in a pita bread with diced tomato, shredded lettuce or cabbage, pickled vegetables, tahini sauce, and zehug.

Makes 16 2½-inch falafels, which will serve 4 to 6

61 CALORIES PER 4 SERVINGS; 3.3 G PROTEIN; .9 G FAT; .1 G SATURATED FAT; 10 G CARBOHYDRATE; 82 MG SODIUM; .03 MG CHOLESTEROL

🐟 Quick Bake-Fried Kreplach 🐟

Let the Italians have ravioli; the Chinese, wontons. I raise my fork for kreplach. These triangular meat-filled dumplings are about the best thing you could find in a bowl of chicken broth or, deep-fried, they make a crackling crisp hors d'oeuvre you'll want to eat more than a few of. So beloved are kreplach they play a symbolic role in three major Jewish holidays: Shavuot (their three corners are said to symbolize the three patriarchs); Yom Kippur eve (the chopping of the filling symbolizes the flagellation to which Jews used to subject themselves to atone for their sins); and even Purim (when Jews eat foods that are chopped or beaten to represent the defeat of the wicked Haman). But that's not to say that kreplach can't be enjoyed other times of year: in my home, they're a perennially popular hors d'oeuvre. To reduce the fat in the traditional recipe, I wrap the kreplach in Chinese wonton wrappers (not egg dough) and bake-fry them in a hot oven. There's another advantage to using this method. The kreplach can be assembled in just a few minutes. Try to make kreplach the day after you've cooked flanken or brisket, so you have the leftover meat on hand.

PREPARATION TIME: 20 MINUTES   COOKING TIME: 10 MINUTES

FOR THE MEAT FILLING:
8 ounces cooked beef (preferably brisket)
1 tablespoon canola oil
1 medium onion, finely chopped
1 clove garlic, finely chopped
Salt and freshly ground black pepper
¼ cup egg substitute or 1 egg or 2 egg whites, lightly beaten

TO FINISH THE KREPLACH:
36 (3-inch) wonton wrappers (thawed if frozen)
2 tablespoons egg substitute or 1 egg white, lightly beaten with a fork
Spray oil

1. Prepare the filling. Finely chop the beef in a meat grinder or food processor. (If using the latter, cut the meat into ½-inch pieces before grinding.) **Note:** Some people like to grind the filling so finely it becomes a paste. I prefer a very fine chop.

2. Heat the oil in a nonstick skillet. Add the onion and garlic and cook over medium heat until lightly browned, about 5 minutes. Grind the onion mixture into the meat. Add salt and pepper to taste; the mixture should be highly seasoned. Mix in the egg substitute.

3. Preheat the oven to 400 degrees.

4. Arrange a few wonton wrappers on a work surface. Lightly brush two adjacent edges of each wrapper with the egg substitute. Place a spoonful of meat mixture (about 2½ teaspoons) in the center. Fold the wrapper in half on the diagonal to make a triangular dumpling, pressing the edges together with your fingertips to seal them. Assemble the remaining kreplach the same way.

5. Spray a nonstick baking sheet with oil. Arrange the kreplach on the baking sheet and spray the tops with oil. Bake the kreplach until crisp and golden brown, 4 to 6 minutes per side. Transfer to a platter and serve at once.

*Makes 32 to 36 kreplach,
enough to serve 6 to 8 as an appetizer*

44 CALORIES PER PIECE; 3 G PROTEIN; 1.2 G FAT; .3 G SATURATED FAT; 5 G CARBOHYDRATE; 55 MG SODIUM; 6.6 MG CHOLESTEROL

VARIATION—BOILED KREPLACH

To make boiled kreplach, prepare the recipe through step 4. Cook the kreplach in boiling salted water for 5 minutes. Transfer the kreplach to chicken broth (page 189), 1 to 1½ cups of broth per person. Simmer the kreplach in the broth for 1 minute before serving.

VARIATION— POTATO KREPLACH

Make a half batch of the potato blintz filling on page 65. Assemble and bake the kreplach as described above.

Makes 24 kreplach

✄ Savory Cheese Kreplach ✄

Fried dumplings may not seem like the stuff of a healthy diet, but these are no ordinary kreplach: I've replaced the traditional egg dough with Chinese wonton wrappers (available in supermarket produce sections) and I bake the wontons in a hot oven instead of deep-frying them. This produces a crisp, low-fat kreplach you can assemble in a matter of minutes. (Remember the old days, when you used to have to roll out and cut kreplach dough by hand?) Below I offer two variations on cheese kreplach suitable for a dairy meal: a savory version flavored with green onion and a sweet kreplach flavored with cinnamon, lemon, and sugar.

PREPARATION TIME: 20 MINUTES   COOKING TIME: 12 MINUTES

FOR THE FILLING:
½ pound (1 cup) dry curd low- or no-fat cottage cheese
3 tablespoons finely chopped scallion greens or green onion
¼ cup egg substitute or 2 egg whites, lightly beaten with a fork
2 tablespoons dried unflavored bread crumbs
Salt and plenty of freshly ground black pepper

TO FINISH THE KREPLACH:
36 (3-inch) wonton wrappers (thawed if frozen)
2 tablespoons egg substitute or 1 egg white, lightly beaten with a fork
Spray oil
1 tablespoon melted butter
1 tablespoon sesame seeds

1. Preheat the oven to 400 degrees.

2. Prepare the filling. In a mixing bowl, combine the cottage cheese, scallion greens, egg substitute, bread crumbs, salt, and pepper and stir to mix.

3. Arrange a few wonton wrappers on a work surface. Lightly brush two adjacent edges of each wrapper with egg substitute. Place a spoonful of cheese mixture (about 2½ teaspoons) in the center. Fold the wrapper in half on the diagonal to make a triangular dumpling, pressing the edges together with your fingertips to seal them. Assemble the remaining kreplach the same way.

4. Lightly spray a nonstick baking sheet with oil. Arrange the kreplach on the baking sheet and brush the tops with melted butter. Sprinkle the kreplach with sesame seeds. Bake the kreplach until crisp and golden brown, 4 to 6 minutes per side. Transfer to a platter and serve at once.

Makes 32 to 36 kreplach,
enough to serve 6 to 8 as an appetizer

36 CALORIES PER PIECE; 2 G PROTEIN; .7 G FAT; .3 G SATURATED FAT; 5.2 G CARBOHYDRATE; 78 MG SODIUM; 1.6 MG CHOLESTEROL

⚔ Sweet Cheese Kreplach ⚔

Jews of European descent have always blurred the line between sweet and savory dishes. Sugar, cinnamon, and lemon zest give the following kreplach a sweet touch, but you could still serve them as an appetizer. Another way to enjoy sweet kreplach is to boil them in milk, toss them with a little butter (1 to 2 tablespoons), and sprinkle them with poppy seeds or cinnamon sugar.

PREPARATION TIME: 20 MINUTES   COOKING TIME: 10 MINUTES

FOR THE FILLING:
½ pound (1 cup) dry curd low- or no-fat cottage cheese
2 tablespoons dried unflavored bread crumbs
1 tablespoon sugar
½ teaspoon vanilla extract
½ teaspoon cinnamon
½ teaspoon lemon zest
¼ cup egg substitute or 2 egg whites, lightly beaten with a fork

TO FINISH THE KREPLACH:
36 (3-inch) wonton wrappers (thawed if frozen)
2 tablespoons egg substitute or 1 egg white, lightly beaten with a fork
Spray oil
1 tablespoon melted butter
1 tablespoon poppy seeds or cinnamon sugar (made by mixing 1 tablespoon sugar with ½ teaspoon cinnamon)

1. Prepare as described above, substituting the sugar, vanilla, cinnamon, and lemon zest for the scallion greens, salt, and pepper. After brushing the assembled kreplach with melted butter, sprinkle with poppy seeds or cinnamon sugar instead of sesame seeds.

*Makes 32 to 36 kreplach,
enough to serve 6 to 8 as an appetizer*

32 CALORIES PER PIECE; 2 G PROTEIN; .2 G FAT; .04 G SATURATED FAT; 5.5 G CARBOHYDRATE; 73 MG SODIUM; .7 MG CHOLESTEROL

⚘ Spinach Turnovers ⚘
(Pasticcini di Spinaci)

Here's the Italian version of kreplach, a pastry turnover stuffed with spinach and provolone cheese. Traditional pasticcini would be made with an oil- and butter-based dough. To slash the fat, I use wonton wrappers, as in the previous recipe for kreplach. If you're used to the meat and cheese kreplach served in most Ashkenazi homes, these crisp spinach turnovers will come as a revelation.

PREPARATION TIME: 20 MINUTES   COOKING TIME: 10 MINUTES

FOR THE FILLING:
10 ounces fresh spinach or 1 (10-ounce) package
   frozen
Salt
1/3 cup finely diced raw potato
1/3 cup grated provolone cheese
1/4 cup egg substitute or 2 egg whites
1/2 teaspoon grated lemon zest
Freshly ground black pepper
Freshly grated nutmeg

TO FINISH THE KREPLACH:
36 (3-inch) Chinese ravioli wrappers or wonton
   wrappers, preferably round (thawed if frozen)
2 tablespoons egg substitute or 1 egg white, lightly
   beaten with a fork
Spray oil
1 tablespoon sesame seeds

1. Preheat the oven to 400 degrees.

2. If using fresh spinach, wash and stem. Bring 2 cups salted water to a boil in a large pot. Add the potato and boil until soft, about 4 minutes. Add the spinach and cook until wilted, about 2 minutes, stirring often. Drain the spinach and potato in a colander, rinse with cold water, and drain again. When cool enough to handle, grab handfuls of spinach and potato and squeeze between your fingers to wring out the water. Coarsely chop the spinach and potato in a food processor or by hand. If using frozen spinach, cook according to the instructions on the package. Drain and dry as described above.

3. Place the spinach in a mixing bowl and stir in the provolone, egg substitute, lemon zest, and salt, pepper, and nutmeg to taste. The filling should be highly seasoned.

4. Arrange a few wonton wrappers on a work surface. Lightly brush two adjacent edges of each wrapper with egg substitute. Place a spoonful of spinach mixture (about 2½ teaspoons) in the center. Fold the wrapper in half on the diagonal to make a triangular dumpling, pressing the edges together with your fingertips to seal them. Assemble the remaining turnovers in the same way.

5. Spray a nonstick baking sheet with oil. Arrange the kreplach on the baking sheet and spray the tops with oil. Sprinkle the turnovers with sesame seeds. Bake until crisp and golden brown, 4 to 6 minutes per side. Transfer to a platter and serve at once.

Makes 32 to 36 kreplach,
enough to serve 6 to 8 as an appetizer

34 CALORIES PER PIECE; 1.7 G PROTEIN; .65 G FAT; .26 G SATURATED FAT; 5.2 G CARBOHYDRATE; 80 MG SODIUM; 1.6 MG CHOLESTEROL

VARIATION—DUMPLINGS

To make spinach dumplings, prepare the recipe through step 4. Cook the kreplach in boiling salted water for 5 minutes. Transfer the kreplach to chicken broth (page 189), 1 to 1½ cups of broth per person. Simmer the kreplach in the broth for 1 minute before serving.

✎ Beef Empanadas ✎

Empanadas are the Sephardic equivalent of that Ashkenazi delicacy: pirogi. Spanish Jews brought them to the Caribbean and Latin America in the years following the Inquisition. To keep empanadas kosher, Jewish cooks eliminated the lard in the dough and pork in the filling. To trim the fat, I've taken to making empanadas with Chinese wonton wrappers, which are available in Asian markets and the produce section of most supermarkets. (If unavailable, use egg roll wrappers and cut them into 3-inch circles or squares.) I bake-fry the pies in a hot oven rather than deep-frying them, which further reduces the fat. Besides the obvious health advantage, you'll love the ease and speed with which these empanadas can be assembled. The juxtaposition of sweet raisins and salty capers and olives in this beef empanada recipe is characteristic of Dutch and Spanish Caribbean Jewish cooking.

PREPARATION TIME: 25 MINUTES   COOKING TIME: 15 MINUTES

FOR THE FILLING:
8 ounces lean beef, such as sirloin or tenderloin
1 clove garlic, finely chopped
½ small onion, finely chopped (about ¼ cup)
½ green bell pepper, cored, seeded, and finely chopped
½ tomato, chopped with juices
1 tablespoon tomato paste
2 tablespoons white wine
½ teaspoon cumin
2 tablespoons raisins
4 pimiento-stuffed green olives, coarsely chopped

2 teaspoons drained capers
1 teaspoon minced fresh cilantro or parsley
Salt and freshly ground black pepper
1 to 2 tablespoons dried bread crumbs (optional)

TO FINISH THE EMPANADAS:
36 (3-inch) Chinese ravioli wrappers or wonton wrappers (if round are not available, use square ones and fold them in half on the diagonal)
1 egg white, lightly beaten with a fork
Spray oil or olive oil for brushing

1. Prepare the filling. Trim any fat off the beef and cut the meat into ½-inch dice. Combine the beef and other ingredients for the filling, minus the bread crumbs, in a saucepan. Simmer the mixture, uncovered, over medium heat until the beef is cooked, about 5 minutes, stirring often.

2. Transfer the mixture to a food processor and coarsely grind. The mixture should be fairly dry: if too wet, add 1 to 2 tablespoons bread crumbs. Correct the seasoning, adding salt and pepper to taste: the filling should be highly seasoned. Refrigerate the filling until cold.

3. Preheat the oven to 400 degrees.

4. Arrange a few ravioli wrappers on a work surface. Lightly brush the edge of each wrapper with egg white. (This acts as glue to make a seal.) Place 2½ teaspoons beef mixture in the center and fold the wrapper in half to make a half-moon-shaped dumpling. Crimp the edges with a fork. Place the empanadas on a cake rack while you finish the others.

5. Arrange the empanadas on a nonstick baking sheet lightly sprayed or brushed with oil. Spray the tops of the empanadas with oil. Bake the empanadas until the pastry is crisp and golden brown, 4 to 6 minutes per side.

Makes 36 empanadas

22 CALORIES PER EMPANADA; 1.5 G PROTEIN; 0.4 G FAT; 0 G SATURATED FAT; 3 G CARBOHYDRATE; 16 MG SODIUM; 6 MG CHOLESTEROL

VARIATION—FISH EMPANADAS

To make empanadas for milchig meals, Hispanic Jews use cooked fish in place of beef. Prepare the preceding recipe, substituting ½ pound cooked white fish or boiled salt cod for the beef.

✂ My Great-grandmother's Pirogi ✂

According to family legend, when my grandmother Ethel Raichlen got married, she didn't know how to cook. (Grammie Ethel was not a little spoiled back in the days before the Depression. She even drove a Cadillac to high school!) So her mother, Bertha Fribush, would cook dinner for her daughter and son-in-law and drive it over to their apartment. Every day! For years on end! I gather that Grandma Fribush was quite a cook. I vividly remember her chocolate roll (page 168) and her pirogi, which she dutifully prepared every Friday night for our Sabbath dinners. Grandma Fribush made meat pirogis. I like the meaty richness of the mushroom filling below. (To make meat pirogis, use the kreplach filling on page 3. To make potato pirogi, use the potato blintz filling on page 65. To make chicken pirogi, use the chicken knish filling on page 71.) **Note:** *Because of the reduced fat in the dough, these pirogi taste best not hot out of the oven, but after they've had a couple of hours to sit and soften. So by all means make them ahead.*

PREPARATION TIME: 1 HOUR (PLUS TIME FOR MAKING THE FILLINGS AND ALLOWING THE DOUGH TO RISE)
COOKING TIME: 20 MINUTES

FOR THE DOUGH:
1 package dry yeast
1 tablespoon sugar
¼ cup warm water
3½ cups flour, plus additional as needed
1½ teaspoons salt
1 cup warm skim milk
3 tablespoons canola oil
1 egg, lightly beaten

FOR THE FILLINGS:
One or more of the following:
   mushroom filling (page 13)
   beef filling (page 3)
   chicken filling (page 71)
   potato filling (page 65)
2 tablespoons egg substitute or 1 egg white, lightly beaten with a fork

1. Prepare the dough. Combine the yeast, sugar, and water in a small bowl and stir to mix. Let stand until the mixture is foamy, about 10 minutes.

2. Place the flour and salt in a food processor fitted with a dough blade. Add the yeast mixture, warm milk, oil, and egg. Process in short bursts to obtain a dough that is soft and pliable, but not sticky, 3 to 4 minutes. (Add flour as needed.) Turn the dough onto your work surface and knead it for a few minutes by hand.

3. Transfer the dough to a lightly oiled bowl and cover with plastic wrap. Let the dough rise in a warm spot until doubled in bulk, 1 to 2 hours.

4. Punch down the dough and divide it in four. Roll out each quarter as thinly as possible (the dough should be no more than ⅛ inch thick). Using a cookie cutter or an inverted glass, cut out 4-inch circles of dough.

5. Preheat the oven to 350 degrees.

6. Assemble the pirogi. Lightly brush the outside edge of each dough circle with water. Place a scant tablespoon of filling in the center of each circle. Fold the circle in half to envelop the filling, pinching the edges to make a seal. (Start pinching at one edge of the pirogi and continue around to the other.) Stand the pirogi upright on a nonstick baking sheet so that the folded side is on the bottom and the pinched side is upright. If you like, you can decoratively pleat the top of the pirogi. Prepare the remaining pirogi the same way. Loosely cover the pirogi with a dishcloth and let sit at room temperature for 20 minutes.

7. Lightly brush the tops of the pirogi with egg glaze, taking care not to drip any on the side. Bake the pirogi until golden brown, 15 to 20 minutes. Transfer the pirogi to a plate to cool slightly. You can serve the pirogi hot out of the oven, but I find they taste better if you let them cool for an hour or so, then rewarm them if desired before serving. (Because the dough

contains relatively little fat, it tends to be hard just out of the oven. It softens as it sits.)

Note: These pirogi freeze well. Freeze them on a baking sheet and store in a plastic bag. To cook, arrange them on a baking sheet and allow them to thaw at room temperature, about 1 hour. Brush with egg glaze and bake at 350 degrees.

Makes about 50 4-inch pirogi

44 CALORIES PER PIROGI (DOUGH ONLY); 1.2 G PROTEIN; 1 G FAT; .1 G SATURATED FAT; 7.2 G CARBOHYDRATE; 73 MG SODIUM; 4.3 MG CHOLESTEROL

46 CALORIES PER PIROGI (WITH MUSHROOM FILLING); 1.5 G PROTEIN; 1.1 G FAT; .13 G SATURATED FAT; 7.5 G CARBOHYDRATE; 74 MG SODIUM; 4.3 MG CHOLESTEROL

⚘ Mushroom Filling ⚘

I love the meaty richness of this strictly vegetarian mushroom stuffing, which makes a great filling for blinzes, kreplach, pirogi, and knishes. It contains only three main ingredients, but the flavor seems to go on forever. For an exotic touch, you could use shiitakes or portobellos (or a mixture of the two). There's also nothing wrong with adding a spoonful of chopped fresh dill.

PREPARATION TIME: 10 MINUTES   COOKING TIME: 10 MINUTES

**1 (14-ounce) package white mushrooms, trimmed
and wiped clean with a damp paper towel
½ medium onion, finely chopped**

**3 tablespoons finely chopped parsley
Salt and freshly ground black pepper
Pinch of cayenne pepper**

1. Cut the large mushrooms in quarters, the smaller ones in half. Finely chop the mushrooms in a food processor, working in small batches, running the machine in short bursts.

2. Transfer the mushrooms to a nonstick frying pan with the onion, parsley, and seasonings. Cook over high heat until most of the mushroom liquid has evaporated and the mixture is intensely flavored and concentrated, 7 to 10 minutes. Correct the seasoning, adding salt and pepper to taste. The cayenne should give it a little bite.

*Makes 1½ cups,
enough to stuff 50 pirogi, 24 knishes, or 8 blintzes*

29 CALORIES PER SERVING; 2.8 G PROTEIN; 4 G FAT; .02 G SATURATED FAT; 373 G CARBOHYDRATE; 513 MG SODIUM; 0 MG CHOLESTEROL

Dips and Spreads

⌨ The Amazing Low-Fat Chopped Liver ⌨

*My Grammie Ethel was best known for her cookies and fudge. But she also made a mean chopped liver, which was mild, light, and fluffy, and didn't taste too much like liver. Her secret was the high proportion of hard-boiled egg whites to liver. And the hand-cranked metal meat grinder she used her whole life to grind the ingredients into a chunky puree. Low-fat chopped liver might seem like an oxymoron. After all, liver is one of the fattiest and most cholesterol-laden substances known to man. By replacing most of the liver with mushrooms (keeping just enough liver for flavor) and by roasting the ingredients in a hot oven instead of sautéing them, we create a chopped liver that explodes with flavor and is mercifully light on fat. I'm sure my grandmother would have approved. **Note:** To be in strict accordance with the kashrut, you would boil, not roast, the chicken liver. (This is considered a more effective way to remove the blood.)*

PREPARATION TIME: 10 MINUTES   COOKING TIME: 20 MINUTES

8 ounces mushrooms
1 medium onion, quartered
1 teaspoon canola or olive oil
Salt and freshly ground black pepper, to taste

2 ounces chicken or turkey liver
5 eggs
2 tablespoons chopped fresh parsley, plus sprigs for garnish

1. Preheat the oven to 450 degrees. Trim the stem ends off the mushrooms and wipe the caps clean with a damp paper towel. Quarter any large mushrooms; halve medium-size ones; leave any small mushrooms whole. Place the mushrooms and onion in a nonstick roasting pan and toss with the oil, salt, and pepper. Roast the mushrooms until lightly browned, 8 to 10 minutes, stirring to ensure even cooking.

2. Add the livers and continue roasting until the mushrooms are well browned and flavorful and the liver is cooked but still pink in the center, 8 to 10 minutes more.

3. Meanwhile, hard-cook the eggs, following the instructions on page 194. (Cook them for 11 min-

utes.) When cool enough to handle, peel and halve the eggs. Remove and discard the yolks. Cut each white half in half.

4. Place the mushrooms, onion, liver, hard-cooked egg whites, and parsley in a food processor and grind to a coarse puree. (Run the machine in short bursts.) Correct the seasoning, adding salt and pepper to taste: the mixture should be highly seasoned. Transfer the chopped liver to a bowl or platter, garnish with parsley sprigs, and serve with crackers or toasted challah.

Note: For a richer chopped liver, keep two of the egg yolks. The fat will still be below 4 grams per serving.

Makes 1½ cups, serves 6 to 8

53.5 CALORIES PER SERVING (BASED ON 6 SERVINGS); 6.2 G PROTEIN; 1.8 G FAT; .28 G SATURATED FAT;
4 G CARBOHYDRATE; 56.2 MG SODIUM; 41.5 MG CHOLESTEROL

Three spreads (clockwise from the top: amazing low-fat chopped liver, smoked fish spread, grilled vegetable spread).

⌇ Not-Chopped-Liver #2 ⌇

Live with a vegetarian long enough and you'll figure out how to make meatless versions of all sorts of dishes you've loved since childhood—even chopped liver. This succulent pâté owes its "livery" flavor to the combination of mushrooms and green beans. (I'm not sure why the combination tastes like liver, but it does.) So why is this recipe #2? In my book High-Flavor, Low-Fat Vegetarian Cooking *(Viking, 1994), you'll find another vegetarian chopped liver—that one made with peas.*

PREPARATION TIME: 20 MINUTES   COOKING TIME: 30 MINUTES

Salt
8 ounces green beans (ends snapped off)
3 eggs
8 ounces mushrooms
1 tablespoon olive oil

1 medium onion, finely chopped
3 tablespoons finely chopped parsley, plus a few
   sprigs for garnish
Freshly ground black pepper
1 to 2 tablespoons dried bread crumbs (optional)

1. Bring 2 quarts salted water to a boil in a saucepan. Cook the beans until very tender, 6 to 8 minutes. (You're not looking for the al dente beans of nouvelle cuisine here.) Transfer the green beans to a colander with a slotted spoon. (Keep the hot water in the pan.) Rinse the beans under cold water to cool, then drain well.

2. Place the eggs in the bean water. Briskly simmer for 11 minutes. Rinse the eggs under cold water until cool enough to handle, then shell. Cut each egg in half. Remove and discard the yolks.

3. Meanwhile, trim the ends off the mushroom stems and wipe the caps clean with a damp paper towel. Thinly slice the mushrooms. Heat the oil in a nonstick frying pan. Cook the onion over medium heat until soft, but not brown, 3 minutes. Increase the heat to high and add the mushrooms and chopped parsley. Cook until the mushrooms are browned and most of the mushroom liquid has evaporated, 3 to 5 minutes. Let the onion-mushroom mixture cool to room temperature.

4. Combine the green beans, hard-cooked egg whites, and onion-mushroom mixture in a food processor fitted with a chopping blade. Finely chop or puree to a coarse paste. Add plenty of salt and pepper: the mixture should be highly seasoned. Transfer the not-chopped-liver to a bowl and garnish with parsley sprigs. Serve with sliced challah, toast points, toasted pita chips, or crackers.

Makes 2 cups, which will serve 4 to 6 generously or 8 when served with other appetizers

103 CALORIES PER 4 SERVINGS; 5 G PROTEIN; 4 G FAT; 0 G SATURATED FAT; 11 G CARBOHYDRATE; 43 MG SODIUM; 0 MG CHOLESTEROL

⌘ Smoked Fish Spread ⌘

As a time-starved cook (and who isn't these days?), I'm always looking for dishes you can make in a matter of minutes that taste like a million bucks. Nothing quite fits the bill like this cream cheese spread made with kippered salmon. For a spread that will make you plotz with pleasure, use the home-kippered salmon on page 79, but even store-bought salmon will produce a great shmeer. Serve this spread on bagels or, for a touch of elegance, pipe rosettes of it onto toast points or cucumber slices, crowning each with a sprig of fresh dill or a spoonful of salmon caviar.

PREPARATION TIME: 5 MINUTES

8 ounces kippered salmon (weighed after all skin, bones, and any visible fat have been removed)

6 ounces low- or no-fat cream cheese
Freshly ground black pepper, to taste

1. Puree the fish in the food processor. Add the cream cheese and pepper and puree until smooth. Transfer to a bowl for serving or pipe the spread onto toast points or cucumber slices as described above.

Makes 1¼ cups, which will serve 4 to 6

148 CALORIES PER 4 SERVINGS; 23 G PROTEIN; 5 G FAT; 1.4 G SATURATED FAT; 3 G CARBOHYDRATE; 477 MG SODIUM; 41 MG CHOLESTEROL

Hummus with Roasted Garlic

Hummus (garlicky chickpea dip) is a Middle Eastern meze (appetizer) that's become one of Israel's national snacks. The traditional version would be made with raw garlic—lots of it. You can certainly prepare the following hummus in this fashion: it will be delicious. (I'd cut back the garlic to 2 or 3 cloves.) I once had the idea to make hummus with roasted garlic: the sweet, complex flavor was an instant hit. **Note:** *Tahini is Middle East sesame paste. I've made it optional, but it is a traditional flavoring for hummus. I've also slashed the olive oil in the traditional recipe, adding the chickpea cooking liquid for moistness.*

PREPARATION TIME: 10 MINUTES   COOKING TIME: 40 TO 60 MINUTES (FOR ROASTING THE GARLIC)

1 head fresh garlic
1 (15-ounce) can chickpeas, drained and rinsed
   (reserve the canning liquid)
1 tablespoon tahini (optional)
½ teaspoon ground cumin

1 tablespoon extra-virgin olive oil
1½ tablespoons lemon juice, or to taste
Salt and freshly ground black pepper
A little sweet or hot paprika for sprinkling
Pita bread cut into wedges for dipping

1. Preheat the oven to 375 degrees. Loosely wrap the whole head of garlic in foil. Bake the garlic until very soft, 40 to 60 minutes. Let cool, then, using a sharp knife, cut the garlic head in half widthwise. Squeeze the soft roasted garlic out of the skins (as you would toothpaste out of a tube) and place in a food processor.

2. Add the chickpeas, tahini, cumin, 2 teaspoons olive oil, and the lemon juice. Grind to a smooth paste. Add enough chickpea liquid to obtain a loose puree. Correct the seasoning, adding additional lemon juice, if desired, and salt and pepper to taste. Transfer the hummus to a shallow bowl or platter for serving. Drizzle the top with the remaining 1 teaspoon olive oil and lightly sprinkle with paprika. Serve with pita wedges for dipping.

Serves 4 to 6

172 CALORIES PER SERVING (BASED ON 4 SERVINGS); 6 G PROTEIN; 5 G FAT; .6 G SATURATED FAT;
28 G CARBOHYDRATE; 320 MG SODIUM; 0 MG CHOLESTEROL

Baba Ganoosh Made the Old-fashioned Way
(Flame-Roasted Eggplant Dip)

Baba ganoosh (eggplant dip) has become such a fixture in the North American diet it's easy to forget the dish originated in the Middle East and that Israelis have enjoyed it for decades. The correct way to prepare it is to char the eggplants over a charcoal fire: this imparts an intense smoky flavor, which makes authentic baba ganoosh one of the most delectable dips ever to cross a wedge of pita bread. You could certainly use a gas grill to char the eggplant. I've even seen Israelis roast the eggplant directly over a burner on the stove. The important thing is to char the skin of the eggplant all over to impart the requisite smoke flavor. **Note:** *Tahini is a chalky paste made from sesame seeds. It's available at Israeli and Middle Eastern markets and at most supermarkets.*

PREPARATION TIME: 5 MINUTES   COOKING TIME: 20 MINUTES

2 to 3 long, slender eggplants (about 2 pounds)
2 cloves garlic, minced
3 tablespoons fresh lemon juice, or to taste
2 tablespoons tahini
2 tablespoons extra-virgin olive oil, plus oil for drizzling

Salt and freshly ground black pepper
1 scallion, minced
2 tablespoons minced flat-leaf parsley

1. Light your grill and build a medium-hot fire. Prick the eggplants in a few spots with a fork. (This keeps them from exploding.) Grill the eggplants until the skin is charred on all sides (I mean really charred—black as coal!) and the flesh is soft. Turn eggplants with tongs to ensure even cooking. This will take about 20 to 30 minutes in all. Transfer the eggplants to a plate to cool.

2. Peel or scrape the burned skin off the eggplants. Place the flesh in a food processor with the garlic. Puree until smooth. Add the lemon juice, tahini, all but 1 teaspoon of the olive oil, salt, and pepper and puree until smooth. Correct the seasoning, adding salt or lemon juice to taste: the baba should be highly seasoned. Add scallion and parsley and pulse the processor just to mix. (Don't overprocess or the parsley will turn the baba green.)

3. Spoon the baba ganoosh into a shallow bowl and drizzle with the remaining olive oil. Serve with wedges of fresh or toasted pita bread for scooping up the dip.

Makes about 2 cups, which will serve 8

93 CALORIES PER SERVING; 3 G PROTEIN; 6 G FAT; .5 G SATURATED FAT; 7.4 G CARBOHYDRATE; 11 MG SODIUM; 0 MG CHOLESTEROL

⚜ Eggplant Caviar ⚜

Eggplant caviar is a popular Russian-Jewish appetizer, not to mention one of the specialties of my late friend Bob Ginn, who was a fabulous cook and fabulous human being. (You can read more about Bob's culinary exploits in the kugel chapter.) This "caviar" won't fool anyone into thinking he's eating beluga, but it does have the soft, crunchy-gooey texture one associates with fish roe and a robust flavor that would do any vorspeis (Russian-Jewish hors d'oeuvre) spread proud. My low-fat version calls for the vegetables to be roasted in a superhot oven—a technique that provides so much flavor you only need a fraction of the oil found in the traditional recipe.

PREPARATION TIME: 10 MINUTES   COOKING TIME: 20 MINUTES

1 medium eggplant (10 to 12 ounces)
4 cloves garlic
1 medium onion, peeled and quartered
½ green bell pepper, cored and seeded
½ red bell pepper, or more green, cored and seeded
1 carrot, peeled, trimmed, and cut into chunks
2 whole celery stalks, peeled and cut into chunks
1 large, ripe red tomato, cut in half

Spray oil
3 tablespoons chopped fresh parsley (preferably flat-leaf)
2 to 3 tablespoons chopped fresh dill or cilantro
1½ tablespoons extra-virgin olive oil
1 tablespoon fresh lemon juice, or to taste
Salt and freshly ground black pepper

1. Preheat the oven to 450 degrees. Make 8 slits in the eggplant with the tip of a paring knife. Cut each garlic clove in half lengthwise and insert each half in a slit in the eggplant. Place the eggplant, onion, peppers, carrot, celery, and tomato halves (cut side up) on a nonstick baking sheet, lightly oiled with spray oil. Roast the vegetables in the oven until very tender, 20 to 30 minutes, stirring once or twice to prevent scorching. Remove the pan from the oven and let the vegetables cool to room temperature.

2. Transfer the onion, carrot, celery, and tomato to a food processor fitted with a metal blade and coarsely chop, running the machine in bursts. Cut the eggplant in half lengthwise, scrape the pulp and garlic out of the skin with a spoon, and add it to the processor with the bell peppers. Coarsely chop, running the machine in bursts. Add the parsley, dill, olive oil, lemon juice, salt, and pepper and process just to mix. Correct the seasoning, adding lemon juice or salt to taste: eggplant caviar should be highly seasoned. Chill well before serving.

3. Serve eggplant caviar with wedges of pita bread or slices of pumpernickel.

Makes about 2½ cups, enough to serve 6 to 8

43 CALORIES PER 6 SERVINGS; 9 G PROTEIN; 1.9 G FAT; .3 G SATURATED FAT; 6.6 G CARBOHYDRATE; 12 MG SODIUM; 0 MG CHOLESTEROL

⋙ Grilled Vegetable Spread ⋘

Of all the flavored cream cheeses arrayed in a delicatessen display case, none looks more inviting than vegetable spread. Alas, looks are all you get with your average veggie spread, as the colorful pieces are actually freeze-dried vegetable bits. Take the time to grill fresh vegetables (you can do it a day ahead, when you're grilling something else) and you'll wind up with one of the most exquisite shmeers ever to grace a bagel.

PREPARATION TIME: 10 MINUTES   COOKING TIME: 10 MINUTES

1 bunch of scallions, roots trimmed off
1 small red bell pepper, cored and quartered
1 small yellow bell pepper, cored and quartered

8 ounces reduced-fat or no-fat cream cheese, at room temperature
Freshly ground black pepper

1. Preheat your grill to high. Grill the scallions and peppers until nicely browned, 4 to 6 minutes per side. Transfer the vegetables to a cutting board and let cool.

2. Very finely chop the vegetables. (This is best done by hand.) Drain in a strainer, then blot dry with paper towels. Beat the cream cheese until light and fluffy in a mixing bowl. Beat in the vegetables and pepper to taste. Transfer the spread to an attractive bowl for serving.

Makes about 2 cups, which will serve 8

42 CALORIES PER 8 SERVINGS; 4.6 G PROTEIN; .5 G FAT; .3 G SATURATED FAT; 5 G CARBOHYDRATE; 157 MG SODIUM; 2.2 MG CHOLESTEROL

Soups

✺ My Grandmother's Chicken Noodle Soup ✺

When I was growing up, we dined weekly with both sets of grandparents. Tuesday night was Goldman night: we had dinner with Grammie Sarah and Grandpa Jack Goldman. (Salmon croquettes were the house specialty here—see recipe on page 77.) Friday night was Raichlen night: dinner with my Grammie Ethel and Dear. After chopped liver on saltine crackers (page 15) and, when we were lucky, my great-grandmother's pirogi (page 11), we would take our seats at a polished mahogany table. The first course rarely varied: a steaming bowl of chicken noodle soup.

Untold generations of Raichlens have enjoyed this golden elixir in times of illness as well as health. I can't think of better relief for a cold, flu, depression, or whatever else ails you. Here's a rich, golden, soothing chicken soup just like my Grammie Ethel used to make. I must note in passing a Raichlen family peculiarity for serving chicken noodle soup. When she was young, my aunt Linda Millison would make a happy face in her bowl of soup with drops of ketchup. I'm not sure I'd recommend the practice for adults, but kids love it.
Note: *Please take the time to make chicken broth from scratch, following the recipe on page 189. Otherwise, you won't get the full effect.*

PREPARATION TIME: 10 MINUTES   COOKING TIME: 10 MINUTES PLUS TIME FOR MAKING THE BROTH

8 ounces thin egg noodles or spaghettini
Salt
10 cups basic chicken broth (page 189)

2 cups diced or shredded cooked chicken
3 tablespoons finely chopped celery leaves
Freshly ground black pepper

1. Cook the noodles in 3 quarts boiling salted water in a large pot until tender, about 8 minutes. Strain, rinse under cold water, and drain.

2. Combine the noodles, broth, chicken, and celery leaves in a large saucepan and simmer for 2 minutes. (The chicken should be heated through.) Season the soup with salt and pepper to taste; it should be highly seasoned. Ladle the soup into bowls for serving.

Makes 10 to 12 cups, enough to serve 8

213 CALORIES PER SERVING; 15 G PROTEIN; 3 G FAT; 1 G SATURATED FAT; 30 G CARBOHYDRATE; 38 MG SODIUM; 29 MG CHOLESTEROL

Aunt Annette's matzo ball soup.

✑ My Aunt Annette's Matzo Ball Soup ✑

Every family has one superlative cook: ours was my great-aunt Annette Farber. Armed with little more than a few battered pots and wooden spoons, she would create exquisite elaborate dinners for forty people. (Without the benefit of food processors, microwave ovens, or a dishwasher, of course.) Her gedemfted chicken (page 89) was the stuff of miracles. Her brisket could make you weep. As for her matzo balls, well, suffice it to say that rabbis would drive from Washington, D.C., to Baltimore just to have a seat at our Passover table. What makes a great matzo ball? It shouldn't be too light. (Heaven forbid!) And it shouldn't be too heavy. Aunt Annette achieved the perfect consistency every time—with nary a measuring cup in sight. To create a low-fat matzo ball, I've made a few small adjustments to Aunt Annette's recipe. Mostly, I've reduced the amount of schmaltz. The club soda acts as a natural (and legal!) leavening agent. You'll be pleased to know that Aunt Annette (age ninety-two) gives the following recipe a thumbs-up!

PREPARATION TIME: 10 MINUTES, PLUS 4 TO 6 HOURS FOR CHILLING THE MATZO BALLS
COOKING TIME: 40 MINUTES

FOR THE MATZO BALLS:
2 eggs plus 2 egg whites
2 tablespoons real schmaltz (page 192) or mock schmaltz (page 193)
3 tablespoons minced onion
3 tablespoons finely chopped parsley
2 teaspoons minced or grated fresh ginger
1 teaspoon salt, or to taste, plus additional as needed
½ teaspoon freshly ground black pepper, plus additional as needed

¼ teaspoon ground allspice
⅛ teaspoon ground nutmeg or mace
¾ cup plus 2 tablespoons club soda or seltzer water
2 cups matzo meal

2 quarts basic chicken broth (page 189)
2 scallions, green part only, finely chopped

1. In a mixing bowl, combine the eggs, egg whites, schmaltz, onion, parsley, ginger, salt, pepper, allspice, and nutmeg and beat with a fork to mix. Beat in the club soda, followed by the matzo meal. The mixture should be thick but pliable (roughly the consistency of soft ice cream). If too thick, add a little more club soda; if too thin, add a little more matzo meal.

2. Wet your hands with cold water and pinch off walnut-size pieces of matzo mixture. Roll them into 1½-inch balls between the palms of your hands. Arrange the matzo balls on a plate lined with plastic wrap and chill for 1 hour.

3. Bring 1 gallon lightly salted water to a rolling boil in a large pot. Drop the matzo balls in one by one. Better still, roll them down on an inclined cutting board into the water. This keeps them perfectly round. Simmer until cooked and tender, 25 to 35 minutes. Using a slotted spoon, transfer the matzo balls to a colander to drain.

4. To serve the soup, heat the broth, adding salt and pepper to taste. Place two matzo balls in each soup bowl and ladle the broth over them. Sprinkle with chopped scallions and serve at once.

Makes 12 matzo balls. Serves 6 as a substantial soup, 12 as a light soup as part of a rich holiday meal

236 CALORIES PER SERVING (2 BALLS PER SERVING); 7.8 G PROTEIN; 6.2 G FAT; 1.8 G SATURATED FAT;
37.1 G CARBOHYDRATE; 440 MG SODIUM; 74.5 MG CHOLESTEROL

⚥ Hot Borscht ⚥

Whenever I'm feeling low and I want some edible comfort, I make a pot of borscht. I love this rib-sticking, crimson-colored soup from Eastern Europe. I love its earthy beet flavor and the way the brassy splash of vinegar offsets the sweetness of the vegetables. I love the tangy garnish of chopped scallions and buttery boiled potatoes. Hot borscht can be made either milchig or fleischig. Below is the meatless version. Instructions for a meat-based borscht are listed as a variation.

PREPARATION TIME: 20 MINUTES   COOKING TIME: 40 MINUTES

1 tablespoon olive oil
1 medium onion, finely chopped
1 carrot, finely diced
1 stalk celery, finely diced
2 cloves garlic, minced
3 tablespoons finely chopped parsley
1 pound beets, peeled and cut into ½-inch dice
5 cups vegetable broth (page 191) or water
1 bay leaf

½ teaspoon caraway seeds (optional)
1 tablespoon balsamic vinegar
Salt and freshly ground black pepper

FOR THE GARNISH:
1 pound small red potatoes, scrubbed
½ cup no-fat sour cream in an attractive serving bowl
4 scallions, finely chopped

1. Heat the oil in a large heavy saucepan. Add the onion, carrot, celery, garlic, and parsley and cook over medium heat until soft but not brown, about 4 minutes.

2. Stir in the beets, vegetable broth, bay leaf, and caraway seeds (if using) and bring to a boil. Reduce the heat and gently simmer the borscht until the beets are tender, 20 to 30 minutes. Stir in the vinegar and simmer for 1 minute. Add salt and pepper to taste: the borscht should be highly seasoned.

3. Meanwhile, prepare the garnish. Place the pota-toes in a pot with cold salted water to cover. Bring the potatoes to a boil, reduce the heat, and simmer until tender, 10 to 15 minutes. Drain the potatoes well. Cut each potato in quarters and place in an attractive serving bowl, and keep warm.

4. To serve the borscht, ladle it into bowls. Have each eater add sour cream, boiled potatoes, and scallions to the soup to taste. Serve with black bread and cucumber salad (page 42).

Serves 4

240 CALORIES PER SERVING; 8 G PROTEIN; 4 G FAT; .5 G SATURATED FAT; 45 G CARBOHYDRATE; 147 MG SODIUM; 0 MG CHOLESTEROL

VARIATION

Take 1 pound trimmed, diced brisket and place in a pot with 6 cups cold water. Briskly simmer the beef until tender, about 1 hour. Skim off any foam or scum that rises to the surface. Transfer the beef to a platter and let cool, then finely chop or shred. Reserve the re-sulting beef broth. Prepare the borscht as described above, using the beef broth in place of vegetable broth. Add the beef to the soup when you add the beets. Omit the sour cream from the garnish.

Greek Egg-Lemon Matzo Soup

This soup is a perfect example of how Jews adapted the dishes of a particular country to their religious and aesthetic needs. Avgolemono (chicken soup thickened with eggs and invigorated with fresh lemon juice) is a mainstay of the Greek table, but usually it's made with rice. Come Passover, the Jews of Salonika enrich the broth with matzo farfel to make a soup that's wonderfully soothing and sustaining. The tang of the lemon juice makes this unlike any chicken soup you've ever tasted. To reduce the fat, I use 1 whole egg instead of the traditional 3 to 4 yolks. Withal, I think you'll find the soup amply rich and endowed with flavor.

PREPARATION TIME: 5 MINUTES   COOKING TIME: 5 MINUTES

1 quart basic chicken broth (page 189)
2 cups matzo farfel
2 tablespoons chopped flat-leaf parsley (optional)

Salt and freshly ground black pepper
1 large egg
3 tablespoons fresh lemon juice

1. Bring the chicken broth to a boil in a heavy saucepan. Add the matzo farfel and parsley and simmer until the farfel is soft, 2 minutes. Add salt and pepper to taste; the broth should be highly seasoned. Remove the pan from the heat.

2. Beat the egg in a small bowl with a fork and strain it into a heatproof medium-size bowl. Beat in the lemon juice. Beat ½ cup of the hot soup into egg mixture, little by little. Very gradually stir this mixture back into the remaining soup.

3. Return the soup to a medium heat and cook until slightly thickened, 1 to 2 minutes, stirring with a wooden spoon. Do not let the soup boil or even simmer or the egg will curdle. Correct the seasoning, adding salt to taste. Ladle the soup into bowls and serve at once.

Serves 4

264 CALORIES PER SERVING; 8 G PROTEIN; 1.5 G FAT; .4 G SATURATED FAT; 55 G CARBOHYDRATE; 23 MG SODIUM; 53 MG CHOLESTEROL

✂ Grandma Raichlen's Cabbage Borscht ✂

To most people "borscht" means beets, but this soulful soup can be made with a multitude of vegetables. The recipe comes from my great grandmother, who brought it to America from her native Riga. Grandma Raichlen and her daughters made the borscht with rich beef broth (page 190), but these days the vegetarians in the family rely on the vegetables to make a rich broth. I dedicate this recipe to my aunt Vivian, who loved cabbage borscht more than anything. (Except Uncle Morty.)

PREPARATION TIME: 20 MINUTES   COOKING TIME: 40 TO 50 MINUTES

1½ tablespoons olive oil
2 leeks, trimmed, washed, and finely chopped
1 large onion, finely chopped
2 carrots, peeled and finely chopped
2 stalks celery, finely chopped
3 cloves garlic, minced
1 large parsnip, peeled and finely chopped
1 small head of green or savoy cabbage, cored and thinly sliced
4 to 5 medium-ripe tomatoes (about 2 pounds), finely chopped, or one 28-ounce can plum tomatoes, finely chopped with juices

2 quarts rich beef, chicken, or vegetable broth, or water, or as needed
5 cloves or ¼ teaspoon ground cloves
1 teaspoon caraway seeds (optional)
Salt and freshly ground black pepper
Approximately ¼ cup brown sugar or to taste
Approximately ¼ cup red wine vinegar or to taste
4 scallions, trimmed and finely chopped
¼ cup chopped flat-leaf parsley

1. Heat the olive oil in a large saucepan. Add the leeks, onion, carrots, celery, garlic, and parsnip and cook over medium heat until soft but not brown, 5 minutes. Stir in the cabbage and cook until soft, 6 to 8 minutes, stirring often. Stir in the tomatoes, broth, spices, salt, and pepper. Bring the soup to a boil, reduce the heat, and simmer, uncovered, until the vegetables are very tender, 30 to 40 minutes. Borscht should be thick but soupy; if it dries out too much, add more stock.

2. Ten minutes before the end, stir in the sugar and vinegar: the borscht should be a little sweet and a little sour. Correct the seasoning, adding salt, sugar, or vinegar to taste. Ladle the cabbage borscht into bowls and garnish with chopped scallion and parsley.

Serves 8 to 10

160 CALORIES PER SERVING; 6 G PROTEIN; 4 G FAT; 0 G SATURATED FAT; 29 G CARBOHYDRATE; 832 MG SODIUM; 0 MG CHOLESTEROL

✎ Polish Vegetable Soup with "Torn" Dumplings ✎

"A good summer soup for a milchig party," is how Esther "Edzia" Korman describes a dish with the tongue-twisting Yiddish name of getsipte klushkilach. *A* klushkilach *is a dumpling, which is getsipte (torn) into tiny pieces and cooked in the soup. But just as remarkable as the dumplings is the soup itself, which is chock-full of vegetables and soulfully flavored with sour cream and fresh dill. Born in Kozienice, Poland, Esther survived the war and now lives in Brooklyn, New York. Her soup has the rich flavor of prewar Jewish life in Poland.*

PREPARATION TIME: 15 MINUTES   COOKING TIME: 30 MINUTES

1 large leek, trimmed, washed, and thinly sliced
1 onion, finely chopped
3 cloves garlic, finely chopped
2 carrots, peeled and cut into ½-inch dice
2 stalks celery, cut into ½-inch dice
1 pound potatoes, peeled and cut into ½-inch dice
⅓ cup chopped fresh dill, plus 8 sprigs for garnish

2 tablespoons butter
10 cups hot water
2 tablespoons quick-cook oatmeal
Salt and freshly ground black pepper
½ cup no-fat sour cream

"Torn" dumplings (opposite)

1. In a large pot, place the leek, onion, garlic, carrots, celery, potatoes, 3 tablespoons dill, butter, and water and bring to a boil. Reduce the heat to medium and gently simmer the vegetables for 10 minutes.

2. Stir in the oatmeal and a little salt and pepper. Continue simmering the soup until the vegetables are tender and the broth is slightly thickened, 10 to 15 minutes more. Make the dumpling dough as described below.

3. Tear or cut the dumpling dough into pea-sized pieces and add them to the soup. Simmer until firm and cooked through, about 10 minutes. Stir in the sour cream and simmer for 5 minutes. The soup should be substantial but not too thick: add a little water if necessary. Stir in the remaining dill and simmer for 1 minute. Correct the seasoning, adding salt and pepper to taste; the soup should be highly seasoned. Ladle the soup into bowls and garnish each with a sprig of dill.

Serves 8

156 CALORIES PER SERVING; 4.5 G PROTEIN; 3.5 G FAT; 1.9 G SATURATED FAT; 2.7 G CARBOHYDRATE; 149 MG SODIUM; 8.2 MG CHOLESTEROL

❧ "Torn" Dumplings ❧

It doesn't take much longer to make these tiny dumplings than it takes to say their name in Yiddish:
getsipte klushkilach. *I can't think of a soup that wouldn't benefit from their addition.*

PREPARATION TIME: 5 MINUTES   COOKING TIME: 10 MINUTES

½ cup flour, plus flour for the board
¼ teaspoon salt

2 tablespoons egg substitute or 1 lightly beaten egg white
1 tablespoon cool water

1. Place the flour and salt in a bowl and mix with your fingertips. Make a well in the center and add the egg substitute and water. Stir the ingredients with your fingertips or a wooden spoon to make a stiff dough. (If the dough is sticky, you can add a little flour.) Cut the dough in quarters and roll each piece into a pencil-thin tube on a lightly floured cutting board.

2. Tear pea-sized pieces off the dough tubes and toss them into the boiling soup as described above. Cook for about 10 minutes.

Note: You can also cook the dumplings in boiling water.

Serves 8

157 CALORIES PER SERVING; 4.5 G PROTEIN; 3.5 G FAT; 2 G SATURATED FAT; 27 G CARBOHYDRATE; 149 MG SODIUM; 8.2 MG CHOLESTEROL

✄ Salonikan Bean Soup ✄

This splendid recipe came from Lily Modiano, a fabulous Sephardic-Greek cook who was ninety-three years old when I wrote this and who happened to be my great-aunt. She described it so lovingly and vividly I could taste it without eating it. (We were speaking at the time in a nursing home.) Sure enough, when I went to make the soup, the earthy flavor of the beans, the meaty richness of the broth, the sweetness of the fried onion, and the tartness of the tomatoes and lemon juice were exactly as Lily described them. They conspired to make this one of the tastiest bean soups on the planet. **Note:** *The spinach is not traditional, but I love the contrasting color and the way it rounds out the flavors. Omit it if you like.*

PREPARATION TIME: 10 MINUTES   COOKING TIME: 1½ TO 2 HOURS

1½ cups dried white beans (navy beans or great
   Northern beans)
1 pound brisket or stew beef
1 bay leaf
Salt and freshly ground black pepper
1 tablespoon olive oil
2 cups chopped onion (approximately 1 large)

1 large, ripe red tomato or 1 (14-ounce) can peeled
   plum tomatoes, drained and chopped
3 tablespoons chopped fresh parsley
3 cups spinach leaves (preferably small young
   leaves from bunch spinach), stemmed and
   washed
6 lemon wedges for serving

1. Spread out the beans on a baking sheet and pick through them, discarding any twigs or stones. Rinse the beans in a colander under cold water and place in a large bowl with water to cover by 2 inches. Soak the beans for at least 6 hours, preferably overnight. Or use the quick-soak method: Place the beans in a large pot with 3 inches water to cover. Boil the beans for 10 minutes. Remove the pan from the heat and let the beans soak for 1 hour.

2. If using brisket, trim off any visible fat. Cut the meat into 1-inch cubes. Place in a deep pot with 9 cups of water. Bring the meat to a boil and skim off any foam or scum that rises to the surface. Reduce the heat to medium and simmer the beef, uncovered, for 30 minutes, skimming often.

3. Add the beans and bay leaf and simmer until the

beans and beef are very tender, about 1 hour. The pan should be loosely covered. Add a little salt and pepper.

4. Meanwhile, heat the oil in a nonstick skillet. Cook the onion over medium heat until nicely browned, 5 to 8 minutes. Increase the heat to high, add the tomato and parsley, and cook until most of the tomato juices are evaporated, 3 minutes.

5. To finish the soup, remove and discard the bay leaf. Stir the onion-tomato mixture into the soup. Simmer for 5 minutes, adding salt and pepper to taste. The soup should be thick, creamy, and highly seasoned. If the soup is too thick, add a little more water. If using spinach, stir it into the soup and cook for 1 minute. Ladle the soup into bowls and serve with lemon wedges.

Serves 6

396 CALORIES PER SERVING; 35 G PROTEIN; 9 G FAT; 3.4 G SATURATED FAT; 37 G CARBOHYDRATE; 84 MG SODIUM; 70 MG CHOLESTEROL

✄ The One and Only Raichlen Family Sauerkraut Soup ✄

Sauerkraut soup. Most people react with horror at the mention of a dish that has been a Raichlen family specialty for generations. We always ate sauerkraut soup at Thanksgiving—a practice that originated with my great-grandfather Isador, who made his own sauerkraut in a barrel under the back porch. (The first batch was ready to eat around November 24.) So great was the demand for this piquant elixir, my aunt Annette would prepare the soup in four-gallon batches. After the holidays, Raichlens would return to their homes all over the country, loaded with jars of sauerkraut soup. (How the potent stuff cleared airport security remains a mystery.)

For the best results, use barrel sauerkraut (the sort sold in bulk at a good deli or ethnic grocery store). However, the supermarket kraut sold in jars or plastic bags will work okay, too. (Use canned sauerkraut only as a last resort.) **Note:** *My family doesn't keep kosher, so we garnished our sauerkraut soup with dollops of sour cream. To keep the soup kosher, use a nondairy sour cream substitute. Or omit the sour cream entirely. If you're in a hurry, you could use canned beef stock, omitting the flanken and bones and steps 1 and 2. Of course, your soup won't be quite so spectacular.*

PREPARATION TIME: 20 MINUTES   COOKING TIME: 1¾ HOURS

FOR THE BROTH:
2 pounds flanken, skirt steak, or brisket
1 pound beef bones
1 onion, skin left on, quartered
2 carrots, cut into 1-inch pieces
2 stalks celery, cut into 1-inch pieces
2 cloves garlic
10 peppercorns, 2 cloves, 1 bay leaf, and 2 sprigs each of thyme and parsley, all tied in cheesecloth

TO FINISH THE SOUP:
2 pounds sauerkraut with juices
Salt and freshly ground black pepper
2 tablespoons lemon juice, or to taste
½ cup brown sugar, or to taste

1. Prepare the broth. Place the flanken, beef bones, onion, carrots, celery, garlic, and herb bundle in a large pot with 3 quarts cold water. Bring the ingredients to a boil and skim off any foam that rises to the surface. Reduce the heat and simmer the broth until the meat is cooked and tender and the broth is reduced to about 2 quarts, 1½ hours. It's important to skim the broth often to remove any fat that rises to the surface.

2. Strain the broth into a large saucepan and let cool to room temperature. Refrigerate the broth until cold. The fat will congeal on the surface; skim it off with a spoon and discard. Tear the meat into shreds, discarding any visible pieces of fat or bone. Return the beef to the broth.

3. Add the sauerkraut with its juices, salt, pepper, the lemon juice, and brown sugar to the broth. Simmer for 15 minutes. Correct the seasoning, adding brown sugar, lemon juice, or salt as needed. The soup should be a little sweet, a little sour, and very highly seasoned.

Serves 8

262 CALORIES PER SERVING; 26 G PROTEIN; 9 G FAT; 4 G SATURATED FAT; 19 G CARBOHYDRATE; 843 MG SODIUM; 46 MG CHOLESTEROL

VARIATION—VEGETARIAN SAUERKRAUT SOUP

For all you vegetarians out there, which includes my cousins Martha and Andy. Now you can use real sour cream for a garnish.

PREPARATION TIME: 20 MINUTES   COOKING TIME: 1½ HOURS

2 onions, skins left on, quartered
2 carrots, cut into 1-inch pieces
2 stalks celery, cut into 1-inch pieces
2 small zucchini, cut into 1-inch pieces
2 tomatoes, cut in half
1 leek, trimmed, washed, and cut into 1-inch
   pieces
½ cabbage, cut into 1-inch wedges
1 head garlic, cut in half

10 peppercorns, 2 cloves, 1 bay leaf, and 2 sprigs
   each of thyme and parsley, all tied in
   cheesecloth

TO FINISH THE SOUP:
2 pounds sauerkraut with juices
Salt and freshly ground black pepper, to taste
2 tablespoons lemon juice, or to taste
½ cup brown sugar, or to taste
1 cup no-fat sour cream

1. Preheat the oven to 400 degrees. Arrange the vegetables on a nonstick baking sheet and roast until darkly browned, 40 to 60 minutes, turning with a spatula to ensure even browning.

2. Transfer the vegetables to a large pot and add the spice bundle and 3 quarts water. Bring to a boil, reduce the heat to medium, and simmer the vegetables to obtain a dark rich broth, about 30 minutes. Strain the broth into another pot. You should have about 2 quarts.

3. Add the sauerkraut with juices, salt, pepper, lemon juice, and brown sugar. Simmer the soup for 15 minutes. Correct the seasoning, adding brown sugar, lemon juice, or salt as needed. The soup should be a little sweet, a little sour, and very highly seasoned. Serve with dollops of sour cream in each bowl.

Serves 8

151 CALORIES PER SERVING; 5.3 G PROTEIN; .6 G FAT; .10 G SATURATED FAT; 33.5 G CARBOHYDRATE; 810 MG SODIUM; 0 MG CHOLESTEROL

❧ Sorrel Soup ❧
(Schav)

*Schav is a cold sorrel soup prized by Jews of Eastern Europe. (My grandparents would eat it several times a week in the summer.) I grew up on bottled schav because the main ingredient—a tart spinachy-looking leaf called sorrel—wasn't available in the United States. (The first time I tasted a fresh sorrel soup was at the La Varenne Cooking School in Paris.) Today, you can buy fresh sorrel at a gourmet shop or specialty greengrocer. If you can't find it, an interesting, not strictly traditional, soup can be made with spinach and lemon juice. Thick, creamy, and bracingly tart, schav makes a perfect refresher on a hot summer day. **Note:** The dill isn't strictly traditional, but I love the way it pops up the flavor.*

PREPARATION TIME: 15 MINUTES   COOKING TIME: 15 MINUTES, PLUS TIME FOR CHILLING

1 tablespoon canola oil
1 bunch of scallions, finely chopped (keep the white and green parts separate)
3 medium white potatoes (about 1 pound), peeled and cut into ¼-inch dice
12 ounces fresh sorrel or spinach, stemmed, washed, and cut into ½-inch strips

5 cups water
1¾ cups no-fat sour cream
Salt and freshly ground black pepper, to taste
1 to 2 tablespoons sugar, or to taste
1 to 2 tablespoons fresh lemon juice, or to taste
2 tablespoons chopped dill (optional)

1. Heat the oil in a large saucepan. Add the scallion whites and all but ¼ cup scallion greens (reserve the latter for garnish) and the potatoes and cook over medium heat until the vegetables are soft but not brown, 5 minutes, stirring with a wooden spoon. Stir in the sorrel and cook for 1 minute.

2. Stir in the water, 1 cup sour cream, salt, pepper, and sugar and bring to a boil. Simmer the soup until the potatoes are very soft, 8 to 10 minutes. Puree the soup in a blender. Strain the soup into a bowl and let cool to room temperature, then refrigerate until cold.

3. Just before serving, stir in the lemon juice and dill. Correct the seasoning, adding sugar, salt, or pepper to taste. The soup should be highly seasoned and tart, but also a little sweet. It should also be thick but pourable. Add a little water if needed. Transfer the remaining scallion greens and sour cream to attractive bowls. Ladle the schav into bowls, passing the scallion greens and sour cream separately for garnish.

Serves 6 to 8

117 CALORIES PER 6 SERVINGS; 2.9 G PROTEIN; 2.8 G FAT; .19 G SATURATED FAT;
21.6 G CARBOHYDRATE; 21.7 MG SODIUM; .84 MG CHOLESTEROL

Salads

❧❧◆❧❧

❧ Israeli Salad ❧

This lively salad epitomizes Israeli cooking—vividly colorful and impeccably fresh, made with vegetables so crisp you can hear yourself take a bite. I first had it at the Kibbutz Kfar Hanassi near Tiberias, where my stepson Jake spent a year after high school. Talk about fresh: the tomatoes, peppers, and cucumbers had been plucked from the garden that very morning. To get the full effect, make this salad in summer or early fall with vegetables from your garden or local farm stand.

PREPARATION TIME: 20 MINUTES

1 English or large American cucumber
1 green bell pepper
1 red bell pepper
2 stalks celery
2 luscious ripe red tomatoes
¾ cup cooked chickpeas
½ red onion, finely chopped

3 tablespoons finely chopped parsley (preferably flat-leaf)
1½ tablespoons extra-virgin olive oil
1½ tablespoons red wine vinegar
Salt and freshly ground black pepper, to taste
6 black Greek-style olives

1. Peel the cucumber, removing the skin in lengthwise strips, leaving a little green on the cucumber for color. If using an American cucumber, cut in half lengthwise and scrape out the seeds with a melon baller. Cut the cucumber into ½-inch dice.

2. Core and seed the peppers and cut into ½-inch dice. Peel the outside of the celery stalks with a vegetable peeler and cut into ½-inch dice. Cut the tomatoes into ½-inch dice, reserving the juices.

3. Combine the diced vegetables and chickpeas in an attractive serving bowl. Add the onion, parsley, oil, vinegar, salt, pepper, and reserved tomato juices, and toss to mix. Correct the seasoning, adding vinegar or salt to taste. The salad should be highly seasoned. Decorate the salad with the olives and serve at once.

Serves 6

100 CALORIES PER SERVING; 3.1 G PROTEIN; 5 G FAT; .6 G SATURATED FAT; 13 G CARBOHYDRATE; 58 MG SODIUM; 0 MG CHOLESTEROL

Five-minute sweet-and-sour cucumber salad with dill (top) and Israeli salad (bottom).

✂ Moroccan Carrot Salad ✂

Carrots have always had important symbolic significance in Judaism: the coinlike appearance of sliced carrots symbolizes money and by extension prosperity, while the Yiddish word for carrot, mehren, also means "to multiply." This unusual carrot salad would be one of the half dozen or more salads served at a Moroccan holiday feast. Orange-flower water is a perfumed flavoring found at Middle Eastern and Indian markets: add a few drops and you'll never think about carrots in quite the same way. (In a pinch, you could substitute rose water or orange liqueur, but the effect won't be quite the same.)

PREPARATION TIME: 5 MINUTES   COOKING TIME: 5 MINUTES

1 pound carrots, peeled and cut crosswise into ¼-inch rounds
2 tablespoons sugar
¼ teaspoon salt, plus ⅛ teaspoon for the final seasoning

3 tablespoons raisins
1 tablespoon lemon juice
1 teaspoon canola oil
1 teaspoon orange-flower water
½ teaspoon ground cinnamon

1. Place the carrots, 1 tablespoon sugar, and ¼ teaspoon salt in a saucepan and add water just to cover. Cook the carrots over high heat until tender, 4 to 6 minutes. Remove the pan from the heat and add the raisins. Let the mixture cool.

2. Drain the carrots and raisins and place in an attractive serving bowl. Stir in the remaining 1 tablespoon sugar, the lemon juice, oil, orange-flower water, cinnamon, and remaining ⅛ teaspoon salt. Correct the seasoning, adding any of the flavorings to taste. The salad should be sweet and perfumy.

Serves 4 to 6

65 CALORIES PER SERVING; .7 G PROTEIN; 1.7 G FAT; 0 G SATURATED FAT; 12.5 G CARBOHYDRATE; 22 MG SODIUM; 0 MG CHOLESTEROL

⚒ Moroccan Grilled Pepper and Tomato Salad ⚒

Here's another of the colorful salads served at the start of a Moroccan holiday meal. Tradition calls for the peppers to be deep-fried, but grilling delivers a delectable smoke flavor and dramatically reduces the fat.

PREPARATION TIME: 10 MINUTES   COOKING TIME: 12 MINUTES

3 green bell peppers
3 medium or 2 large ripe tomatoes
¼ cup finely chopped parsley (preferably flat-leaf)
3 tablespoons chopped fresh mint
1 clove garlic, minced
1½ tablespoons extra-virgin olive oil

1 tablespoon red wine vinegar
½ teaspoon sweet paprika
½ teaspoon ground coriander
¼ teaspoon ground cumin
Salt and freshly ground pepper, to taste

1. Preheat the grill or broiler to high. Char the peppers until the skins are black all over. (This will take 3 to 4 minutes per side, 12 to 16 minutes in all.) Alternatively, you can char the peppers by placing them directly over a gas or electric burner on the stove. Place the charred peppers in a bowl, cover with plastic wrap, and let cool. (The resulting steam will loosen the pepper skins.)

2. Meanwhile, cut the tomatoes in half widthwise and wring out the liquids and seeds. Cut the tomatoes into ½-inch dice. When the peppers are cool, scrape off the burned skins with a paring knife. Cut the peppers in half lengthwise and scrape out the seeds. Cut the peppers into ½-inch dice.

3. Combine the peppers, tomatoes, parsley, mint, garlic, olive oil, vinegar, spices, salt, and pepper in a salad bowl and toss to mix. Correct the seasoning, adding salt, vinegar, or any of the spices to taste.

Serves 6

66 CALORIES PER SERVING; 1.3 G PROTEIN; 4 G FAT; .5 G SATURATED FAT; 8.1 G CARBOHYDRATE; 9 MG SODIUM; 0 MG CHOLESTEROL

⚔ Tabouleh with Pomegranate Syrup ⚔
(Cracked Wheat Salad with Parsley and Mint)

This vibrant, nourishing salad is one of the best ways I know to beat the summer heat. That's because, although it's based on grain, it requires no cooking. The cracked wheat is soaked in water overnight to soften it and make it palatable. Tabouleh owes its explosive flavor to the addition of fresh lemon juice, flat-leaf parsley, and fresh mint, and this is probably how you've enjoyed it in North America. But Armenian and Syrian Jews sometimes add a fillip of pomegranate syrup (also known as pomegranate molasses), an exotic, sweet-sour condiment made by boiling down fresh pomegranate juice into a thick, fragrant syrup. Pomegranate syrup is available at Middle East grocery stores and via the mail order sources at the back of this book. Don't worry too much if you can't find it: your tabouleh will be perfectly tasty without it.

PREPARATION TIME: 15 MINUTES
COOKING TIME: NO COOKING, BUT SOAK THE BULGHUR AT LEAST 4 HOURS AHEAD

1 cup bulghur (cracked wheat)
4 cups cold water
1 large ripe red tomato, cut into ¼-inch dice
1 cucumber, peeled, seeded, and cut into ¼-inch dice
4 scallions, finely chopped
1 cup chopped flat-leaf parsley
½ cup chopped fresh mint leaves, plus 6 sprigs for garnish

¼ cup fresh lemon juice, or to taste
2 tablespoons extra-virgin olive oil
1 tablespoon pomegranate syrup, or to taste
Salt and plenty of freshly ground black pepper, to taste
6 romaine lettuce leaves for garnish

1. Place the bulghur in a fine-meshed strainer and rinse well under cold water. Transfer it to a large bowl and add the water. Let soak for at least 4 hours or as long as overnight in the refrigerator.

2. Drain the bulghur in a strainer, pressing firmly to extract all the water. Squeeze handfuls of bulghur between your fingers to wring out the water. Transfer the bulghur to a mixing bowl.

3. Stir in the tomato, cucumber, scallions, parsley, mint, lemon juice, olive oil, pomegranate syrup, salt, and pepper. Toss to mix. The tabouleh should be highly seasoned; add salt, lemon juice, or pomegranate syrup to taste.

4. Line 6 salad plates with lettuce leaves and mound the tabouleh on top. Garnish with mint sprigs and serve at once.

Makes about 6 cups, which will serve 6

140 CALORIES PER SERVING; 4 G PROTEIN; 5 G FAT; .7 G SATURATED FAT; 22 G CARBOHYDRATE; 15 MG SODIUM; 0 MG CHOLESTEROL

Syrian Cracked Wheat Salad
(Bazerghane)

I like to think of this Syrian wheat salad as tabouleh (opposite) that's been to finishing school. It contains an offbeat ingredient most North American Jews don't think of as Jewish: tamarind. But this tropical fruit (actually, it's the pulp of a curved seedpod) is mentioned by name in the Bible and its tart, fruity flavor (think prunes soaked in lime juice) is appreciated by Sephardic Jews from the Caribbean to Calcutta. Look for tamarind at Caribbean and Middle Eastern markets. The easiest way to buy it is as frozen tamarind puree (available at Hispanic and Caribbean markets). Instructions for making tamarind puree from tamarind pulp are found below. Bulghur (cracked wheat) comes in several grades of coarseness: you want the finest you can find.

PREPARATION TIME: 20 MINUTES   COOKING TIME: NONE, BUT ALLOW 1 HOUR FOR SOAKING

6 ounces (1 cup) fine bulghur (cracked wheat)
¼ cup tamarind puree
2½ tablespoons ketchup
1½ tablespoons olive oil
3 tablespoons grated onion
1½ tablespoons toasted pine nuts, plus 1 tablespoon for garnish
2 tablespoons chopped walnuts

½ teaspoon ground cumin
¼ teaspoon cayenne pepper (optional)
3 tablespoons chopped parsley (preferably flat-leaf), plus 6 whole parsley sprigs for garnish
Salt and freshly ground black pepper

6 Boston lettuce leaves for serving

1. Place the bulghur in a fine-meshed strainer and rinse well under cold water. Transfer it to a large bowl with cold water to cover. Agitate the water with your fingers and pour it off, leaving the bulghur in a bowl. Repeat several times, adding fresh water until the water runs clear. Add water to cover and let the bulghur soak in the refrigerator for at least 4 hours, or as long as overnight.

2. Drain the bulghur in a strainer. Wring it dry by grabbing handfuls and squeezing between your fingers.

3. Combine the tamarind puree, ketchup, and oil in a mixing bowl and whisk to mix. Stir in the bulghur, onion, 1 tablespoon pine nuts, the walnuts, cumin, cayenne if using, 3 tablespoons chopped parsley, and salt and pepper to taste. The salad should be highly seasoned. If a stronger tamarind flavor is desired, add more tamarind.

4. To serve, line 6 plates with lettuce leaves. Mound the salad on top and decorate with the parsley sprigs and remaining pine nuts. Serve at room temperature.

Serves 6

174 CALORIES PER SERVING; 5 G PROTEIN; 7 G FAT; .9 G SATURATED FAT; 25 G CARBOHYDRATE; 82 MG SODIUM; 0 MG CHOLESTEROL

⚔ Homemade Tamarind Puree ⚔

If you live in an area with a large Hispanic or West Indian community, you may be able to find frozen tamarind puree.
If not, you'll need to make it, using tamarind pulp (peeled pods with the seeds), which are sold at
ethnic markets and many supermarkets. Here's how to make tamarind puree.

PREPARATION TIME: 10 MINUTES

½ cup peeled tamarind pulp, with seeds

1¾ cups hot water

1. Break the pulp into 1-inch pieces and place in the bowl of a blender with 1 cup hot water. Let the tamarind soften for 5 minutes.

2. Run the blender in short bursts at low speed for 15 to 30 seconds to obtain a thick brown liquid. Do not overblend, or you'll break up the seeds. Pour the resulting liquid through a strainer, pressing hard with a wooden spoon to extract the juices, scraping the bottom of the strainer with a spatula.

3. Return the pulp in the strainer to the blender and add ¾ cup hot water. Blend again and pour the mixture through the strainer, pressing well to extract the juices.

Tamarind water will keep for up to 5 days in the refrigerator and can be frozen for several months. I like to freeze it in plastic ice cube trays, so I have convenient premeasured portions on hand.

Makes 1½ cups, 12 servings

🖎 Five-Minute Sweet-and-Sour Cucumber Salad with Dill 🖎

Embarrassingly easy to make, this crisp, tart, tangy salad is an Eastern European Jewish staple. It takes about 5 minutes to prepare, which makes it a perennial favorite at my house. **Note:** *When fresh dill is available, I like to use it to jazz up the salad.*

PREPARATION TIME: 5 MINUTES

1 European or 2 American cucumbers
1 small or ½ medium sweet white onion (like a Maui or Vidalia)
3 tablespoons distilled white vinegar

1 tablespoon sugar, or to taste
Salt and freshly ground black pepper, to taste
2 tablespoons chopped fresh dill (optional)

1. Wash the cucumber. Partially remove the peel in lengthwise strips, using a vegetable peeler, leaving a little skin between each strip. (This gives you pretty green stripes on the cucumber slices.) Thinly slice the cucumber widthwise. Thinly slice the onion and break into rings.

2. Place the vinegar, sugar, salt, and pepper in a bowl and whisk until the sugar is dissolved. Add the cucumber and onion and toss to mix. Stir in the dill. You can serve the salad immediately, but it will taste even better if you let it sit for 15 minutes to allow the flavors to blend.

Serves 4

38 CALORIES PER SERVING; 1 G PROTEIN; 0 G FAT; 0 G SATURATED FAT; 10 G CARBOHYDRATE; 5 MG SODIUM; 0 MG CHOLESTEROL

⚘ Cucumber Salad with Yogurt and Mint ⚘

Variations on this tangy, creamy salad are enjoyed throughout the Middle and Near East. Both Jewish and Arab Israelis
would enjoy it as part of a meze (hors d'oeuvre/salad) platter. Traditionally, you'd use drained whole-milk yogurt.
To achieve the richness of the original without the fat, I use a mixture of no-fat yogurt and no-fat sour cream.

PREPARATION TIME: 10 MINUTES

2 large cucumbers
2 cloves garlic, finely chopped
½ teaspoon salt, or to taste
1 cup no-fat yogurt

1 cup no-fat sour cream
½ cup chopped fresh spearmint
Freshly ground black pepper, to taste
1 tablespoon extra-virgin olive oil

1. Peel the cucumber, removing the skin in lengthwise strips with a vegetable peeler, leaving a little green on the cucumber for color. Cut it in half lengthwise and scrape out the seeds with a melon baller. Cut the cucumber into ½-inch dice.

2. Place the garlic and salt in the bottom of an attractive serving bowl and mash to a paste with the back of a wooden spoon. Stir in the yogurt, sour cream, cucumbers, mint, and pepper. Correct the seasoning, adding salt to taste. The salad should be highly seasoned. Drizzle the salad with the olive oil and serve at once with wedges of pita bread for scooping.

Serves 4 to 6

147 CALORIES PER 4 SERVINGS; 10 G PROTEIN; 5 G FAT; 0 G SATURATED FAT; 16 G CARBOHYDRATE; 107 MG SODIUM; 12 MG CHOLESTEROL

⚙ Green Onion Salad ⚙

Here's another salad you might find on an Israeli meze platter. No, you don't need to worry about onion breath:
parsley and sumac are natural breath fresheners, counterbalancing the pungency of the green onions.
Sumac is a tart purple seasoning made from a Middle East berry. Look for it in Middle East markets.

PREPARATION TIME: 10 MINUTES

1 clove garlic, finely chopped
½ teaspoon salt
3 tablespoons fresh lemon juice, or to taste
1 bunch of green onions or 2 bunches of scallions, trimmed and thinly sliced

1 bunch flat-leaf parsley, stemmed and coarsely chopped
Freshly ground black pepper, to taste
1 tablespoon extra-virgin olive oil
1½ teaspoons ground sumac (optional)

1. Place the garlic and salt in the bottom of an attractive serving bowl and mash to a smooth paste. Stir in the lemon juice, green onions, parsley, and pepper. Correct the seasoning, adding salt and/or lemon juice to taste.

2. Drizzle the salad with olive oil and sprinkle with sumac. Serve with wedges of pita bread for scooping.

Serves 4 to 6

82 CALORIES PER 4 SERVINGS; 1 G PROTEIN; 7 G FAT; 0 G SATURATED FAT; 6 G CARBOHYDRATE; 10 MG SODIUM; 0 MG CHOLESTEROL

⚡ Hannah's Two-"Egg" Salad ⚡
(Hatsulina—Eggplant Egg Salad)

*Here's an egg salad that's mercifully low in fat and cholesterol. The secret? Hannah Kuperstock replaces most of the eggs with roasted eggplant. Born in Kozienice, Poland, Hannah is a wonderful cook who learned to make this salad in Israel, where she emigrated after World War II. The salad reflects the culinary fusion that took place in Israel after the war: hard-boiled eggs and egg salad are Ashkenazi fare, while roasted eggplant is strictly Israeli. Put them together and you get an egg salad that's long on flavor but light on fat. **Note:** I like a more pronounced smoke flavor, so I grill the eggplant. For a milder flavor, roast the eggplant in a 400-degree oven until soft, 40 to 60 minutes.*

PREPARATION TIME: 10 MINUTES   COOKING TIME: 20 TO 30 MINUTES

2 long, slender eggplants (1½ pounds)
4 eggs
¼ cup chopped sweet onion, or to taste
3 tablespoons chopped fresh parsley (preferably flat-leaf), plus 1 tablespoon for garnish

1 scallion, finely chopped
1½ tablespoons mayonnaise
½ teaspoon Dijon-style mustard
Salt and freshly ground black pepper

1. Preheat the grill or broiler to high. Prick the eggplants in 6 or 8 places with a fork. Grill or broil the eggplants until the skin is charred and the flesh is very soft, 20 to 30 minutes, turning with tongs. Transfer the eggplants to a plate and let cool. Scrape off the skin. Coarsely chop the eggplant flesh and transfer to a mixing bowl. Alternatively, roast the eggplants in the oven as described above.

2. Meanwhile, place the eggs in a pot with cold water to cover. Gradually bring to a boil. Simmer the eggs for 11 minutes. Rinse under cold water until cool enough to handle, then shell the eggs and cut in half. Remove and discard the yolks. Chop the whites and add them to the eggplant.

3. Stir in the onion, 3 tablespoons parsley, scallion, mayonnaise, mustard, and salt and pepper to taste. Mash the ingredients into a coarse puree with a fork or coarsely puree in the food processor. Transfer the salad to a serving dish and sprinkle with the remaining parsley. Serve with wedges of pita or slices of pumpernickel. Or serve in lettuce cups.

Makes 2¼ cups, which will serve 6 as an appetizer

108 CALORIES PER SERVING; 5.5 G PROTEIN; 6.3 G FAT; 1.4 G SATURATED FAT; 8.2 G CARBOHYDRATE; 68 MG SODIUM; 142 MG CHOLESTEROL

⚔ Barbara's Sour Cream Salad ⚔

In my wife's family, this colorful salad is always served at a Yom Kippur break-fast. You can serve it with wedges of fresh pita bread or chunks of challah. The dill isn't strictly traditional, but I like the way it pumps up the flavor.

PREPARATION TIME: 10 MINUTES

8 large red radishes, trimmed and washed
1 cucumber, peeled and seeded
1 tomato, seeded and chopped
4 scallions, finely chopped

2 tablespoons chopped fresh dill (optional)
1 cup no- or low-fat sour cream
Salt and freshly ground black pepper

1. Cut the radishes, cucumber, and tomato into ½-inch dice. Transfer them to an attractive bowl and stir in the scallions, dill (if using), and sour cream. Add salt and pepper to taste.

Serves 6

57 CALORIES PER SERVING; 3.1 G PROTEIN; .14 G FAT; .014 G SATURATED FAT; 10 G CARBOHYDRATE; 39 MG SODIUM; 0 MG CHOLESTEROL

Breads

❧❧❀❧❧

❧ Janice and Michael's Honey-Vanilla Challah ❧

This golden bread, rich with eggs and sweet with honey, is one of the glories of Jewish baking. Sabbath dinner—indeed, any holiday except Passover—would seem downright impoverished without it. The following recipe comes from a family dear to my heart—the Freemans, Hasidic Jews who lived next door to my grandparents. Although they had four young children to care for, Janice and Michael looked after my grandparents in health and sickness. They were always there with a kind word, a helping hand, or a loaf of challah, and when my grandparents passed away, Michael's prayers sped them on to heaven. This book wouldn't be complete without a recipe from them. Janice's challah owes its inviting sweetness to honey and one unexpected ingredient: vanilla extract. Janice forms her challah from six braids, which has symbolic significance in the Kabbalah. You can certainly use the traditional three braids. By the way, this recipe works great in a bread machine.

PREPARATION TIME: 30 MINUTES, PLUS 2 TO 2½ HOURS FOR RISING   COOKING TIME: 40 MINUTES

1 package dry yeast
2 tablespoons sugar
1 cup warm water
2 eggs, lightly beaten
¼ cup honey
¼ cup vegetable oil, plus oil for the bowl

2 teaspoons vanilla extract
2 teaspoons salt
4 to 4½ cups unbleached all-purpose flour
2 tablespoons egg substitute or 1 egg white, lightly beaten with a fork
1 tablespoon poppy seeds

1. Place the yeast and sugar in a small bowl and add ¼ cup warm water. Stir to mix and let sit until the mixture becomes foamy, about 10 minutes.

2. *To make the dough by hand*, place the yeast mixture, remaining water, eggs, honey, oil, and vanilla in a large, heavy mixing bowl. Stir in the salt and 4 cups flour with a wooden spoon to obtain a dough stiff enough to come away from the sides of the mixing bowl. Turn the mixture onto a work surface and knead until pliable and smooth, about 10 minutes. Add flour as needed; the dough should be soft but not sticky.

To make the dough in a mixer, place the yeast mixture, remaining water, eggs, honey, oil, and vanilla in the mixing bowl. Using the dough hook, work in the salt and 4 cups flour, mixing at low speed to obtain a smooth, pliable dough that comes away from the sides

of the mixing bowl. Add flour as needed; the dough should be soft but not sticky. You'll need about 10 minutes of mixing.

To make the dough in a food processor, place the salt and 4 cups flour in the bowl of a food processor fitted with a dough blade. With the machine running, add the yeast mixture, remaining water, eggs, honey, oil, and vanilla. Process until the dough comes together into a smooth ball, 1 to 2 minutes. (If the dough is too wet, add more flour.) Knead the dough in the processor until smooth and springy, 3 to 4 minutes, running the machine in spurts. Turn the dough onto a floured surface and knead it a little by hand.

3. Transfer the dough to a large, clean, lightly oiled bowl and cover with plastic wrap. Let rise in a warm, draft-free spot until doubled in bulk, 1 to 2 hours.

Janice and Michael's honey-vanilla challah.

4. Punch down the dough and cut it into 3 or 6 even pieces. Roll each into a 14-inch rope. Arrange the ropes in front of you so that they join at the end away from you and spread out like the fingers of your hand toward you. Braid the ropes into a loaf.

5. Transfer the loaf to a baking sheet and cover with a clean dishcloth. Let rise until soft and puffy, 30 to 60 minutes.

6. Meanwhile, preheat the oven to 350 degrees.

7. Brush the challah with egg substitute and sprinkle with poppy seeds. Place on the middle rack of the oven and bake until a deep golden brown, 30 to 40 minutes. When done, the loaf will sound hollow when tapped.

8. Transfer the challah to a cake rack to cool and cut into slices or tear into chunks for serving.

Makes 1 12-inch extremely beautiful loaf,
which will serve 8 to 10

292 CALORIES PER 8 SERVINGS; 7.3 G PROTEIN; 7.4 G FAT; 1 G SATURATED FAT; 48 G CARBOHYDRATE; 485 MG SODIUM; 42 MG CHOLESTEROL

🔀 Pita Bread 🔀

These soft, flat, puffy breads are the staff of life in Israel, and while it's easy to find commercial pita bread in the United States, it's fun to make your own. This recipe comes from my stepson, Jake Klein, who learned to make it on the Kibbutz Kfar Hanassi in Rosh Pina near the Golan Heights. **Note:** *Sometimes I like to overbake the pita until they become golden brown and crackling crisp. Break them into shards and enjoy them as you would potato chips.*

PREPARATION TIME: 30 MINUTES, PLUS 1 HOUR FOR RISING   COOKING TIME: 10 MINUTES

1 package dry yeast
3½ cups flour, or as needed
1¼ cups warm water

2 tablespoons olive oil
Scant 2 teaspoons salt
¼ teaspoon sugar

1. Combine the yeast and 1½ cups flour in the bowl of a mixer. Mix in the water, oil, salt, and sugar. Mix on low speed for 3 minutes, then on high speed for 3 minutes. Turn off the mixer.

2. Add the remaining flour and mix at medium-low speed until the dough is smooth and comes away from the sides of the bowl. This will take 6 to 8 minutes. (If the dough is too sticky to come away from the sides of the bowl, add a little more flour.) Cover the dough with plastic wrap and let rise until doubled in bulk, 45 minutes to 1 hour.

3. Preheat the oven to 400 degrees.

4. Punch the dough down and cut it into 12 even pieces. Roll each into a ball. Cover the dough balls with plastic wrap and let rest for 10 minutes.

5. Flatten each ball into a disk, using the palm of your hand, then roll it out into a 5-inch circle, using a rolling pin. Use flour as needed, but as little as possible to keep the dough from sticking. Transfer the pita breads to baking sheets, 6 to a sheet.

6. Bake the pita breads until puffed and lightly browned, about 10 minutes. Remove from the oven and serve at once.

Makes 12, which will serve 6

155 CALORIES PER PITA; 4 G PROTEIN; 3 G FAT; .4 G SATURATED FAT; 28 G CARBOHYDRATE; 388 MG SODIUM; 0 MG CHOLESTEROL

✂ Zibulnikas ✂
(Cottage Cheese Buns with Green Onions)

My grandfather Samuel "Dear" Raichlen was an inveterate raconteur and nothing delighted him more than telling about growing up in an immigrant household. His eyes would glow when he spoke of his mother's cooking: her sauerkraut soup (page 31), her ptscha (braised calves' trotters), and chocolate roll (page 168). But no dish was as beloved as zibulnikas, flaky buns stuffed with cottage cheese, sour cream, and green onions. "You could smell them down the block," he recalled nostalgically as he explained how Grandma Raichlen would put a pat of butter on top of each bun before baking. As it turns out, zibulnikas are relatively easy to make. Using the new no-fat dairy products, you can dramatically slash the fat.

PREPARATION TIME: 40 MINUTES   COOKING TIME: 30 MINUTES

2 cups no- or low-fat small curd cottage cheese

FOR THE DOUGH:
1 package dry yeast
1 teaspoon sugar
1 cup warm water
3½ cups flour, plus flour for rolling out
1½ teaspoons salt
2 tablespoons oil, plus oil for the bowl
1 egg, lightly beaten

TO FINISH THE FILLING:
½ cup no-fat sour cream
¼ cup egg substitute or 2 egg whites, lightly beaten
1 bunch of scallions, trimmed and finely chopped
Freshly ground black pepper
Salt

Spray oil
2 tablespoons egg substitute or 1 egg white beaten with a pinch of salt, for glaze
1 tablespoon butter

1. The night before, or at least 4 hours ahead of time, place the cottage cheese in a strainer lined with a paper towel or cheesecloth over a bowl in the refrigerator. Drain for at least 4 hours or as long as overnight.

2. Combine the yeast, sugar, and ¼ cup water in a small bowl and stir to mix. Let stand until the mixture is foamy, 10 minutes.

3. Place the flour and salt in a food processor fitted with a dough blade. Add the yeast mixture, remaining ¾ cup water, the oil, and egg. Process in short bursts to obtain a dough that is soft and pliable but not sticky, 3 to 4 minutes. (Add flour as needed.) Turn the dough onto a clean work surface and knead a few minutes by hand.

4. Transfer the dough to a lightly oiled bowl and cover with plastic wrap. Let the dough rise in a warm spot until doubled in bulk, 1 to 2 hours.

5. Meanwhile, prepare the filling. Combine the drained cottage cheese, sour cream, egg substitute, scallions, and pepper in a mixing bowl and stir to mix. Correct the seasoning, adding salt and pepper to taste. The mixture should be highly seasoned.

6. Punch down the dough and divide it into 12 pieces. Roll each into a ball, cover with plastic wrap, and let rest for 5 minutes. Flatten each ball with the palm of your hand, then, using a rolling pin, roll it into a 6-inch circle. Place 3 tablespoons cheese mixture in the center. Lightly brush the edges of the dough with water and gather them together in pleats to form what looks like a beggar's purse or old-fashioned money bag. Pinch or twist the top to seal in

the filling. Arrange the rolls on a nonstick baking sheet lightly sprayed with oil. Loosely cover the rolls with plastic wrap and let rise until soft and puffy, about 30 minutes.

7. Preheat the oven to 350 degrees.

8. Brush the zibulnikas with egg glaze. Place a little piece of butter on top of each. Bake the zibulnikas un-til puffed and golden brown, about 30 minutes. Let cool for at least 10 minutes before serving. Have nap-kins on hand when you take a bite: the filling is very juicy.

Makes 12 4-inch zibulnikas,
which will serve 12 as a side dish or 6 as a snack

219 CALORIES PER ZIBULNIKA; 11 G PROTEIN; 4.3 G FAT; 1.1 G SATURATED FAT; 32 G CARBOHYDRATE; 457 MG SODIUM; 20 MG CHOLESTEROL

Passover Rolls

This recipe is dedicated to my uncle Ted, who may well be the kindest, gentlest man on the planet. Although pushing ninety, he visits his sister, my Grammie Sarah, daily and still does volunteer work at nursing homes several times a week. When he learned I was writing a Jewish cookbook, he offered to find the recipe for Passover rolls he used to enjoy at the home of a former neighbor, Mrs. Marion Schenker of Baltimore. Sure enough, a week later, a letter came in Uncle Ted's shaky handwriting with Mrs. Schenker's recipe. The very notion of Passover "rolls" is a paradox, seeing how flour and leavening agents are forbidden during this holiday. These rolls are actually a sort of cream puff that take their leavening power from eggs. To trim the fat in the traditional recipe, I've reduced the oil and replaced most of the whole eggs with egg whites. You still get light, crusty, drop-dead beautiful rolls that are a pleasure at the Passover table.

PREPARATION TIME: 10 MINUTES   COOKING TIME: 1 HOUR

1 cup water
⅓ cup canola oil
1 teaspoon sugar

1 scant teaspoon salt
1½ to 2 cups matzo meal
1 egg plus 8 egg whites or 1 cup egg substitute

1. Preheat the oven to 375 degrees.
2. Combine the water, oil, sugar, and salt in a saucepan and bring to a boil. Remove the pan from the heat and stir in the matzo meal, using a wooden spoon.
3. Stir in the egg, then the whites, two by two. (If using egg substitute, add it in four batches.) Beat until the mixture is smooth before adding more egg.

4. Using two spoons, form the dough into 2-inch balls and arrange them on a lightly greased baking sheet with 3 inches between each. Using a fork dipped in water, smooth the tops of the rolls.
5. Bake the rolls until puffed and golden brown, 40 to 50 minutes. Do not open the oven door during baking. Serve at once.

Makes 12 rolls

152 CALORIES PER ROLL; 4.4 G PROTEIN; 6.5 G FAT; .55 G SATURATED FAT; 19 G CARBOHYDRATE; 228.8 MG SODIUM; 17.7 MG CHOLESTEROL

✄ Onion Rolls ✄

They fill the bread baskets of Jewish-style restaurants from Brooklyn to Miami. Some are consumed on the spot; the remainder leave the restaurant in a doggie bag—to be enjoyed the following day for lunch. They're soft, chewy, Jewish-style onion rolls and no "early bird" dining experience would be quite complete without them. Here are two versions on a theme of onion roll—one from North America and the other from Central Asia.

PREPARATION TIME: 30 MINUTES, PLUS 1½ HOURS FOR RISING   COOKING TIME: 20 MINUTES

1 package dry yeast
1 teaspoon sugar
1½ cups warm water
4 cups flour, or as needed
2 teaspoons salt
2 tablespoons melted butter or vegetable oil, plus a

little oil for the dough bowl
½ cup dried onion flakes
¼ cup poppy seeds
Spray oil for the baking sheet
¼ cup egg substitute or 2 egg whites, lightly beaten with a fork, for glaze

1. Combine the yeast, sugar, and ¼ cup warm water in a small bowl and stir to mix. Let stand until the mixture is foamy, 10 minutes.

2. Place the flour and salt in a food processor fitted with a dough blade. Add the yeast mixture and remaining 1¼ cups water. Process in short bursts for 2 to 4 minutes to obtain a dough that is soft and pliable but not sticky. (Add flour as needed.)

3. Transfer the dough to a lightly oiled bowl and cover with plastic wrap. Let the dough rise in a warm spot until doubled in bulk, about 1 hour.

4. Punch down the dough and roll it into a large (14 by 8-inch) rectangle. Arrange the rectangle so that one long end is facing you. Brush the top with the melted butter or oil and sprinkle with half the dried

onion flakes and poppy seeds. Starting with the long end, roll up the dough into a tight cylinder. Using a sharp knife, cut the cylinder widthwise into 24 slices.

5. Mold each slice into a ball with your hands. Arrange the balls on a lightly oiled nonstick baking sheet, gently flattening each with the palm of your hand. Cover the rolls with a sheet of plastic wrap. Let rise until doubled in bulk, 30 to 45 minutes.

6. Meanwhile, preheat the oven to 350 degrees.

7. Brush the tops of the rolls with egg glaze and sprinkle with the remaining onion flakes and poppy seeds. Bake the rolls until golden brown and cooked through, 15 to 20 minutes. Transfer to a cake rack to cool. Serve the rolls warm or at room temperature.

Makes 24 rolls

100 CALORIES PER ROLL; 3 G PROTEIN; 2 G FAT; .75 G SATURATED FAT; 17 G CARBOHYDRATE; 474 MG SODIUM; 3 MG CHOLESTEROL

✄ Bukharan Steamed Buns with Cilantro and Chives ✄

North American Jews have long had a special fondness for Chinese food. (After all, who else fills all those Chinese restaurants on Christmas Day and Easter?) I was intrigued to learn of another Judeo-Chinese food relationship: that of the Jews of Bukhara in Central Asia. According to Rabbi Gil Marks, author of The World of Jewish Cooking *(Simon & Schuster, 1996), yutangza are herb-flavored buns beloved by Bukharan Jews and steamed in the style of the Chinese. I've taken a few liberties with Marks's recipe, but I think you'll find these buns as tasty as they are offbeat.* **Note:** *When making buns for a meat meal, substitute water for the milk and use oil, not butter.*

PREPARATION TIME: 30 MINUTES, PLUS 1½ HOURS FOR RISING   COOKING TIME: 30 TO 45 MINUTES

FOR THE DOUGH:
1 package dry yeast
1 teaspoon sugar
¾ cup warm water
4 cups flour, or as needed
2 teaspoons salt
1 teaspoon baking powder
¾ cup warm skim milk
1 teaspoon Asian sesame oil or vegetable oil, plus a little oil for the dough bowl

TO FINISH THE BUNS:
1½ tablespoons sesame oil, vegetable oil, or melted butter
½ cup chopped fresh cilantro
¼ cup chopped chives or scallion greens
24 3-inch-square pieces of parchment paper

1. Combine the yeast, sugar, and ¼ cup warm water in a small bowl and stir to mix. Let stand until the mixture is foamy, 10 minutes.

2. Place the flour, salt, and baking powder in a food processor fitted with a dough blade. Add the yeast mixture, milk, sesame oil, and remaining ½ cup water. Process in short bursts for 2 to 4 minutes to obtain a dough that is soft and pliable but not sticky. (Add flour as needed.)

3. Transfer the dough to a lightly oiled bowl and cover with plastic wrap. Let the dough rise in a warm spot until doubled in bulk, about 1 hour.

4. Punch down the dough and roll it into a large (14 by 8-inch) rectangle. Arrange the rectangle so that one long end is facing you. Brush the top with the oil and sprinkle with the cilantro and chives. Starting with the long end, roll up the dough into a tight cylinder. Using a sharp knife, cut the cylinder widthwise into 24 slices.

5. Mold each slice into a flat ball with your hands. Arrange the balls on the squares of parchment paper, 1 ball per square. Cover the buns with a sheet of plastic wrap. Let rise until doubled in bulk, 30 minutes.

6. Place 4 cups of water in a wok and set a bamboo steamer on top. Bring the water to a boil. Place the rolls in the steamer, tightly covered, and steam until puffed and cooked through, 15 to 20 minutes. Steam the rolls in several batches if needed. Serve the buns warm. Warn your guests not to eat the paper.

Makes 24 buns, which will serve 8 to 12

90 CALORIES PER BUN; 2.5 G PROTEIN; 1.2 G FAT; .19 G SATURATED FAT; 17 G CARBOHYDRATE; 199 MG SODIUM; .14 MG CHOLESTEROL

⚥ Matzo "Muffins" ⚥

The following "muffins" resulted from an attempt to make a matzo meal popover. I never was able to get the puffs to soar to popover grandure, but I did create a highly tasty breakfast pastry with the steamy lightness of a hot muffin.

PREPARATION TIME: 5 MINUTES   COOKING TIME: 20 MINUTES

Spray oil
1 cup skim milk
½ teaspoon sugar
½ teaspoon salt, or to taste

1 egg plus 2 egg whites, or ½ cup egg substitute
1 tablespoon canola oil
¾ cup matzo meal

1. Preheat the oven to 400 degrees. Spray a muffin tin or popover mold (preferably nonstick) with spray oil.

2. In a mixing bowl, combine the milk, sugar, salt, egg substitute, and oil and whisk to mix. Whisk in the matzo meal. (Or combine the ingredients in the blender.) Pour the mixture into the muffin tins, filling each about halfway.

3. Bake the muffins until puffed and golden brown, 20 to 30 minutes. Unmold and serve at once. My wife likes to eat these with jelly.

Makes 8 puffs, which will serve 4

171 CALORIES PER SERVING; 8.2 G PROTEIN; 5 G FAT; .5 G SATURATED FAT; 24 G CARBOHYDRATE; 380 MG SODIUM; 1.4 MG CHOLESTEROL

Egg and Matzo Dishes

❧❧❀❧❧

❧ Lox, Eggs, and Onions ❧

My grandfather didn't do much cooking (how many men of his generation did?), but he dearly loved food and his eyes would glow with pleasure when he described the dishes he grew up on. He did have a small repertory of specialties, and when he decided to make one, it was a great thrill for his grandchildren. He excelled at making breakfast. (I suspect that this was the only time my grandmother would let him into the kitchen, so she'd have all day to clean up the mess.) One of his masterpieces was lox, eggs, and onions. He'd make it with lox "wings," the tough but flavorful fins of the salmon that he ate as a child, probably because they were inexpensive. Over time, he'd convinced us all that lox wings had the best flavor. Lox wings are hard to find these days and are rather fatty, so I've recrafted the recipe, using the kippered salmon on page 79. (Alternatively, you can buy ready-made kippered salmon at a deli.) To trim the fat in the recipe, I've replaced most of the eggs with egg substitute: if your fat budget allows, include 1 whole egg for richness. But even with no egg yolks, this dish fairly explodes with flavor.

PREPARATION TIME: 5 MINUTES   COOKING TIME: 20 MINUTES

1 tablespoon canola oil
1 medium white onion, finely chopped
4 ounces kippered salmon
1¼ cups (10 ounces) egg substitute or 10 egg whites

1 large egg, lightly beaten with a fork, or ¼ cup additional egg substitute
Salt and freshly ground black pepper
2 tablespoons finely chopped chives or scallion greens

1. Heat the oil in a large nonstick frying pan. Add the onion and cook until caramelized (a rich golden brown), stirring often with a wooden spoon. Start the onions on a medium-high heat and reduce the flame to medium, then to low, as the onions brown. The caramelization process will take 8 to 12 minutes. Don't let the onions burn.

2. Pick through the salmon, feeling for and removing any skin or bones. Crumble the salmon into the onions. Stir in the egg substitute, egg, and salt and pepper to taste. (You won't need much salt, as the salmon is quite salty. On the other hand, this is a dish that cries for lots of black pepper.) Cook the eggs over medium heat until scrambled (I like them fairly wet), 2 minutes, stirring and scraping with a wooden spoon. Transfer the eggs to plates or a platter. Sprinkle with chives and serve at once.

Serves 4

184 CALORIES PER SERVING; 20 G PROTEIN; 9.5 G FAT; 2 G SATURATED FAT; 4.3 G CARBOHYDRATE; 279 MG SODIUM; 73 MG CHOLESTEROL

Fritada.

⚱ Chopped Eggs and Onions ⚱

This tangy egg spread has been part of my wife's family's Yom Kippur break-fast tradition as long as anyone can remember. Barbara uses mayonnaise to bind and flavor the mixture. To slash the fat, I discard three of the hard-cooked egg yolks and substitute no-fat sour cream for the mayonnaise. But there's no lack of flavor, thanks to a blast of sweet white onion and fresh dill. We often add chopped tomato for color and succulence. Here, then, are chopped eggs and onions that are as good for you as they taste.

PREPARATION TIME: 5 MINUTES   COOKING TIME: 15 MINUTES

4 large eggs
1 baking potato, peeled and cut into ½-inch dice
Salt
¼ cup diced sweet white onion
3 tablespoons no-fat sour cream
1 teaspoon Dijon-style mustard
2 tablespoons chopped fresh dill

1 scallion, finely chopped
1 large tomato, peeled, seeded, and diced
  (see below)
Freshly ground black pepper

Lettuce leaves for serving (optional)

1. Place the eggs in a pot with cold water to cover. Gradually bring to a boil. Reduce the heat slightly and simmer the eggs for exactly 11 minutes. Transfer the eggs to a colander and rinse with cold water. When cool enough to handle, shell the eggs. Cut the eggs in half and discard 3 of the yolks. Cut each half egg white in half again.

2. Meanwhile, place the potato in a pot with ½ teaspoon salt and cold water to cover. Gradually bring to a boil. Reduce the heat to a simmer and cook the potato until soft, 8 to 10 minutes. Drain in a colander and let cool.

3. Place the eggs, potato, and onion in a food processor fitted with a metal blade. Run the machine in short bursts to chop the mixture. Do not puree too much, or the mixture will become a gummy mess. (You can also chop the eggs and onions by hand.) Transfer the mixture to a mixing bowl and stir in the sour cream, mustard, dill, scallion, tomato, and salt and pepper to taste.

4. Transfer the mixture to plates or a platter (we like to mound it on lettuce leaves, using an ice cream scoop to obtain an attractive shape). Serve with crackers, melba toast, toast points, or sliced challah.

Serves 4 to 6

130 CALORIES PER 4 SERVINGS; 8.1 G PROTEIN; 5.2 G FAT; 1.5 G SATURATED FAT; 12 G CARBOHYDRATE; 85 MG SODIUM; 212 MG CHOLESTEROL

TO PEEL AND SEED A TOMATO

To peel a tomato, bring 1 to 2 quarts water to a boil in a saucepan. Using the tip of a paring knife, cut a shallow X in the rounded end opposite the stem. Boil the tomato until the skin is loose, 15 to 30 seconds. (The riper the tomato, the shorter the cooking time required.)

Let the tomato cool on a plate until you can handle it comfortably, then pull off the skin with your fingers. It should slip off in broad strips. Cut out the stem end with a paring knife.

To seed the tomato, cut it in half widthwise and squeeze each half in the palm of your hand, cut side down, to wring out the seeds and liquid. If you like, reserve the tomato liquid for broth.

⚔ Sephardic Scrambled Eggs ⚔

I like to think of this dish as Sephardic huevos rancheros. Variations on the recipe are found throughout the Sephardic world, with each community adding its signature flavorings. Thus, the Tunisian version (called chakchouka) would feature cumin, cayenne, and green bell peppers; the Syrian version, fresh mint and parsley; the Macedonian version, marjoram, rosemary, and hot paprika. Here's the Salonikan version, called strapatsata in Ladino. **Note:** *If your fat budget allows it, use 2 whole eggs, plus the whites. The scramble will taste richer.*

PREPARATION TIME: 10 MINUTES   COOKING TIME: 10 MINUTES

1 tablespoon extra-virgin olive oil
1 white onion, thinly sliced
1 green bell pepper, finely chopped
3 cloves garlic
2 scallions, finely chopped (reserve a little of the green for garnish)
1 teaspoon sweet or hot paprika

½ teaspoon ground cumin
3 tomatoes, seeded and finely chopped
3 tablespoons chopped fresh parsley
Salt and freshly ground black pepper
2 whole eggs plus 8 egg whites or 1½ cups egg substitute

1. Heat the oil in a large nonstick frying pan. Add the onion, pepper, garlic, and scallions and cook over medium heat until the vegetables are lightly browned and soft, 5 minutes, stirring with a wooden spoon. Lower the heat if the vegetables start to burn. Add the paprika and cumin and cook for 1 minute.

2. Stir in the tomatoes and parsley and increase the heat to high. Cook until the tomatoes have disintegrated into a thick sauce and most of the tomato liquid has evaporated. Add salt and pepper to taste. Reduce the heat to medium.

3. Lightly beat the eggs and egg whites and stir into the tomato mixture. Cook until scrambled (the eggs should remain quite loose), 1 to 2 minutes. If using egg substitute, you'll need to be especially careful, lest the scramble overcooks and becomes watery. Correct the seasoning, adding salt or paprika to taste. The scramble should be highly seasoned. Sprinkle with the reserved scallion greens and serve at once, with crusty bread for mopping up the eggs.

Serves 4

155 CALORIES PER SERVING; 12 G PROTEIN; 6.4 G FAT; 1.3 G SATURATED FAT; 13 G CARBOHYDRATE; 155 MG SODIUM; 106 MG CHOLESTEROL

⚔ Fritada ⚔
(Sephardic Pepper and Cheese Frittata)

Turkey generally has treated Jews well, which is not something you can say about many of the countries in the world. When Spain expelled its Jews in 1492 at the height of the Inquisition, Sultan Bayazid II of Turkey welcomed the outcasts. His gesture may have been humanitarian, but it brought to the Ottoman Empire a highly educated and motivated class of scientists, physicians, and merchants. Turkey would become and remain the preeminent power of the Near East for another four hundred years. In 1992, Turkey acknowledged the Jewish contribution to its culture on the five hundredth anniversary of the Spanish expulsion. All of which is a lengthy prologue to this popular Sephardic egg dish that's bursting with the bold Turkish flavors of garlic, peppers, tomatoes, and tangy feta cheese. Moreover, it's quick and easy to prepare, which makes it a perfect centerpiece for an impromptu brunch.

PREPARATION TIME: 20 MINUTES   COOKING TIME: 10 TO 15 MINUTES

2 tomatoes, seeded and finely chopped
1 red or green bell pepper, finely chopped
1 bunch of scallions, finely chopped
2 cloves garlic, minced
1 teaspoon hot paprika
¼ cup chopped fresh parsley

Salt and freshly ground black pepper
2 whole eggs plus 6 egg whites or 1¼ cups egg substitute
1 to 2 ounces crumbled or grated feta cheese (4 to 6 tablespoons)
1 tablespoon extra-virgin olive oil

1. Preheat the broiler.

2. Combine the tomatoes, pepper, scallions, garlic, paprika, and parsley in a large nonstick frying pan. Cook over medium heat until the vegetables are soft and most of the tomato juices have evaporated, 5 to 8 minutes. Add salt and pepper to taste.

3. In a large mixing bowl, beat the eggs and egg whites to mix. Beat in the cheese and vegetable mixture. Add salt and pepper to taste. The mixture should be highly seasoned.

4. Wipe out the frying pan with a paper towel. Add the oil and heat over a medium flame. Add the egg mixture and cook over medium heat until the mixture is set on the bottom, about 2 minutes.

5. Place the fritada under the broiler and continue cooking until set and the top is lightly browned, 2 to 4 minutes. Let the fritada cool for a couple of minutes.

Using a spatula or thin, flexible knife, loosen the fritada from the sides of the pan. Invert it onto a round platter. Cut fritada into wedges for serving. It can be served either hot or at room temperature.

Serves 4 for brunch

145 CALORIES PER SERVING; 11 G PROTEIN; 8 G FAT; 2.3 G SATURATED FAT; 9 G CARBOHYDRATE; 204 MG SODIUM; 112 MG CHOLESTEROL

🖂 Matzo Brei 🖂

It's silly, really. I could make fried matzo any time of the year. But I always wait until Passover; then I eat it once, often twice, a day. Fried matzo is the Passover equivalent of French toast and there are almost as many versions as there are cooks to make it. My grandfather, for example, would soak his matzo in hot water, making fried matzo that was soft and fluffy like a pancake. My mother went in for a crispier consistency, hardly wetting her matzo at all, so it remained hard and crunchy. (This is the style I prefer.) If you don't have real or mock schmaltz, use olive oil, adding 3 tablespoons minced onion.

PREPARATION TIME: 10 MINUTES   COOKING TIME: 6 MINUTES

5 pieces matzo
2 eggs and 6 egg whites (or ¾ cup egg substitute)
   or 1 cup egg substitute
Salt and freshly ground black pepper

1 tablespoon schmaltz (page 192), mock schmaltz
   (page 193), or olive oil
3 tablespoons finely chopped onion (optional)

1. *To make crisp fried matzo,* hold each sheet of matzo under warm running water for 10 seconds per side. Shake off the excess water and break the matzo into 2-inch pieces in a mixing bowl.

To make soft fried matzo, break the matzo into 1-inch pieces in a colander. Pour boiling or very hot water over them until soft. Let stand for 5 minutes. Transfer the matzo to a mixing bowl.

2. Stir in the eggs and egg whites (or egg substitute) and salt and pepper to taste. The mixture should be highly seasoned.

3. Heat the schmaltz or oil in a large nonstick frying pan. If using oil, add the onions and cook over medium heat for 30 seconds. Add the matzo mixture and pan-fry until golden brown on the bottom, 2 to 3 minutes. Flip the matzo brei by giving the pan a deft flick of the wrist. Or, to play it safe, place a plate over the pan, invert the matzo brei onto it, then slide it back into the pan. Continue cooking until the bottom is brown and the matzo brei is cooked through, another 2 to 3 minutes. Slide the matzo brei onto a platter, cut into wedges, and serve.

Serves 4

231 CALORIES PER SERVING; 12 G PROTEIN; 6 G FAT; 2 G SATURATED FAT; 30 G CARBOHYDRATE; 114 MG SODIUM; 108 MG CHOLESTEROL

VARIATION—SELDIN FAMILY MATZO SCRAMBLE

Matzo scramble was a popular dish in my wife's family, where cream cheese and green onions were added for extra richness. Use mock schmaltz or oil, not real schmaltz, on account of the cream cheese.

PREPARATION TIME: 10 MINUTES   COOKING TIME: 4 MINUTES

5 pieces matzo
4 ounces low- or no-fat cream cheese, cut into ½-inch dice
½ cup finély chopped green onions or scallions
2 eggs and 6 whites (or ¾ cup egg substitute) or 1 cup egg substitute

Salt and freshly ground black pepper
1 tablespoon mock schmaltz (page 193) or olive oil

1. Hold each sheet of matzo under warm running water until it begins to soften, about 1 minute per side. Shake off the excess water and break the matzo into 2-inch pieces in a mixing bowl.

2. Stir in the cream cheese, green onions, eggs and egg whites (or egg substitute), and salt and pepper to taste. The mixture should be highly seasoned.

3. Heat the mock schmaltz or oil in a large non-stick frying pan. Add the matzo mixture and cook as you would scrambled eggs, stirring with a wooden spoon, until the mixture is set and the cream cheese is slightly melted, 3 to 4 minutes. Serve at once.

Serves 4

261 CALORIES PER SERVING; 16 G PROTEIN; 7 G FAT; 1.5 G SATURATED FAT; 33 G CARBOHYDRATE; 270 MG SODIUM; 108 MG CHOLESTEROL

⚄ Matzo Meal Pancakes ⚄

I love fried matzo and can eat it happily for all eight days of Passover. But after five or six mornings of fried matzo,
my family clamors for a break. So I invented these matzo meal pancakes, which owe their airy lightness to the
addition of stiffly beaten egg whites. If you like a sweet pancake, you can add the vanilla; otherwise, omit it.

PREPARATION TIME: 10 MINUTES   COOKING TIME: 10 MINUTES

1 cup matzo meal
1 teaspoon sugar
½ teaspoon salt, or to taste
1 cup skim milk
1 egg yolk (or a third egg white—see below)
1 teaspoon oil, plus 1 to 2 teaspoons for frying (for

even lower-fat pancakes, grease the pan with
  spray oil)
½ teaspoon vanilla (optional)
2 egg whites
¼ teaspoon cream of tartar

1. Combine the matzo meal, sugar, and salt in a mixing bowl. Whisk in the milk, egg yolk, 1 teaspoon oil, and vanilla (if using).

2. Meanwhile, beat the egg whites with the cream of tartar until firm and glossy but not dry, starting the mixer on slow speed, then medium, then high. The whole beating process will take about 8 minutes. Do not overbeat the whites, or they'll collapse. Gently fold the egg whites into the matzo meal–milk mixture, using a rubber spatula.

3. Heat a nonstick frying pan over a medium flame. Add 1 teaspoon oil and swirl the pan or grease the pan with spray oil. Add spoonfuls of batter to form 3-inch pancakes. Fry until lightly browned on both sides and cooked through, about 2 minutes per side, turning with a spatula. Add oil as needed to keep the pan greased. You can serve the pancakes with maple syrup, American-style, or with applesauce and sour cream, Eastern European–style.

Makes 16 3-inch pancakes, which will serve 4

180 CALORIES PER SERVING; 7.7 G PROTEIN; 2.6 G FAT; .5 G SATURATED FAT; 31 G CARBOHYDRATE; 355 MG SODIUM; 54 MG CHOLESTEROL

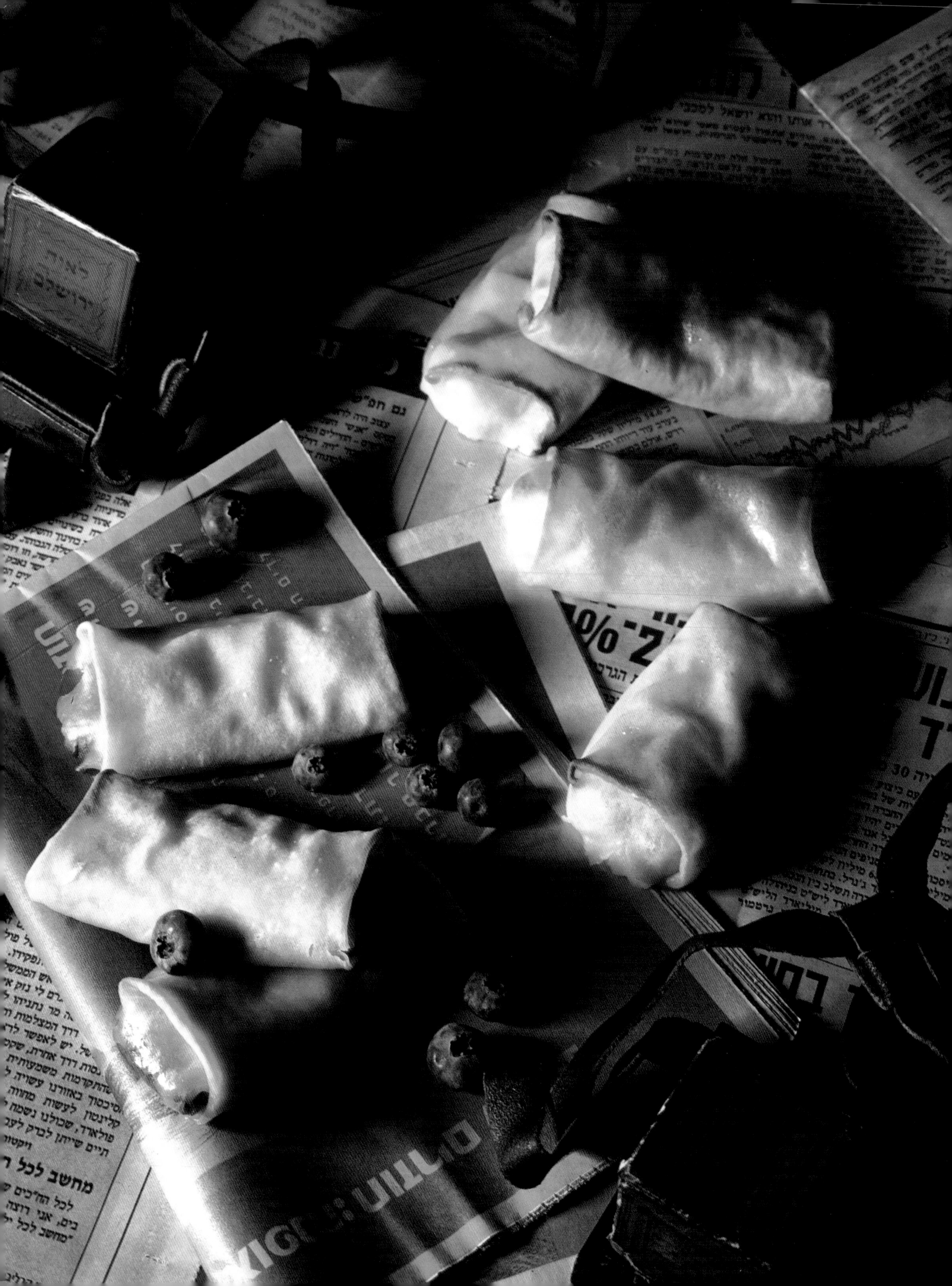

Knishes and Blintzes

❧❧❧◆❧❧

❧ Potato Blintzes ❧

Cheese or potato? That's the question whenever the topic of blintzes comes up in my family. I love the delicate play of sweetness and piquancy of a cheese blintz. My wife prefers the smooth texture and earthy flavor of a potato blintz. The sour cream in the filling isn't traditional, but I like the tangy finish it gives the potatoes. If you prefer a more straightforward potato flavor, use skim milk instead. (You'll probably need less skim milk than sour cream.) Speaking of potatoes, I like to use Yukon golds, which have a naturally buttery flavor.

PREPARATION TIME: 15 MINUTES   COOKING TIME: 30 MINUTES

FOR THE FILLING:
1¼ pounds potatoes (preferably Yukon golds),
    peeled and cut into 1-inch pieces
Salt
1 tablespoon canola oil or mock schmaltz
    (page 193)
1 large onion, finely chopped
3 tablespoons chopped fresh parsley

2 teaspoons sweet paprika
½ cup no-fat sour cream or ¼ to ½ cup skim milk
Freshly ground black pepper

TO FINISH THE BLINTZES:
16 blintz pancakes (page 66)
Spray oil
1 teaspoon melted butter

1. Place the potatoes in a pot with cold salted water to cover. Gradually bring to a boil. Reduce heat to medium and gently simmer the potatoes until very tender, about 10 to 15 minutes. Drain in a colander and return to the pan. Dry the potatoes out over medium heat, 1 to 2 minutes. Mash the potatoes with a potato masher or fork.

2. Meanwhile, heat the oil in a nonstick frying pan. Add the onion and cook until a deep golden brown, 8 to 10 minutes. Start the onions over medium heat, reducing the heat to medium-low, then low, to keep the onions from burning. Stir in the parsley and paprika after 5 minutes.

3. Add the onions to the mashed potatoes. Stir in the sour cream (if using) or enough skim milk to make a creamy but firm puree. Add salt and pepper to taste.

4. Lay one of the pancakes dark side up on a work surface and place a mound of potato mixture (about 3 tablespoons) in the center. Fold the bottom of the pancake over the filling, then fold in the sides. Fold down the top of the pancake to make a rectangular package about 3 inches long and 2 inches wide. Place the blintz seam side down on a plate you've lined with plastic wrap. Assemble the remaining blintzes the same way.

5. Preheat the oven to 375 degrees.

6. Arrange the blintzes in a baking dish or baking sheet that's been lightly oiled with spray oil. Spray the tops with oil or brush with melted butter. Bake the blintzes until puffed and lightly browned, 15 to 20 minutes. Serve the blintzes at once with applesauce (page 147), sour cream, or both.

Makes 16 blintzes, which will serve 4 to 5

96 CALORIES PER BLINTZ; 3.2 G PROTEIN; 2 G FAT; .4 G SATURATED FAT; 16 G CARBOHYDRATE; 103 MG SODIUM; 14 MG CHOLESTEROL

Assorted blintzes.

✂ Pancakes for Blintzes ✂

A blintz is a crepe that's been bar mitzvahed. The stuffings are limited only by your imagination. Cheese blintzes are the most famous, but potato, meat, kasha, and even blueberry blintzes have their partisans. In the following pages, you'll find recipes for these and other blintzes. But before you start thinking about fillings, you need to know how to make the wrapper, a soft, thin pancake that resembles a French crepe. To slash the fat in the pancake, I replace most of the eggs with egg whites, using a nontraditional ingredient—low-fat buttermilk—to make the batter rich and tender. Blintz pancakes freeze well. I always try to keep some on hand.

PREPARATION TIME: 5 MINUTES   COOKING TIME: 15 MINUTES

1 egg
¼ cup egg substitute or 1 egg or 2 whites
½ cup low-fat buttermilk
¾ to 1 cup water
½ teaspoon sugar
½ teaspoon salt, or to taste
1 teaspoon canola oil
1 cup unbleached white all-purpose flour

Spray oil

One or more crepe or omelette pans (7 inches in diameter)

1. Combine the crepe ingredients in a blender and blend just to mix. (Run the blender at medium speed in short bursts.) If the batter looks too thick, add a little more water.

2. Lightly spray the crepe pan(s) with oil and heat over a medium flame. (When the pan is the proper temperature, a drop of water will evaporate in 2 to 3 seconds.) Off the heat, add about 3 tablespoons pancake batter to the pan in one fell swoop. Gently tilt and rotate the pan to coat the bottom with a thin layer of batter. (Pour back any excess—the pancake should be as thin as possible.)

3. Cook the pancake until done but not brown, 1 to 2 minutes per side, turning with a spatula. As the pancakes are done, stack them on a plate on top of one another. You won't need to spray the pan between every crepe, but if the third or fourth crepe starts to stick, spray the pan again. The pancakes can be prepared up to 24 hours ahead to this stage and refrigerated. Let them cool to room temperature before separating and wrapping.

Makes 14 to 16 pancakes

42 CALORIES PER PANCAKE; 2 G PROTEIN; .8 G FAT; .2 G SATURATED FAT; 6.5 G CARBOHYDRATE; 91 MG SODIUM; 13 MG CHOLESTEROL

⌘ Cheese Blintzes ⌘

Is there anything more comforting than a plate of cheese blintzes? There they sit on your plate, as inviting as a pile of plump pillows. Your fork glides through a delicate pancake to reveal a snow-white cheese filling that's sweet but not sugary and delicately flavored with lemon zest and vanilla. Tradition calls for the blintzes to be served with sour cream and jam. By the time you're finished, you feel as if you've died and gone to heaven. To trim the fat, I use low-fat cottage cheese and bake the blintzes instead of pan-frying them. The light brushing of butter makes the blintzes taste far more fattening than they really are.
Note: Low-fat cottage cheese tends to be a bit watery, so I add some bread crumbs to absorb the excess liquid.

PREPARATION TIME: 15 MINUTES, PLUS THE TIME IT TAKES TO MAKE THE PANCAKES
COOKING TIME: 15 TO 20 MINUTES

FOR THE FILLING:
1½ pounds low- or no-fat dry-style small curd
    cottage cheese
¼ to ½ cup unflavored bread crumbs
¼ cup egg substitute or 1 egg
3 tablespoons sugar
1½ teaspoons vanilla extract
1 teaspoon grated lemon zest
½ teaspoon ground cinnamon (optional)

TO FINISH THE BLINTZES:
16 blintz pancakes (opposite)
Spray oil
1 tablespoon melted butter (optional)
1 cup no-fat sour cream
1 cup strawberry jam

1. Place the cottage cheese in a yogurt strainer or strainer lined with a paper towel and drain for at least 6 hours, preferably overnight, in the refrigerator. (Place a large bowl under it.)

2. Preheat the oven to 375 degrees.

3. In a mixing bowl, combine the cottage cheese, ¼ cup bread crumbs, egg substitute, sugar, vanilla, lemon zest, and cinnamon (if using) and stir to mix. The mixture should be as thick as soft ice cream. If too wet, add more bread crumbs.

4. Lay one of the pancakes dark side up on a work surface and place a mound of cheese mixture (about 3 tablespoons) in the center. Fold the bottom of the pancake over the filling, then fold in the sides. Fold down the top of the pancake to make a rectangular package about 3 inches long and 2 inches wide. Place the blintz seam side down on a plate you've lined with plastic wrap. Assemble the remaining blintzes the same way.

4. Arrange the blintzes in a baking dish or baking sheet that's been lightly oiled with spray oil. Brush the tops with melted butter (if using). Bake the blintzes until puffed and lightly browned and the filling is set, 15 to 20 minutes. Serve the blintzes at once with sour cream and jam on the side.

Makes 12 blintzes, which will serve 4

167.9 CALORIES PER BLINTZ; 9.4 G PROTEIN; 1.25 G FAT; .28 G SATURATED FAT;
27.9 G CARBOHYDRATE; 317 MG SODIUM; 18.36 MG CHOLESTEROL

VARIATION—SAVORY CHEESE BLINTZES IN THE STYLE OF VILNA

Green onions and cottage cheese make wonderful companions. (See zibulnikas recipe on page 50.) Here's a savory cheese blintz with a delicate onion flavor for people who don't like sweet blintzes.

Prepare the preceding blinzes, omitting the sugar, vanilla, lemon zest, and cinnamon, adding 1 cup finely chopped green onions or scallions instead. Season the mixture with salt and pepper to taste. Prepare the blintzes as described above. Serve with sour cream, omitting the jam.

VARIATION—GOAT CHEESE BLINTZES

Here's a contemporary twist on an Eastern European classic. Prepare either of the preceding recipes, adding 2 to 3 ounces soft goat cheese, like Montrachet.

✂ Blueberry Blintzes ✂

I did not grow up on blueberry blintzes. (In fact, I'd never heard of blueberry blintzes.) But, apparently, they were part of the Miami Jewish tradition and my wife remembers them from her childhood. Now, I'm a blueberry freak, so it didn't take much coaxing for me to try making blueberry blintzes. We Raichlens didn't know what we were missing! You can certainly use the large, high-bush blueberries, but the tiny low-bush blueberries from Maine have even more flavor.

PREPARATION TIME: 15 MINUTES   COOKING TIME: 20 MINUTES

FOR THE FILLING:
2 pints fresh blueberries
⅓ cup sugar, or to taste
2 tablespoons cornstarch
1 teaspoon grated fresh lemon zest

TO FINISH THE BLINTZES:
16 (7-inch) blintz pancakes (page 66)
Spray oil
2 teaspoons melted butter

1. Prepare the filling. Pick through the blueberries, removing any stems, leaves, or underripe berries. Combine the berries, sugar, cornstarch, and lemon zest in a saucepan and stir to mix.

2. Simmer the blueberries over medium-high heat until the berries burst and the juices form a thick sauce, 3 to 5 minutes, stirring with a wooden spoon. Don't overcook: you should be able to see the individual berries. Transfer the blueberry mixture to a bowl and let cool to room temperature. You should have about 2½ cups filling.

3. Arrange a pancake on your work surface, dark side up. Spoon 3 tablespoons blueberry mixture in the center. Fold the bottom of the pancake over the filling, then fold in the sides. Fold down the top of the pancake to make a rectangular package about 2½ inches square. Place the blintz seam side down on a plate you've lined with plastic wrap. Assemble the remaining blintzes the same way.

4. Preheat the oven to 400 degrees.

5. Arrange the blintzes in a baking dish or baking sheet that's been lightly oiled with spray oil. Spray the tops with oil or brush with melted butter. Bake the blintzes until puffed and lightly browned, 10 to 15 minutes. Serve the blintzes at once. My wife likes to accompany them with maple syrup; I like sour cream.

Makes 16 blintzes, which will serve 4 to 6

86 CALORIES PER BLINTZ; 2 G PROTEIN; 1.5 G FAT; .5 G SATURATED FAT; 16 G CARBOHYDRATE; 99 MG SODIUM; 15 MG CHOLESTEROL

❧ Fat Grandma's Potato Knishes ❧

I never knew "Fat Grandma" (my wife's ex-mother-in-law—the moniker was affectionate, not descriptive), but I've often eaten her fabulous potato knishes. What's nice about these knishes is that they're free-form: you pat the filling into shape with your hands. You don't need to fuss with a crust. To trim the fat, I've eliminated some of the chicken fat and egg yolks, adding fresh herbs to achieve a vibrant Old World flavor without fat. Note: Fat Grandma made these knishes without any sort of crust or crumb coating. I almost caused a riot in my family when I added the crust. For the sake of authenticity, I've made the crust optional— I can name at least three people who will never, ever use it: my wife and her children, Betsy and Jake.

PREPARATION TIME: 15 MINUTES   COOKING TIME: 50 MINUTES

1 tablespoon olive oil or schmaltz
1 large onion, minced (about 2 cups)
2 cloves garlic, minced
1 tablespoon Hungarian sweet paprika
2½ pounds baking potatoes (3 to 4 potatoes), peeled and cut into ½-inch dice
Salt
3 tablespoons chopped fresh herbs, including chives, parsley, basil, and/or or dill
¼ cup egg substitute or 1 egg or 2 whites

Freshly ground black pepper
3 to 4 tablespoons flour or bread crumbs, or as needed
Spray oil

FOR THE CRUST (OPTIONAL):
1 cup dried unflavored bread crumbs
2 teaspoons sweet paprika
1 teaspoon each onion powder and garlic powder

1. Preheat the oven to 350 degrees.

2. Heat the oil in a large nonstick frying pan over medium heat. Add the onion and cook until nicely caramelized, 12 to 15 minutes. Start the onion on medium heat, lowering the temperature to prevent burning. Stir in the garlic and paprika in the last 5 minutes. Set the onion mixture aside to cool.

3. Meanwhile, place the potatoes in a large pot with cold salted water to cover. Bring to a boil, reduce the heat, and simmer the potatoes until soft, 8 to 10 minutes. Drain the potatoes in a colander and return them to the pan. Cook the potatoes over medium heat for 1 to 2 minutes to evaporate any excess liquid. Remove the pot from the heat and let cool slightly.

4. Mash the potatoes in the pot with a potato masher or pestle. (I like to leave a few small lumps for texture.) Stir in the onion mixture, herbs, egg substitute, and salt and pepper to taste. The mixture should be highly seasoned. Add 3 to 4 tablespoons flour, or enough to obtain a mixture you can shape with your hands. Wet your hands and form the potato mixture into patties 1½ inches thick and 3 inches across.

5. Optional: Place the bread crumbs in a shallow bowl and mix in the paprika, onion powder, and garlic powder. Lightly dredge each knish in the crumbs, shaking off the excess.

6. Arrange the knishes on a nonstick baking sheet, lightly sprayed with oil. Spray the tops and sides of the knishes with oil. The knishes can be prepared ahead to this stage, covered with plastic wrap and refrigerated.

7. Bake the knishes until golden brown and hot in the center (an inserted skewer will come out hot to the touch), 30 to 40 minutes, turning the knishes with a spatula after 15 minutes.

Serve the knishes by themselves, or with applesauce (page 147), no-fat sour cream, or, if you're feeling particularly indulgent, both.

Makes 8 knishes, serves 8

177 CALORIES PER SERVING (2 KNISHES); 4 G PROTEIN; 3 G FAT; 0 G SATURATED FAT;

35 G CARBOHYDRATE; 22 MG SODIUM; 0 MG CHOLESTEROL

☙ Chicken Knishes ☙

Long before anyone in America had heard of burgers or wraps, Jews were eating knishes. Talk about the perfect snack or finger food: knishes are self-contained bundles of edible bliss, featuring a rich, moist, meaty filling in a savory crust. I recently discovered a trick for forming perfectly round knishes: I bake them in muffin tins. You could also make these knishes as half-moon-shaped turnovers, following the instructions in the kasha knish recipe on page 73. **Note:** *Chicken knishes are a great way to use up the boiled chicken you'll have left over from making chicken broth (page 189).*

PREPARATION TIME: 30 MINUTES   COOKING TIME: 1 HOUR

FOR THE CHICKEN FILLING:
1 tablespoon olive oil
1 medium onion, finely chopped (½ cup)
1 clove garlic, minced
2 teaspoons paprika
3 cups shredded or diced cooked chicken
3 tablespoons matzo meal or bread crumbs
½ cup chicken broth
Salt and freshly ground black pepper

TO FINISH THE KNISHES:
1 batch reduced-fat knish-dough (page 72)
Spray oil
2 tablespoons egg substitute or 1 egg white, lightly beaten with a fork

1. Prepare the filling. Heat the olive oil in a non-stick skillet. Add the onion and garlic and cook over medium heat until just beginning to brown, 4 minutes.

2. Stir in the paprika and chicken and cook for 1 minute. Stir in the matzo meal and cook for 1 minute. Stir in the chicken broth and bring to a boil for 3 minutes: the mixture should be thick and creamy. Add salt and pepper to taste. Transfer the mixture to a bowl or plate and let cool to room temperature.

3. Preheat the oven to 350 degrees.

4. Roll out the knish dough to a thickness of ³⁄₁₆ inch. Using a cookie cutter or pot lid as a template, cut out 4½-inch circles. Gather up the scraps and reroll. You should ultimately wind up with 12 circles.

5. Lightly spray a small muffin tin (the one I use makes 2½-inch muffins) with spray oil. Line the muffin molds with circles of knish dough; the excess will hang over the edges. Place ¼ cup chicken filling in each hole and bring the edges over the top of the knish to encase the filling. Gather the edges in the center, twisting and pinching, to seal the knish.

6. Lightly brush the tops of the knishes with egg glaze, taking care not to drip any into the molds. Bake the knishes until golden brown, 30 to 40 minutes. Let cool until warm, then unmold.

Makes 12 small knishes, about 2 to 3 per person

197.4 CALORIES PER KNISH; 13.5 G PROTEIN; 7.3 G FAT; 2 G SATURATED FAT; 18.8 G CARBOHYDRATE; 199 MG SODIUM; 50.1 MG CHOLESTEROL

VARIATION— MUSHROOM KNISHES

Prepare as described above, substituting a double batch of mushroom filling (page 13) for the chicken.

VARIATION—MEAT KNISHES

Prepare as described above, substituting a triple batch of beef filling (page 3) for the chicken.

✄ Reduced-Fat Knish Dough ✄

The world's best knishes may well be Mrs. Stahl's, made in a bakery of the same name in Brighton Beach, New York. They're plump and greasy, as a knish should be, and they're best eaten right out of the bag when still warm. This is not Mrs. Stahl's dough. (How could it be in a low-fat cookbook?) But I think you'll find it makes highly tasty knishes that are within the bounds of modern health precepts.

PREPARATION TIME: 5 MINUTES, PLUS 10 MINUTES FOR ROLLING AND CUTTING THE DOUGH
COOKING TIME: 30 TO 40 MINUTES

2 cups flour
1 teaspoon paprika
1 teaspoon baking powder
¾ teaspoon salt

2 tablespoons butter or margarine, cut into pieces
1 egg
2 to 3 tablespoons canola oil
5 to 6 tablespoons ice water, or as needed

1. Combine the flour, paprika, baking powder, salt, and butter in a food processor fitted with a chopping blade. Pulse the machine to cut in the butter; the mixture should feel like cornmeal.

2. Add the egg, oil, and water. Run the machine in short bursts until the dough comes together into a smooth ball, about 3 minutes. If the mixture looks too dry, add water as needed.

3. Gather the dough into a ball, flatten it into a disk 1 inch thick, and wrap in plastic. Chill the dough until firm enough to handle, 1 to 2 hours.

4. To make the knishes, roll out the dough to a thickness of ⅛ inch. Using a cookie cutter or pot top as a template, cut out circles of dough the desired size. Make the knishes as described on page 66, using the desired filling.

Makes enough for 12

121 CALORIES PER SERVING; 3 G PROTEIN; 5 G FAT; 1.5 G SATURATED FAT; 16 G CARBOHYDRATE; 172 MG SODIUM; 23 MG CHOLESTEROL

✠ Kasha Knishes ✠

*I love the earthy flavor of these kasha knishes—the pungency of the onions and mushrooms
counterpointing the grainy sweetness of the kasha. (For a complete discussion of kasha, see page 127.)*

PREPARATION TIME: 30 MINUTES   COOKING TIME: 1 HOUR

FOR THE FILLING:
1 tablespoon olive oil
1 small onion, finely chopped (½ cup)
6 ounces button mushrooms, trimmed, wiped clean
  with a damp paper towel, and thinly sliced
Salt and freshly ground black pepper
½ cup kasha
2 tablespoons egg substitute or 1 egg white

1 cup water

TO FINISH THE KNISHES:
1 batch reduced-fat knish dough (page 72)
Spray oil
2 tablespoons egg substitute or 1 egg white, lightly
  beaten with a fork, for glaze

1. Make the filling. Heat the oil in a large, non-stick frying pan. Add the onion and mushrooms and cook over medium heat until the mixture is nicely browned and the mushroom juices have evaporated, 5 to 8 minutes. Add salt and pepper to taste. Transfer the mixture to a plate and let the pan cool.

2. Place the kasha and 2 tablespoons egg substitute in the pan and stir with a wooden spoon to coat the grains. Place the pan over a medium flame and cook for 2 to 3 minutes, stirring steadily. First the kasha grains will stick together; then the egg will dry and the kasha will separate into individual grains.

3. Stir in the onion-mushroom mixture and water and bring to a boil. Reduce the heat to low and tightly cover the pan. Cook the kasha until tender and all the liquid has been absorbed, 8 to 10 minutes. Remove the pan from the heat and fluff the kasha with a fork. Season to taste with salt and pepper. Transfer the

kasha to a plate and let cool to room temperature.

4. Preheat the oven to 350 degrees.

5. Roll out the knish dough to a thickness of ³⁄₁₆ inch. Using a cookie cutter or pot lid as a template, cut out 4½-inch circles. Gather up the scraps and reroll. You should ultimately wind up with 12 circles. Lightly brush the edges of the dough circles with water.

6. Place ¼ cup kasha filling in the center of each circle. Fold the circle in half to make a half-moon-shaped turnover. Crimp the edges with your fingers or a fork to seal them, or, for a fanciful touch, pleat them. Arrange the resulting knishes on a nonstick baking sheet you've lightly sprayed with oil. Brush the tops of the knishes with egg glaze.

7. Bake the knishes until golden brown, about 30 minutes. Let cool until warm, then serve.

Makes 12 knishes

165 CALORIES PER KNISH; 5 G PROTEIN; 7 G FAT; 2 G SATURATED FAT; 22 G CARBOHYDRATE; 182 MG SODIUM; 23 MG CHOLESTEROL

Fish Dishes

Charmoula Grilled Salmon
(with Moroccan "Vinaigrette")

This lively grilled salmon takes its inspiration from Morocco, particularly from a tangy herb sauce called charmoula, which Moroccan Jews like to serve with fish. To trim the fat, I've reduced the oil in the charmoula, substituting vegetable broth instead. The traditional fish for this dish is fried sardines. I like to use salmon and I love the smoke flavor (not to mention the savings in fat grams) provided by the grilling.

PREPARATION TIME: 10 MINUTES   COOKING TIME: 10 MINUTES, PLUS 1 TO 4 HOURS FOR MARINATING THE FISH

FOR THE CHARMOULA:
1 cup chopped fresh parsley
1 cup chopped fresh cilantro
3 cloves garlic, minced
½ teaspoon salt
1 teaspoon sweet paprika
½ teaspoon black pepper

½ teaspoon ground cumin
½ teaspoon hot pepper flakes, or to taste
3 tablespoons fresh lemon juice
⅓ cup vegetable or chicken broth
1½ tablespoons extra-virgin olive oil

4 (6-ounce) pieces salmon fillet or steaks

1. Make the charmoula. Combine the parsley, cilantro, and garlic in a food processor and finely chop. Add the salt, paprika, pepper, cumin, hot pepper flakes, lemon juice, vegetable broth, and olive oil, and grind to a coarse puree, running the machine in short bursts. Correct the seasoning, adding salt and/or lemon juice to taste. The charmoula should be highly seasoned.

2. Run your fingers over the pieces of fish, feeling for bones. Remove any you may find with tweezers. Pour one third of the charmoula over the bottom of a baking dish just large enough to hold the salmon. Arrange the salmon pieces on top. Spoon another third of the charmoula over the fish. Let marinate in the refrigerator for 1 to 4 hours. (The longer you marinate, the richer the flavor.)

3. Preheat your grill (or broiler) to high. Oil the grill grate (see below). Grill the fish until cooked, 4 to 6 minutes per side, turning with a spatula. Transfer the fish to plates or a platter and spoon the remaining charmoula over it. *Serves 4*

231 CALORIES PER 6 SERVINGS; 25 G PROTEIN; 13 G FAT; 2.1 G SATURATED FAT; 2.3 G CARBOHYDRATE; 255 MG SODIUM; 70 MG CHOLESTEROL

HOW TO OIL A GRILL GRATE

Place a few tablespoons of oil in a small bowl. Fold up a paper towel into a pad and dip it in the oil. Hold the pad with tongs and rub it over the bars of the grate to oil them. The oil burns off, so it will not add extra fat to your dinner.

Charmoula grilled salmon.

⟡ Grilled Salmon with Taratoor ⟡
(Sesame Sauce)

Grilled seafood with taratoor (sesame sauce) is enjoyed throughout the Middle East. The Israeli version would be made with fish, of course, not shrimp (as is commonly done in neighboring Lebanon). You'll love the speed and ease of this recipe, not to mention the way the creamy, lemony taratoor jazzes up otherwise commonplace grilled fish. Tahini (sesame paste) is widely available at Middle Eastern markets, natural foods stores, and most supermarkets.

PREPARATION TIME: 10 MINUTES, PLUS 30 MINUTES TO MARINATE THE FISH
COOKING TIME: 10 MINUTES, PLUS TIME TO PREHEAT THE GRILL

4 (5-ounce) pieces boneless, skinless salmon fillet
Coarse sea salt and freshly ground black pepper
2 teaspoons hot paprika
3 tablespoons minced fresh parsley (preferably flat-leaf)
2 cloves garlic, minced
¼ cup fresh lemon juice

FOR THE TARATOOR (SESAME SAUCE):
3 tablespoons tahini

2 cloves garlic, minced
3 tablespoons fresh lemon juice
2 tablespoons minced fresh parsley (preferably flat-leaf)
3 to 5 tablespoons water
½ teaspoon each salt and white pepper, or to taste
Hot paprika for sprinkling

1 tablespoon oil for oiling the grill grate

1. Season the salmon pieces on both sides with salt, pepper, and paprika. Place the fish in a baking dish and sprinkle on both sides with the parsley and garlic. Pour the lemon juice over the fish and marinate for 30 minutes, turning once. Meanwhile, build a hot fire in your barbecue grill or preheat the broiler.

2. Prepare the sauce. In a mixing bowl, whisk together the tahini, garlic, and lemon juice: the sauce will thicken. Whisk in the parsley and enough water (3 to 5 tablespoons) to obtain a pourable but still quite thick sauce. Correct the seasoning, adding salt and pepper to taste. The taratoor should be highly seasoned.

3. Oil the grill grate (see box on page 75). Place the fish on the grill and grill until cooked, 4 to 6 minutes per side. Rotate each piece of fish 90 degrees after 2 minutes: this will give you an attractive crosshatch of grill marks.

4. Transfer the fish to plates or a platter and spoon the taratoor over them. Dust with paprika and serve at once.

Serves 4

258.7 CALORIES PER SERVING; 35.2 G PROTEIN; 11.1 G FAT; 2.2 G SATURATED FAT;
6.6 G CARBOHYDRATE; 438 MG SODIUM; 53.9 MG CHOLESTEROL

🐟 Grammie Sarah's Salmon Croquettes 🐟

When I was growing up, we had weekly dinners with my grandparents: Friday nights with Grammie and Dear and Tuesday nights with Grammie Sarah and Grandpa Jack. Grammie Sarah wasn't a great cook (as she herself would be the first to admit)— in fact, we once almost came to fisticuffs when I tried to get her to serve my lamb chops medium-rare. But there was one dish she excelled at—and made almost every Tuesday night: salmon croquettes. Who knew from fresh salmon back in those days? No, Grammie Sarah's croquettes (actually, more patty-shaped) were made from lurid red canned salmon and they were crusty on the outside, moist inside, and irresistible whether you ate them hot that evening or cold in your school lunchbox the next day. Here's a recipe that's potently seasoned with nostalgia.

PREPARATION TIME: 10 MINUTES   COOKING TIME: 15 MINUTES

Spray oil
1 tablespoon canola oil
1 medium onion, finely chopped
2 (14¾-ounce) cans chum or pink salmon

3 tablespoons finely chopped fresh parsley
¼ cup cracker crumbs, or as needed
½ cup egg substitute or 1 egg plus 2 egg whites
Salt and freshly ground black pepper

1. Lightly spray a nonstick baking sheet with spray oil. Place the baking sheet in the oven and preheat to 400 degrees.

2. Heat the oil in a nonstick frying pan. Add the onion and cook over medium heat until soft but not brown, 3 minutes.

3. Drain the salmon and flake it into a mixing bowl, discarding any skin. (Include the bones—they're edible and interesting in texture, not to mention a good source of calcium.) Stir in the onion, parsley, cracker crumbs, egg substitute, and salt and pepper. The mixture should be highly seasoned.

(**Note:** You won't need much salt—the salmon is already quite salty.) If the mixture feels too wet, add more cracker crumbs.

4. Wet your hands and form the salmon mixture into eight 3-inch balls. Remove the baking sheet from the oven and arrange the balls on top, gently flattening each with the palm of your hand. Lightly spray the tops of the croquettes with oil.

5. Bake the salmon croquettes until lightly browned and firm, 12 to 15 minutes. Serve at once.

*Makes 8 croquettes,
which will serve 4 as a main course*

191 CALORIES PER SERVING; 25 G PROTEIN; 7.4 G FAT; 1.6 G SATURATED FAT; 5 G CARBOHYDRATE; 537 MG SODIUM; 41 MG CHOLESTEROL

✂ Fresh Salmon Croquettes with Dill ✂

This recipe demonstrates the difference between two generations. My grandmother knew only canned salmon;
I virtually use only fresh. The following croquettes are for the purist who insists on using fresh fish.

PREPARATION TIME: 10 MINUTES   COOKING TIME: 15 MINUTES

Spray oil
2 slices white bread
1½ pounds boneless, skinless salmon fillets
4 scallions, finely chopped
2 tablespoons chopped fresh dill

2 tablespoons finely chopped fresh parsley
1 clove garlic, minced
½ teaspoon freshly grated lemon zest
½ cup egg substitute or 1 egg and 2 whites
Salt and freshly ground black pepper

1. Lightly spray a nonstick baking sheet with spray oil. Place the baking sheet in the oven and preheat to 400 degrees.

2. Soak the bread in warm water for 3 minutes. Squeeze the bread in your fingers to wring out the excess liquid. Place the bread in a mixing bowl.

3. Finely chop the salmon. In the best of all possible worlds, you'd chop it by hand. Or use a hand-crank meat grinder. If you do the chopping in a food processor (as most people will), cut it into 1-inch pieces before chopping. Run the processor in short bursts. Don't overprocess, or you'll wind up with a spongy puree.

4. Transfer the salmon to the mixing bowl. Stir in

the scallions, dill, parsley, garlic, lemon zest, egg substitute, and salt and pepper to taste. If you're really careful, you can do the mixing in the processor. Just run the machine in short bursts.

5. Wet your hands and form the salmon mixture into eight 3-inch balls. Remove the baking sheet from the oven and arrange the balls on top, gently flattening each with the palm of your hand. Lightly spray the tops of the croquettes with oil.

6. Bake the salmon croquettes until lightly browned and firm, 10 to 15 minutes, turning the croquettes after 5 minutes. Serve at once.

Makes 8 croquettes,
which will serve 4 as a main course

270 CALORIES PER SERVING; 42 G PROTEIN; 6.3 G FAT; 1 G SATURATED FAT; 8 G CARBOHYDRATE; 294 MG SODIUM; 88 MG CHOLESTEROL

⚹ Kippered Salmon ⚹

Every Saturday evening, I have a little ritual. I buy a side of salmon, cure it with vodka, salt, and brown sugar, and smoke it over apple or cherry. The next morning, we wake up to bagels and freshly kippered salmon—the gastronomic high point of the week. Smoking salmon sounds like a complicated procedure, so you may be surprised to learn that the actual preparation time is under 15 minutes. You don't need any special equipment (at least no more special than a wok). As for the results, well, Sunday brunch just went from black and white to Technicolor. For the best results, buy a center or head end cut of salmon (not the tail end). Ask the fishmonger to remove the skin and bones. You may wish to make extra, as other recipes in this book call for kippered salmon.

PREPARATION TIME: 10 MINUTES, PLUS 4 HOURS FOR CURING THE FISH　　COOKING TIME: 20 MINUTES

1½-pound piece boneless, skinless salmon fillet
1 cup vodka
1 cup brown sugar (dark or light—your choice)
½ cup kosher salt

2 tablespoons ground black pepper
1 tablespoon hickory, oak, cherry, alder, or other hardwood sawdust

1. Wash the fish and blot dry. Run your fingers over the top of the fillet, feeling for bones. (Even though your ordered boneless fillets, there may be a few bones.) Pull out any you find with a needlenose pliers. Place the fish in a glass pie pan or baking dish and pour the vodka over it. Let marinate for 10 minutes, turning once. Drain the fish well and wipe out the dish.

2. Make the cure. In a mixing bowl, combine the sugar, salt, and pepper and whisk or mix with your fingers to blend. Spread one third of the cure over the bottom of the pie pan or baking dish. (The mixture should cover an area just slightly larger than the fish.) Place the salmon on top and sprinkle the remaining cure over it. Pile any spillover against the edges. Cover the fish with plastic wrap and let cure in the refrigerator for 4 hours. The salt will draw out some of the liquid.

3. If you have a stovetop smoker (see below), place the sawdust in the bottom. Line the drip tray with foil. Or rig up a smoker, using a wok or Dutch oven, following the instructions below. Rinse the sugar mixture off the salmon and blot the fish dry with paper towels. Arrange it on the wire rack of the smoker. Place the smoker over high heat just until the first wisps of smoke appear. Lower the heat to medium and tightly cover the smoker.

4. Smoke the salmon over medium heat until cooked, 18 to 20 minutes. (When cooked, the fish will feel firm and will break into flakes when pressed. Another test is to insert a metal skewer: it will feel very hot to the touch.) Using a large spatula, transfer the salmon to a plate to cool, then wrap it in foil, and refrigerate until cold. Kippered salmon will keep in the refrigerator for up to 5 days and it freezes well.

Note: Cookware shops sell stovetop smokers, which look like a rectangular metal box, and hardwood sawdust. If sawdust is unavailable, use 2 tablespoons hardwood chips. Stovetop smokers and sawdust can be purchased from C. M. International, P.O. Box 60220, Colorado Springs, CO 80960-0220, (888) 563-0227.

Alternatively, rig up a smoker, using a wok or Dutch oven. Line the bottom of the wok or oven with foil. Place the sawdust on top. Set a round metal cake rack in the middle of the wok or Dutch oven at least 2 inches above the sawdust. Place the fish on the rack. Tightly cover when smoking.

Serves 6 to 8

146 CALORIES PER 6 SERVINGS; 26 G PROTEIN; 4.2 G FAT; 1 G SATURATED FAT; .7 G CARBOHYDRATE; 280 MG SODIUM; 43 MG CHOLESTEROL

✄ My Grandmother's Pickled Herring ✄

I have a confession to make. I've never acquired a taste for pickled herring. Which doesn't bother my family members too much, for this means that there's more fish for them. Especially when the fish in question is herring pickled from scratch the way my Grammie Ethel used to do it. If you're used to pickled herring from a jar, the following recipe will come as a revelation.
Note: *The recipe is easy to make, but you must start soaking the herrings the day before.*

PREPARATION TIME: 10 MINUTES
COOKING TIME: 5 MINUTES, PLUS 1½ DAYS FOR SOAKING AND PICKLING THE FISH

4 salted herrings
3½ cups distilled white vinegar
½ cup water
2 tablespoons pickling spice

1 tablespoon sugar
½ teaspoon black peppercorns
4 large sweet onions, thinly sliced

1. The day before, wash the herrings under cold running water, taking care to rinse out the insides. Place the fish in a large jar or bowl with enough cold water to cover by 2 inches. Let soak overnight in the refrigerator, changing the water once or twice.

2. The next day, combine the vinegar, ½ cup water, pickling spice, sugar, and peppercorns in a saucepan and bring to a boil. Reduce the heat and simmer the mixture for 5 minutes. Let cool to room temperature.

3. Drain the soaked herring in a colander and rinse well under cold water. Cut each piece of herring into 2-inch pieces. Arrange a layer of herring in a clean jar or bowl and top with a layer of onions. Repeat with the second herring and onion, then the third and fourth. Pour the vinegar mixture over the fish. Let the fish pickle at room temperature for 4 hours or overnight in the refrigerator. Refrigerate until serving. (The fish will keep in the refrigerator for several weeks.) Serve pickled herring with chunks of challah. Don't forget to eat the onions.

Serves 8 as an appetizer, 4 as a light entrée

259.4 CALORIES PER 4 SERVINGS; 21.7 G PROTEIN; 10.4 G FAT; 2.4 G SATURATED FAT;
1.4 G CARBOHYDRATE; 111 MG SODIUM; 68 MG CHOLESTEROL

🖾 Grilled Sea Bass with Zataar 🖾

If you like the Mediterranean flavors of oregano, thyme, and summer savory, you'll love this simple, summery grilled fish. Zataar is a spice mix popular throughout the Middle East. The Israeli version features thyme, oregano, summer savory, sesame seeds, and sumac. You can buy zataar ready-made at an Israeli or Middle East market (see mail order sources), or follow the simple recipe on page 154. I've called for sea bass in the following recipe, but cod, snapper, or tuna would work equally well.

PREPARATION TIME: 5 MINUTES   COOKING TIME: 10 MINUTES, PLUS TIME TO PREHEAT THE GRILL

4 (6-ounce) sea bass fillets
3 tablespoons zataar
1 tablespoon extra-virgin olive oil, plus oil for the grate

2 tablespoons fresh lemon juice
Coarse sea salt and freshly ground black pepper
Lemon wedges for serving

1. Wash the fish fillets and blot dry. Rub the fish on both sides with the zataar. Place in a baking dish and drizzle with the olive oil and lemon juice. Season on both sides with salt and pepper. Let marinate for 30 minutes.

2. Build a hot fire in your grill. Oil the grate (see box on page 75). Grill the fish until cooked, 4 to 6 minutes per side, turning with a spatula. If you have a fish basket, you may wish to grill the fillets in it. (It's easier to turn the basket than the individual fillets.)

3. Transfer the fish to plates or a platter. Serve with lemon wedges for squeezing over the fish.

Serves 4

225 CALORIES PER SERVING; 32 G PROTEIN; 10 G FAT; 2 G SATURATED FAT; .6 G CARBOHYDRATE; 118 MG SODIUM; 116 MG CHOLESTEROL

✄ Fish (Plaki) with Greek Tomato Sauce ✄

Say the word plaki *to a Greek Jew and his eyes will light with pleasure. This traditional fish dish from the north of Greece and Turkey features Aegean fish baked under rich thick tomato sauce perfumed with cinnamon and bell peppers. The traditional fish would be mullet, which isn't particularly easy to find in the United States. I like to use snapper fillets, but any flavorful fresh fish will do.*

PREPARATION TIME: 10 MINUTES   COOKING TIME: 35 MINUTES

1½ tablespoons extra-virgin olive oil
1 medium onion, finely chopped
2 cloves garlic, minced
1 green bell pepper, cored and finely chopped
¼ cup chopped flat-leaf parsley
2 tablespoons tomato paste
¼ cup dry white wine

1 (28-ounce) can plum tomatoes
½ teaspoon dried oregano
½ teaspoon ground cinnamon
Salt and freshly ground black pepper
Spray oil
4 (6-ounce) boneless, skinless snapper fillets or
    4 fish steaks, washed and blotted dry

1. Preheat the oven to 400 degrees.

2. Heat 1 tablespoon oil in a nonstick frying pan. Add the onion, garlic, pepper, and 3 tablespoons parsley. Cook over medium heat until just beginning to brown, about 4 minutes. Stir in the tomato paste and sauté for 1 minute. Add the wine and boil for 2 minutes.

3. Coarsely chop the tomatoes (this is most easily done in a food processor) and add them with the can juices, the oregano, and cinnamon to the pan. Simmer the tomato sauce until thick and richly flavored, about 10 minutes, adding salt and pepper to taste.

4. Lightly oil an attractive baking dish with spray oil. Spoon one third of the tomato sauce into the bottom of the dish. Salt and pepper the fish and arrange on top. Spoon the remaining tomato sauce on top. Drizzle the remaining ½ tablespoon olive oil on top. Bake the fish until cooked through, about 20 minutes. Sprinkle the remaining 1 tablespoon parsley over the fish and serve at once. The red rice on page 125 makes a great accompaniment.

Serves 4

307 CALORIES PER SERVING; 38 G PROTEIN; 7.5 G FAT; 1.1 G SATURATED FAT; 15 G CARBOHYDRATE; 542 MG SODIUM; 62 MG CHOLESTEROL

✄ Hot and Spicy Sea Bass ✄

This recipe comes from my friends Sonya and Robin Azoulay, Jews from Casablanca, Morocco, who moved to Miami twenty-four years ago. The recipe is quite simple, but the flavors are electrifying—the result of braising the fish on the stove with cilantro, garlic, hot paprika, and pepper flakes. I've given a range for the spices: use as much hot paprika and pepper flakes as you dare.
Note: *This recipe calls for sea bass, but you could also use cod, snapper, grouper, mahimahi, tilapia, or halibut.*

PREPARATION TIME: 10 MINUTES   COOKING TIME: 20 MINUTES

4 (6-ounce) pieces sea bass fillets
Salt and freshly ground black pepper
4 teaspoons vegetable oil
3 cloves garlic, minced
1 to 3 teaspoons hot paprika

½ to 1 teaspoon hot pepper flakes
½ teaspoon ground cumin
3 tablespoons fresh lemon juice
½ cup chopped fresh cilantro

1. Run your fingers over the fish feeling for bones: remove any you find with tweezers or needlenose pliers. Generously season the fish on both sides with salt and pepper.

2. Heat the oil in a sauté pan or deep skillet (preferably nonstick). Add the garlic, paprika, pepper flakes, and cumin and cook over medium heat until the oil is reddish and fragrant, 2 minutes. Add the fish and lightly brown on both sides, 2 minutes per side, turning with a spatula.

3. Stir in the lemon juice, cilantro, and 1 cup water. Cover the pan, increase the heat to high, and boil the fish for 3 minutes. Uncover the fish and continue cooking until the fish is cooked, most of the water has evaporated, and the pan juices have cooked down to a thick sauce, 4 to 8 minutes. Turn the fish with a spatula to ensure even cooking. Correct the seasoning, adding salt and pepper to taste. Couscous would make a good accompaniment.

Note: If the fish is cooked before the sauce is completely reduced, transfer it to a platter and keep warm. Reduce the sauce and pour it over the fish.

Variation: Sometimes Sonya will add sliced carrots, chickpeas, or blanched Moroccan cracked olives to the fish.

Serves 4

214 CALORIES PER SERVING; 32 G PROTEIN; 8 G FAT; 1.3 G SATURATED FAT; 2.2 G CARBOHYDRATE; 117 MG SODIUM; 70 MG CHOLESTEROL

✄ Aunt Annette's Gefilte Fish ✄

*When I was growing up, I didn't like gefilte fish. I didn't like its robust assertiveness and I certainly didn't like the gelatinous juices spooned over it. As a result, I spent eighteen years not eating some of the most glorious gefilte fish ever to grace a holiday table. Our family's gefilte fish maker was my aunt Annette Farber (the same Annette who had such a way with matzo balls and strudel—pages 25 and 173) and her fish had the bold flavors of a Beethoven symphony. She achieved this effect by grinding her fish in an old hand-cranked meat grinder, using seasonings no more complex than onion, carrot, salt, and pepper. (The secret lay in using four different types of fish.) The fish should be chopped, not pureed, and while I'm not going to ask you to trade in your food processor for a hand-cranked meat grinder, I will ask you to follow the instructions below carefully, so you don't overgrind your fish. **Note:** I call for boneless, skinless fish, but ask your fishmonger for the bones, heads, and skins, so you can use them to flavor the cooking liquid.*

PREPARATION TIME: 20 MINUTES   COOKING TIME: 1 HOUR

2 pounds fresh boneless, skinless freshwater fish
  (ideally, ½ pound each carp, pike, whitefish,
  and trout)
1 medium potato, peeled and grated
1 medium onion, very finely chopped
1 tablespoon minced or grated fresh ginger
2 tablespoons canola oil
1 tablespoon sugar
1 teaspoon salt
½ teaspoon freshly ground black pepper
1 egg plus 1 egg white

TO COOK THE FISH:
fish skin, fish bones, and/or heads
3 large carrots, peeled and cut into ¼-inch slices
3 stalks celery, cut into ¼-inch slices
1 large onion, thinly sliced
Salt and pepper
Lettuce leaves for serving
Red or white horseradish sauce for serving
  (page 148)

1. Wash the fish and blot dry. Cut each piece of fish into ½-inch cubes. As you do so, feel for bones and remove any you find with tweezers or pliers. Place the fish in a food processor, filling the processor bowl not more than a quarter of the way. Add some grated potato, chopped onion, and ginger. Finely chop the fish by running the processor in short bursts. Do not overgrind. The texture should be coarse, like ground beef. Transfer the ground fish to a mixing bowl. Continue grinding the fish, potato, and onion in this fashion until all is used up.

2. Add the oil, sugar, salt, pepper, egg, and egg white. Mix well with your fingers or a wooden spoon. Boil a spoonful of the mixture to taste for seasoning. The mixture should be highly seasoned.

3. Line the bottom of a large pot with the fish skins, bones, and head (if using). Arrange half the sliced carrots, celery, and onions on top. Wet your hands with cold water and form oval balls of fish mixture: each should be about 3½ inches long and 2 inches wide. Gently lay the fish balls on the sliced vegetables. Arrange the remaining sliced carrots, celery, and onions on top. Add water to cover by 4 inches and salt and pepper to taste and gradually bring to a boil.

4. Reduce the heat to a gentle simmer. Gently simmer the gefilte fish until firm and cooked through, 1 hour. Remove the pan from the heat. Using a slotted spoon, transfer the fish balls to a baking dish or platter and let cool to room temperature. Arrange some of the carrots, celery, and onions over the fish and strain some of the cooking liquid on top. Discard the skin and bones. Refrigerate the gefilte fish until cold. The cooking liquid will gel.

5. To serve, place 1 ball of gefilte fish per person on a plate lined with a lettuce leaf. Garnish with a few of the carrot and celery slices and a spoonful of the jellied cooking liquid on top. Serve the horseradish sauce on page 148 on the side.

Makes 8 pieces of gefilte fish, which will serve 8

223.9 CALORIES PER SERVING; 23.1 G PROTEIN; 8.7 G FAT; 1.4 G SATURATED FAT; 12.8 G CARBOHYDRATE; 387.3 MG SODIUM; 96.9 MG CHOLESTEROL

Chicken and Turkey Dishes

✄ Roumanian Chicken Fricassee ✄

This rib-sticking fricassee is modeled on a specialty of Sammy's Roumanian in New York. If you haven't been to this Jewish restaurant on the Lower East Side, run, don't walk, to an experience that could be described as a never-ending bar mitzvah that's open to the public. From the pitchers of schmaltz on the table to complimentary egg creams served when you get your check, a meal at Sammy's is the ultimate Jewish-American dining experience. As for the fricassee, it owes its rich flavor to a triple blast of tomatoes: whole tomatoes, tomato sauce, and tomato paste.

PREPARATION TIME: 20 MINUTES   COOKING TIME: 40 MINUTES

1½ pounds boneless, skinless chicken breast, washed, blotted dry, and cut into 2-inch pieces
1 to 2 cloves garlic, minced
½ teaspoon each salt and freshly ground black pepper, or to taste

FOR THE SAUCE:
1 tablespoon vegetable oil
1 medium onion, finely chopped
1 green bell pepper, seeded and cut into thin strips

1 to 2 cloves garlic, finely chopped
1 teaspoon sweet paprika
½ teaspoon hot pepper flakes
2 tablespoons tomato paste
1 (28-ounce) can peeled tomatoes with juices
¼ cup canned tomato sauce
3 tablespoons chopped fresh parsley (preferably flat-leaf)
½ teaspoon brown sugar (optional)

1. Place the chicken in a bowl and toss with the garlic, salt, and pepper. Let marinate for 15 minutes while you make the sauce.

2. Heat the oil in a large, heavy saucepan. Add the onion and pepper and cook until soft but not brown, about 3 minutes. Add the garlic, paprika, and hot pepper flakes and cook for 1 minute. Add the tomato paste and fry for 30 seconds.

3. Coarsely puree the canned tomatoes with their juices in a food processor. Add this mixture to the pan along with the tomato sauce and 2 tablespoons parsley. Simmer the sauce until thick and richly flavored, 10 to 15 minutes, stirring often. Taste the sauce: if too acidic, add the sugar. If you like a smooth fricassee, return the sauce to the processor and puree. (I prefer a chunky fricassee, so I generally don't bother.)

4. Stir the chicken into the sauce and simmer until cooked and richly flavored, 10 to 15 minutes. Correct seasoning, adding salt and pepper to taste. Transfer the fricassee to a platter and garnish with the remaining 1 tablespoon parsley.

Serves 4

111 CALORIES PER SERVING; 3.1 G PROTEIN; 4 G FAT; .4 G SATURATED FAT; 16 G CARBOHYDRATE; 415 MG SODIUM; 0 MG CHOLESTEROL

Roumanian chicken fricassee.

⚥ Chicken with Eggplant—a New "Shepherd's Pie" ⚥

At first glance, this traditional Jewish holiday dish from Syria would not seem a likely candidate for a heart-healthy makeover.
After all, what could be worse than a layered casserole of fried eggplant and roast chicken? But I like a challenge
(I also like the haunting flavors of cinnamon and allspice), so I decided to make the recipe with
grilled eggplant instead of fried. The result may not be traditional, but it sure is delicious.

PREPARATION TIME: 30 MINUTES   COOKING TIME: 1 HOUR

3 eggplants (3½ to 4 pounds—try to choose
   eggplants that are relatively long, slender, and
   cylindrical in shape)
9 cloves garlic, cut lengthwise in half
⅓ cup finely chopped flat-leaf parsley
Salt and freshly ground black pepper, to taste
4 teaspoons extra-virgin olive oil
1 large onion, thinly sliced
1 clove garlic, minced

½ to 1 teaspoon ground cinnamon
¼ to ½ teaspoon ground allspice
4 cups shredded cooked chicken (preferably
   breast—reserved from making broth on page
   189)
½ cup chicken broth
Spray oil
¼ cup unflavored dried bread crumbs

1. Build a hot fire in your barbecue grill. Make 6 slits in each eggplant, using the tip of a paring knife. Insert a half clove of garlic in each. Grill the eggplants until the skins are charred black and the flesh is very tender, 20 to 30 minutes in all, turning with tongs. Transfer the eggplants to a plate to cool.

2. Scrape the burned skin off the eggplant. Coarsely chop the eggplant flesh with the garlic cloves by hand or in a food processor. Add half the parsley and salt and pepper to taste. The mixture should be highly seasoned.

3. Heat the olive oil in a nonstick frying pan. Add the onion, minced garlic, remaining parsley, cinnamon, and allspice and cook over medium heat until the onion is golden brown, 4 to 6 minutes, stirring with a wooden spoon. Stir in the chicken and chicken broth. Simmer until most of the broth is absorbed, 5

minutes. Add salt, pepper, and, if desired, additional cinnamon and allspice to taste. The mixture should be highly seasoned.

4. Lightly spray an attractive baking dish (I use a 10-inch oval) with oil. Arrange half the eggplant mixture over the bottom of the dish. Spread the chicken mixture on top. Arrange the remaining eggplant mixture on top and smooth the top with a fork. The "shepherd's pie" can be prepared ahead to this stage and refrigerated.

5. Preheat the oven to 400 degrees. Sprinkle the bread crumbs over the "shepherd's pie" and lightly spray with oil. Bake until the top is crusty and golden and the "pie" is bubbling hot, 10 to 15 minutes. Serve at once.

Serves 4 to 6

430 CALORIES PER 4 SERVINGS; 49 G PROTEIN; 10.7 G FAT; 2.2 G SATURATED FAT;
35 G CARBOHYDRATE; 179 MG SODIUM; 119 MG CHOLESTEROL

🐦 Aunt Annette's Gedemfted Chicken 🐦

Demfting refers to a venerable Eastern European Jewish cooking technique: braising a chicken or a roast in a sealed heavy pot on the stove. And no one does it better than my great-aunt, Annette Farber. The secret to making a rich brown gravy is to let the onions "catch" and caramelize several times, before adding more water. **Note:** *I like to use bone-in chicken breasts for this recipe: the bones provide extra flavor. But you could certainly use boneless breasts, in which case you'd need 1½ pounds.*

PREPARATION TIME: 15 MINUTES   COOKING TIME: 1 HOUR

1¾ pounds bone-in but skinless chicken breasts
Salt and freshly ground black pepper, to taste
3 cloves garlic, thinly sliced
1 tablespoon vegetable oil
2 medium onions, peeled and cut into ¼-inch slices (about 2 cups)

2 carrots, scrubbed and cut into ¼-inch slices
2 stalks celery, washed and cut into ¼-inch slices
1½ pounds potatoes, peeled and cut into 1½-inch pieces
3 tablespoons chopped flat-leaf parsley

1. Wash the chicken breasts and blot dry. Cut each breast into 3-inch pieces. Place the chicken breasts in a bowl and toss with the salt, pepper, and garlic. Let marinate for 20 minutes.

2. Pour the oil on the bottom of a large, heavy, nonstick sauté pan with a tightly fitting lid. Arrange the sliced onions, carrots, celery, and half the parsley over the bottom. Place the chicken pieces on top. Add 3 tablespoons water to the pan and tightly cover.

3. Cook the chicken over medium-high heat until the onions "catch" and are dark golden brown, 10 to 15 minutes. You'll need to check the onions often (you want them to brown, not burn), stirring as needed to ensure even browning.

4. Add ¼ cup water and stir to dissolve the dark onion juices. Continue cooking the chicken until the onions catch and brown again, 5 to 10 minutes.

5. Stir in the potatoes, half the parsley, and 1½ cups water. Tightly cover the pot and simmer until the chicken and potatoes are cooked, 20 to 30 minutes. (Stir from time to time to ensure even cooking.) Lower the heat as needed, to keep the mixture from burning. When the chicken is ready, the pan juices will be thick and gravylike. Add water as needed. Correct the seasoning, adding salt and pepper to taste.

Serves 4

427 CALORIES PER SERVING; 44 G PROTEIN; 6 G FAT; 1 G SATURATED FAT; 48 G CARBOHYDRATE; 162 MG SODIUM; 98 MG CHOLESTEROL

Chicken Cutlets with Mushroom Stuffing

These crusty chicken cutlets were one of the comfort foods of my childhood. In the old days, we pan-fried them in oil (or even deep-fried them). Today, I use a technique called bake-frying: the cutlets are sprayed with a little oil and baked until crisp in a hot oven. To make up for the lost richness, I add a mushroom stuffing to the chicken breasts. You won't miss the fat for a minute. **Note:** *To make a Passover version of these cutlets, replace the flour and bread crumbs with matzo meal. (You dip twice in the matzo meal.)*

PREPARATION TIME: 15 MINUTES   COOKING TIME: 25 MINUTES

FOR THE MUSHROOM STUFFING:
8 ounces button mushrooms, trimmed and wiped
  clean with a damp paper towel
1 shallot, coarsely chopped
1 clove garlic, coarsely chopped
3 tablespoons chopped parsley (preferably flat-leaf)
Salt and freshly ground black pepper

4 large boneless, skinless half chicken breasts with the tenderloins (the long, slender strip of muscle loosely attached to the breast) removed (each piece should weigh 5 to 6 ounces)
Salt and freshly ground black pepper, to taste
¾ cup flour for dredging
½ cup egg substitute
1 cup bread crumbs or cracker crumbs
Spray oil
Lemon wedges for serving

1. Prepare the stuffing. Cut the mushrooms in quarters and place in a food processor. Add the shallot, garlic, and parsley. Finely chop the vegetables by running the processor in short bursts. Do not over-process, or the mixture will become mushy.

2. Transfer the mushroom mixture to a nonstick frying pan and cook over medium-high heat, stirring with a wooden spoon, until the mushroom liquid has evaporated and the stuffing is thick and dry. Add salt and pepper to taste. The stuffing should be highly seasoned. Transfer the stuffing to a plate and let cool to room temperature.

3. Wash the chicken breasts and blot dry. Trim off any visible fat. Lay a breast at the edge of your cutting board and, holding it flat with the palm of your hand, cut a deep pocket in the side. Pocket the remaining chicken breasts the same way. Place a spoonful of mushroom stuffing in each chicken breast and pin shut with a toothpick. Season the outside of the chicken breasts with salt and pepper.

4. Place the flour in a shallow bowl, the egg substitute in another, and the bread crumbs in a third. Place a baking sheet in the oven and preheat oven to 400 degrees.

5. Just before serving, dip each breast first in flour, shaking off the excess, then in egg substitute, and finally in bread crumbs, shaking off the excess. Spray the preheated baking sheet with oil and arrange the chicken breasts on top. Lightly spray the tops of the breasts with oil.

6. Bake the chicken breasts until golden brown and cooked, 10 to 15 minutes, turning twice. Serve the chicken cutlets with lemon wedges. Remind the eaters to watch out for toothpicks. If desired, with these chicken breasts you could serve the tomato sauce on page 95.

Serves 4

397 CALORIES PER SERVING; 44 G PROTEIN; 5.5 G FAT; 1.1 G SATURATED FAT; 41 G CARBOHYDRATE; 385 MG SODIUM; 82 MG CHOLESTEROL

⚞ Israeli Spiced Turkey Cutlets ⚟

Here is a tasty variation on the preceding recipe. Turkey cutlets are common currency in Israel—served as a quick on-the-run snack or as the centerpiece of a proper meal. A quick spice rub adds flavor while bake-frying controls the fat.

PREPARATION TIME: 10 MINUTES   COOKING TIME: 12 MINUTES, PLUS 15 MINUTES FOR MARINATING

4 broad, thin slices turkey breast (each 5 to 6 ounces and about ¼ inch thick)

FOR THE SPICE MIX:
1 teaspoon ground cumin
1 teaspoon ground coriander
1 teaspoon sweet paprika
1 teaspoon ground turmeric

1 teaspoon black pepper
1 teaspoon salt

¾ cup flour for dredging
½ cup egg substitute
1 cup bread crumbs or cracker crumbs
Spray oil
Lemon wedges for serving

1. Wash the turkey and blot dry. If any pieces are thicker than ¼ inch, place between two sheets of plastic wrap and pound with the side of a cleaver.

2. Combine the spices and salt in a bowl and stir to mix. Rub the turkey slices on both sides with spice mix. Let marinate for 15 minutes.

3. Place the flour in a shallow bowl, the egg substitute in another, and the bread crumbs in a third. Place a nonstick frying pan in the oven and preheat oven to 400 degrees.

4. Just before serving, dip each slice of turkey first in flour, shaking off the excess, then in egg substitute, and finally in bread crumbs, shaking off the excess. Spray the preheated baking sheet with oil and arrange the turkey cutlets on top. Lightly spray the tops of the cutlets with oil. Bake until golden brown and cooked through, 8 to 12 minutes, turning twice. Serve the turkey cutlets with lemon wedges. For Passover, substitute matzo meal for the flour and bread crumbs.

Serves 4

383 CALORIES PER SERVING; 44 G PROTEIN; 3.8 G FAT; .9 G SATURATED FAT; 38 G CARBOHYDRATE; 941 MG SODIUM; 99 MG CHOLESTEROL

✒ Moroccan Chicken with Dried Fruits and Caramelized Onions ✒

Friday night is chicken night throughout much of the Jewish world. In my Ashkenazi family, the arrival of Sabbath meant chicken soup, capon, or gedempfted chicken. In Morocco, a Friday-night chicken dinner would mean this lively chicken stew—fragrant with saffron and turmeric—served over couscous. The pairing of fruit and meat, the fusing of sweet and savory flavors, is characteristic of Jewish cooking from North Africa to Eastern Europe.

PREPARATION TIME: 30 MINUTES   COOKING TIME: 40 MINUTES

2 pounds boneless, skinless chicken breasts

4 sprigs each parsley and cilantro, tied into a bundle (a bouquet garni)

2 tomatoes, cut in half, seeded, and grated

1 small onion, thinly sliced

2 cloves garlic, minced

2 teaspoons minced fresh ginger or ½ teaspoon ginger powder

1 teaspoon ground coriander

½ teaspoon turmeric

¼ teaspoon saffron threads

1 tablespoon olive oil

1 pound potatoes (2 medium potatoes), peeled and cut into 1-inch pieces

1 pound carrots, peeled and cut into 1-inch pieces

18 pitted prunes

Salt and freshly ground black pepper

FOR THE CARAMELIZED ONION TOPPING:

8 dried figs (about 4 ounces)

3 medium onions (about 12 ounces), peeled and cut into thin wedges

½ cup raisins

¼ cup sugar

1 to 2 tablespoons canola oil

1 teaspoon ground cinnamon, or to taste

Couscous (page 131)

3 tablespoons chopped flat-leaf parsley

1. Wash the chicken breasts and blot dry. Cut each breast into 2-inch diamond shapes. Place the chicken, the parsley and cilantro bundle, tomatoes, onion, garlic, ginger, coriander, turmeric, saffron, and oil in the bottom of a couscoussière or large, deep, heavy pot. Place over high heat and cook until the chicken is shiny and golden, about 5 minutes.

2. Add 2 quarts water and bring to a boil. Reduce the heat and gently simmer the chicken until very tender, about 20 minutes, adding the potatoes and carrots after 5 minutes, the prunes after 15 minutes. Skim the surface of the broth to remove any fat that rises to the surface. Add salt and pepper to taste.

3. Meanwhile, prepare the topping. Cut the stems off the figs and cut the figs in half. Cook the figs and onions in boiling salted water to cover in a saucepan until tender, about 5 minutes. Drain off the water. Add the raisins, sugar, oil, and cinnamon. Cook over high heat for 3 minutes. Add 3 tablespoons water and continue cooking until the mixture is thick and caramelized, 3 to 6 minutes more.

4. To serve, mound the couscous on a large platter. Make a depression in the center and place the chicken on top. Strain the broth (the chicken cooking liquid) into a bowl for serving on the side. Spoon the vegetables and prunes around the chicken. Spoon the caramelized onion mixture over the chicken and sprinkle with parsley. Let each guest ladle the broth over his couscous, chicken, and vegetables.

Serves 6

589 CALORIES PER SERVING; 41 G PROTEIN; 7.4 G FAT; 1.1 G SATURATED FAT; 94 G CARBOHYDRATE; 145 MG SODIUM; 88 MG CHOLESTEROL

Note: Grating a tomato is a terrific way to obtain the tomato flesh without the skin. Cut the tomato in half; grate it on the large-hole side of a grater, cut side to the grater. The flesh will fall into the bowl. The skin will remain on the outside of the grater.

✄ Sweet-and-Sour Turkey Stuffed Cabbage Rolls ✄

Golubtsis. Golabki. Holishkes. Praakes. Yaprakes. Sarmali. Gefullted kraut. The sheer multiplicity of names suggests the enormous popularity of stuffed cabbage rolls. Jews in virtually every corner of the world have a version—many made with ground beef or ground veal. To lighten the traditional recipe, I use ground turkey. Not all ground turkeys are equal, however, and unless you seek out lean ground turkey breast, you may be getting meat that's 20 percent fat. The following recipe comes from Mama Drevich, concentration camp survivor and mother of my dear friend, Shirley. I love the play of sweet and sour in a dish that's nearly as old as Judaism itself.

Note: There are two ways to soften the cabbage leaves—by freezing and by boiling. The former is easier, but you need to remember to start the recipe the night before. (The boiling method is described in the vegetarian stuffed cabbage on page 111.)

PREPARATION TIME: 30 MINUTES   COOKING TIME: 2 HOURS

1 medium green cabbage

FOR THE FILLING:
1 pound lean ground turkey
¼ cup uncooked rice
¼ cup grated or finely chopped onion
1 clove garlic, minced
¼ cup club soda

¼ cup egg substitute or 2 egg whites
1 tablespoon ketchup
1 tablespoon chopped fresh dill (optional)
Salt and freshly ground black pepper, to taste

TO FINISH THE STUFFED CABBAGE:
1 small onion, thinly sliced
Sweet and sour tomato sauce (see below)

1. The night before, place the cabbage in the freezer and freeze until hard. The next day, leave the cabbage out in a bowl at room temperature until thawed.

2. Prepare the filling. Combine the turkey, rice, onion, garlic, club soda, egg substitute, ketchup, dill (if using), salt, and pepper in a mixing bowl and stir to mix. (Actually, I find the best way to mix is to squeeze the meat with my fingers.)

3. Preheat the oven to 325 degrees.

4. Peel off and discard any tough, dark green, exterior leaves from the cabbage. Peel off a leaf and lay it flat on your work surface, cupped side up. Using the side of a cleaver or a scaloppine pounder, flatten the stem to make the leaf pliable. Place 3 tablespoons turkey mixture in the center of the leaf toward the bottom (the stem end). Roll the leaf up one third of the way to encase the filling, fold in the sides, and

continue rolling to obtain a neat bundle. (The cabbage is rolled the same way you'd fold a crepe to make a blintz.) Repeat until all the filling is used up: you should wind up with 12 cabbage rolls.

5. Thinly slice a little of the cabbage core (the part left over) and arrange the slices over the bottom of a 9 by 12-inch baking dish. Arrange the sliced onion on top. Arrange the stuffed cabbage rolls, seam side down, on top. Pour the sweet and sour sauce over the cabbage. Cover the dish with foil. The recipe can be prepared several hours ahead to this stage and refrigerated.

6. Bake the cabbage for 1 hour covered. Remove the foil and continue baking uncovered until the cabbage rolls are tender and the sauce is thick and flavorful, about 1 hour longer.

Makes 12 cabbage rolls, which will feed 4 to 6

525 CALORIES PER 4 SERVINGS; 29 G PROTEIN; 11 G FAT; 2.8 G SATURATED FAT; 84 G CARBOHYDRATE; 1,315 MG SODIUM; 90 MG CHOLESTEROL

⚥ Sweet-and-Sour Tomato Sauce ⚥

This sweet and sour sauce is of relatively new coinage. (Tomato ketchup didn't become commercially available until 1875.)
But the interplay of sweet and sour has struck a chord in the sensibilities of Jews around the world.

PREPARATION TIME: 5 MINUTES   COOKING TIME: 2 HOURS (INCLUDED IN THE PREVIOUS RECIPE)

1 cup canned tomato sauce
1 cup tomato ketchup
2 cups water or chicken broth or beef broth
½ cup raisins
6 pitted prunes, finely chopped

1 small onion, finely chopped
3 cloves garlic, minced
¼ cup brown sugar, or to taste
2 tablespoons lemon juice
Salt and freshly ground black pepper

1. Combine the ingredients in a large bowl and stir to mix. Pour this mixture over the cabbage and bake as described above.

Serves 4 to 6

219 CALORIES PER 4 SERVINGS; 3.2 G PROTEIN; .5 G FAT; .09 G SATURATED FAT; 56 G CARBOHYDRATE; 1,090 MG SODIUM; 0 MG CHOLESTEROL

Meat Dishes

❧❧❧◆❧❧

🐟 Holiday Brisket with Dried Fruits and Sweet Wine 🐟

In our family, a holiday simply isn't a holiday without a brisket dinner. Lengthy cooking transforms this tough, flavorful cut of meat into fork-tender bites of heaven. Especially when the brisket is braised in sweet red wine with a fruity entourage of raisins, prunes, and apricots. It's customary to serve brisket with fruit at Rosh Hashanah, the Jewish New Year. (The fruit symbolizes a hope for sweetness and plenty in the coming year.) Note two offbeat techniques in this recipe. The first is braising the brisket without browning it first. I've tried it both ways: browning adds fat and mess to the preparation without any significant improvement of flavor. Note, too, how the brisket is sliced midway through the cooking process. This is a trick I learned from my wife: you get neater slices when you carve the meat before it's fully cooked.

PREPARATION TIME: 15 MINUTES   COOKING TIME: 3 TO 4 HOURS

1 (3-pound beef brisket), trimmed of all visible fat
Salt and freshly ground black pepper, to taste
1½ tablespoons canola oil
1 large onion, finely chopped
2 carrots, finely chopped
2 stalks celery, finely chopped
2 cloves garlic, finely chopped
¼ cup chopped parsley (preferably flat-leaf)

1½ cups Concord grape wine
2½ cups beef or chicken broth or water, or as needed
2 bay leaves
1½ cups dried apricots (8 ounces)
1½ cups pitted prunes
1 cup golden raisins

1. Preheat the oven to 350 degrees.

2. Lightly score the brisket on both sides in a cross-hatch pattern, using a sharp knife. Season the brisket all over with salt and pepper. Heat the oil in a non-stick frying pan. Add the onion, carrots, celery, garlic, and 3 tablespoons parsley and cook over medium heat until lightly browned, about 5 minutes.

3. Spoon half this mixture into a roasting pan or baking dish just large enough to hold the brisket. Lay the brisket on top and spoon the remaining vegetables over it. Add the wine, broth, and bay leaves. Tightly cover the pan and bake the brisket for 1½ hours.

4. Transfer the brisket to a cutting board and thinly slice it across the grain. (An electric knife works great for slicing.) Stir half the dried fruits into

roasting pan juices. Lay the sliced brisket on top. Arrange the remaining dried fruits on top. Season with salt and pepper. Add broth as needed to cover the meat and fruit.

5. Continue baking the brisket until the meat is tender enough to cut with a fork, an additional 1½ to 2 hours. Add broth or water as needed to keep the meat and fruits moist. If there's too much cooking liquid, uncover the pan the last half hour to allow some of it to evaporate.

6. Transfer the brisket to a platter. Using a slotted spoon, transfer the fruits to the platter around the meat. Discard the bay leaf. Pour the pan juices into the sort of gravy boat that allows you to pour the broth off from the bottom, leaving the fat on top. If you

Holiday brisket with dried fruits and sweet wine.

don't have one of these, pour the gravy into a bowl or measuring cup and skim the fat off the top with a ladle. Spoon some of the gravy over the meat and fruit, serving the rest on the side. Sprinkle the remaining 1 tablespoon parsley over the meat and serve at once.

Serves 8

469 CALORIES PER SERVING; 31 G PROTEIN; 12 G FAT; 3.7 G SATURATED FAT; 51 G CARBOHYDRATE; 134 MG SODIUM; 84 MG CHOLESTEROL

⚰ Wine Country Brisket ⚰

Not everyone likes a sweet, Eastern European–style brisket. A few years ago, my wife and I were in the Napa Valley and we happened to have a holiday brisket braised in zinfandel and roasted with baby onions and potatoes—without the least trace of sugar. I don't need to tell you, it was delicious. When possible, use fingerling potatoes and baby red onions.

PREPARATION TIME: 20 MINUTES   COOKING TIME: 3 TO 4 HOURS

1 (3-pound beef brisket), trimmed of all visible fat
Salt and freshly ground black pepper, to taste
1 tablespoon canola oil
4 shallots, finely chopped (about 1 cup)
2 stalks celery, finely chopped
2 cloves garlic, finely chopped
¼ cup chopped parsley (preferably flat-leaf)
1 bottle zinfandel wine

1 cup beef or chicken broth or water, or as needed
1 bay leaf
1 sprig of thyme
2 pounds fingerling potatoes or small red or white potatoes, scrubbed
1 pound baby red onions, white onions, or cipollini, peeled
1 pound baby carrots, peeled and trimmed

1. Preheat the oven to 350 degrees.

2. Lightly score the brisket on both sides in a crosshatch pattern, using a sharp knife. Season the brisket all over with salt and pepper. Heat the oil in a nonstick frying pan. Add the shallots, celery, garlic, and 3 tablespoons parsley and cook over medium heat until lightly browned, about 5 minutes.

3. Spoon half this mixture into a roasting pan or baking dish just large enough to hold the brisket. Lay the brisket on top and spoon the remaining vegetables over it. Add the wine, broth, bay leaf, and thyme. Tightly cover the pan and bake the brisket for 1½ hours.

4. Transfer the brisket to a cutting board and thinly slice it across the grain. (An electric knife works great for slicing.) Discard the sprig of thyme and bay leaf. Pour the pan juices and chopped vegetables into a blender and puree until smooth. Return the meat to the roasting pan and arrange the potatoes, onions, and carrots around it. Season the pureed pan juices with salt and pepper and pour over the meat and vegetables.

5. Continue baking the brisket until the meat is tender enough to cut with a fork, an additional 1½ to 2 hours. Add broth or water as needed to keep the meat and vegetables moist. If there's too much cooking liquid, uncover the pan the last half hour to allow some of it to evaporate.

6. Transfer the brisket to a platter. Using a slotted spoon, transfer the vegetables to the platter around the meat. Correct the seasoning of the sauce, adding salt and pepper to taste. Pour the sauce over the meat and vegetables. (For a more refined presentation, strain the sauce over the meat.) Sprinkle with the remaining 1 tablespoon parsley and serve at once.

Serves 10 to 12

394 CALORIES PER 10 SERVINGS; 32 G PROTEIN; 12.3 G FAT; 3.7 G SATURATED FAT; 26 G CARBOHYDRATE; 141 MG SODIUM; 84 MG CHOLESTEROL

⊠ Mama Drevich's Veal Meat Loaf ⊠

Seema "Sylvia" Salzberg came from a long line of bakers in the town of Kozienice, Poland (a town whose rabbis were immortalized in Isaac Bashevis Singer's novels). But when her daughter, my friend Shirley Drevich, remembers her mother's cooking, it's the meat loaf she misses the most. And what meat loaf! The delicacy of lean ground veal punctuated with pungent fresh dill and garlic. A loaf that's crusty and brown on the outside, yet meltingly moist within. The shot of club soda acts as a leavening agent, producing an uncommonly light meat loaf. If you've always thought of meat loaf as a leaden, plebeian dish, wait until you taste this one!

PREPARATION TIME: 10 MINUTES   COOKING TIME: 45 MINUTES

Spray oil
2 slices white bread
1½ pounds lean ground veal
3 egg whites or ⅓ cup egg substitute
3 cloves garlic, minced
¾ cup diced onion

3 tablespoons finely chopped fresh parsley
3 tablespoons finely chopped fresh dill
⅓ cup club soda
Salt (I'd use 1 teaspoon) and freshly ground black pepper

1. Preheat the oven to 375 degrees. Preheat a non-stick loaf pan you've lightly sprayed with oil.

2. Soak the bread in warm water for 3 minutes. Squeeze the bread in your fingers to wring out the excess liquid. Place the bread in a mixing bowl and stir in the veal, egg whites, garlic, onion, parsley, and dill. Mix well with your hands or a wooden spoon. Stir in the club soda and salt and pepper to taste. (If you don't like tasting raw meat, fry a little pancake of veal in a nonstick frying pan.) The meat loaf should be highly seasoned.

3. Spoon the veal mixture into the preheated loaf pan. Bake the meat loaf until crusty and golden brown on top and cooked through, 50 minutes. (Use an instant-read meat thermometer to test for doneness. The internal temperature should be 165 degrees.) Remove the pan from the oven and let cool for 2 minutes, then invert the meat loaf onto a platter. Cut into slices for serving.

Serves 4

259.2 CALORIES PER SERVING; 38.6 G PROTEIN; 6.2 G FAT; 1.8 G SATURATED FAT;
9.9 G CARBOHYDRATE; 270.9 MG SODIUM; 136.2 MG CHOLESTEROL

Greek Lamb Stew with Romaine Lettuce and Dill

My aunt Rosa Miller is an extraordinary Sephardic cook. But because I was a finicky eater when I was young, I used to dread going to her house for dinner. Rosa was forever serving "weird" foods, like feta cheese or chickpeas, and as she was European (Greek to be precise), one simply did not leave food left one's plate. In my later years, I have come to cherish Aunt Rosa's cooking and that of her mother, Lily. This hearty stew was popular among Greek Jews in the springtime, when the first of the year's romaine lettuce crop came in season. The lettuce and dill offset the richness of the lamb, making this one of the most refreshing stews you'll ever taste.

PREPARATION TIME: 20 MINUTES   COOKING TIME: 1¼ HOURS

1¾ pounds lean lamb (from the leg)
Salt and freshly ground pepper
1 tablespoon extra-virgin olive oil
4 large heads romaine lettuce, separated into leaves, washed and spun dry
1 bunch of fresh dill, finely chopped (leave 6 sprigs whole for garnish)

1 bunch of scallions, trimmed and finely chopped
6 tablespoons fresh lemon juice (2 lemons), or to taste
1 teaspoon sugar

1. Trim any fat and sinews off the lamb and cut it into 1½-inch cubes. Season well with salt and pepper. Heat the olive oil in a large nonstick sauté pan and thoroughly brown the lamb on all sides over high heat, working in several batches so as not to crowd the pan. Pour off and discard the fat in the pan.

2. Return the lamb to the pan and add 1 inch water (about 2 cups). Bring the lamb to a boil, reduce the heat, cover the pan, and gently simmer the lamb until tender, about 1 hour. (Add water as needed to keep the lamb moist.) Transfer the lamb to a platter with a slotted spoon, reserving the cooking liquid in the pan.

3. Cut the lettuce leaves into 2-inch squares, leaving 6 large leaves whole for garnish. Add the diced lettuce, dill, scallions, and lemon juice to the pan with the lamb cooking liquid. Briskly simmer these ingredients, covered, until the lettuce is tender, about 5 minutes. You should have about 1¾ cups cooking liquid. (You may need to uncover the pan after a few minutes to evaporate any excess liquid.)

4. Return the lamb to the pan and simmer until thoroughly heated. Add the sugar and salt and pepper to taste. (If extra tartness is desired, you can add a little extra lemon juice as well.) Arrange the whole lettuce leaves on a platter and mound the stew in the center. Garnish with whole sprigs of dill. Aunt Rosa suggests serving the stew with crusty Greek or French bread (or matzo during Passover) for dipping, or rice pilaf.

Serves 6

238 CALORIES PER SERVING; 29 G PROTEIN; 11 G FAT; 3 G SATURATED FAT; 5 G CARBOHYDRATE; 93 MG SODIUM; 87 MG CHOLESTEROL

⛧ Lamb Tagine ⛧

Lamb has deep religious significance for Jews—particularly for the Jews of North Africa and the Middle and Near East. Being a spring food, lamb is the traditional fare of Passover. Lamb blood marked the doorways of the Israelites when the Angel of Death flew over to slay the firstborn sons of Egypt—an event commemorated by the lamb shank bone that appears on the Seder plate. A tagine is a lamb stew from North Africa—named for the conical earthenware dish in which it's traditionally cooked. Serve this savory tagine over couscous. You'll never again think about lamb in quite the same way.

PREPARATION TIME: 20 MINUTES   COOKING TIME: 1½ TO 2 HOURS

2 pounds lean leg of lamb, cut into 2-inch cubes
1 teaspoon turmeric
1 teaspoon ground cumin
1 teaspoon ground coriander
1 teaspoon paprika
1 teaspoon black pepper
1 teaspoon salt, or to taste
½ pound turnips, cut into 1-inch pieces
½ pound carrots, cut into 1-inch pieces
½ pound parsnips, cut into 1-inch pieces
½ pound potatoes, cut into 1-inch pieces (optional)
1½ tablespoons olive oil
1 large onion, finely chopped

3 cloves garlic, minced
1 tablespoon minced fresh ginger
¼ cup chopped parsley (preferably flat-leaf)
10 cups water
1 cinnamon stick
¼ teaspoon saffron threads, soaked in 1 tablespoon warm water
½ cup raisins
½ cup cooked chickpeas

Couscous (page 131), for serving
Harissa (North African hot sauce—page 152), for serving

1. Place the lamb in a mixing bowl and toss with the turmeric, cumin, coriander, paprika, pepper, and salt. Let marinate for 20 minutes. Meanwhile, prepare all the vegetables.

2. Heat the olive oil in a large, heavy pot (preferably nonstick). Brown the lamb, working in several batches. This will take 4 to 6 minutes per batch. Transfer the lamb to a platter with a slotted spoon. Pour out all but 1½ tablespoons fat.

3. Add the onion and cook over medium heat for 3 minutes. Add the garlic, ginger, and 2 tablespoons parsley and continue cooking rest of parsley until the onion begins to brown, 2 to 3 minutes more.

4. Return the lamb to the pot and stir in the water, cinnamon stick, and saffron. Gently simmer the lamb for 1 hour.

5. Add the turnips, carrots, parsnips, and potatoes. Simmer the tagine until the vegetables and lamb are very tender, about 30 minutes more. Add the raisins and chickpeas 10 minutes before the end. If the tagine starts to dry out (it should be quite soupy), add more water. The tagine should be highly seasoned; add salt or pepper as needed.

Serve the tagine over couscous sprinkled with the remaining parsley and served with the with harissa as a condiment. (One traditional way to serve couscous is to stir the harissa into 1 cup of the tagine broth and spoon it over the lamb.)

Serves 8

356.8 CALORIES PER SERVING; 34.6 G PROTEIN; 11 G FAT; 3 G SATURATED FAT;
30.5 G CARBOHYDRATE; 530 MG SODIUM; 96.8 MG CHOLESTEROL

✍ Shish Kebab with North African Seasonings ✍

It's a scene that's as old as Judaism itself: beef or lamb flavored with cumin and garlic, cooked on a spit or skewer over a campfire. Grilling wasn't really part of my Ashkenazic heritage, but in North Africa and the Middle East, it's one of the preferred ways to cook and socialize. Variations on a theme of kebab can be found in Jewish communities from Casablanca to Cochin. **Note:** *These kebabs are equally delicious made with lamb.*

PREPARATION TIME: 15 MINUTES, PLUS 1 TO 2 HOURS FOR MARINATING   COOKING TIME: 12 MINUTES

1½ pounds lean beef (such as sirloin or
   tenderloin)
1 tablespoon extra-virgin olive oil
3 cloves garlic, minced
1½ teaspoons paprika
1½ teaspoons ground coriander
1 teaspoon ground cumin, plus a little dish of
   cumin for sprinkling on the cooked meat
1 teaspoon each salt and freshly ground black
   pepper, or to taste
1 green bell pepper, cut into 1-inch squares
1 red bell pepper, cut into 1-inch squares

FOR THE RELISH:
1 large cucumber, peeled, seeded, and cut into ½-
   inch dice

1 large ripe tomato, cut into ½-inch dice (with
   juices)
2 stalks celery, cut into ½-inch dice
1 green bell pepper, cut into ½-inch dice
½ red onion, finely chopped
3 tablespoons chopped flat-leaf parsley
1 tablespoon capers
1 tablespoon red wine vinegar, or to taste
1 tablespoon extra-virgin olive oil

6 pita breads
Zehug (Yemenite hot sauce—page 151)
   (optional)

1. Cut the beef into 1½-inch cubes and place in a mixing bowl. Stir in 1 tablespoon oil, the garlic, paprika, coriander, cumin, salt, and pepper. Let the meat marinate for 1 to 2 hours in the refrigerator.

2. Combine the ingredients for the relish in an attractive serving bowl and toss to mix. Correct the seasoning, adding salt, pepper, and vinegar to taste. The relish should be highly seasoned.

3. Build a hot fire in your grill. Thread the beef cubes onto skewers, placing a square of bell pepper between each. Grill the kebabs to taste: 2 to 3 minutes per side (8 to 12 minutes in all) for medium rare.

4. Serve the kebabs with pita breads. Have each guest fold a pita bread around the meat and pull out the skewer. Sprinkle the meat with additional cumin if desired. Spoon relish (and zehug if desired) over the meat and eat like a wrap.

Serves 6

285.8 CALORIES PER SERVING; 36 G PROTEIN; 11.5 G FAT; 3.8 G SATURATED FAT;
8.6 G CARBOHYDRATE; 145.7 MG SODIUM; 100.8 MG CHOLESTEROL

⚘ Three B's Cholent ⚘
(Sabbath Baked Beans, Beef, and Barley)

"Sabbath without cholent is like a king without a throne," runs an old Yiddish saying. Hyperbole, perhaps, but the dictum reflects the importance of this supremely comforting casserole in traditional Jewish life. Cholent (sometimes spelled tscholent) was to Eastern European Jews what baked beans were to nineteenth-century New Englanders and what cassoulet remains to the French. Imagine a soulful stew of beans, barley, beef, and root vegetables slowly baked for hours to rib-sticking perfection. Traditionally, cholent would be placed in the oven on Friday afternoon and left to bake overnight as the oven cooled, so it could be eaten on the Sabbath without requiring any cooking.

Cholent (which seems to take its name from the French word chaleur—"heat") has fallen out of fashion among many modern American Jews, which is a shame, because few dishes offer so much flavor, nutrition, and satisfaction for so little work. As a nation of health-conscious eaters, we know we should eat ample portions of beans and grains, using meat sparingly, as a condiment. You couldn't find a better description of cholent. I've trimmed the fat a little, but otherwise left the recipe as it's been prepared for centuries.

Below is a basic recipe, which you should feel free to adapt to your taste. Some people add a sweet note in the form of prunes, raisins, or dried apricots. Others like the richness of goose or kishka, or the earthy flavor of chickpeas. Don't be intimidated by the long ingredient list. This cholent can be assembled quite literally in less than 20 minutes (although it does take 5 to 6 hours to bake). The bread crumb crust isn't strictly traditional, but I love the way it adds texture.

PREPARATION TIME: 20 MINUTES   COOKING TIME: 5½ TO 6½ HOURS, PLUS TIME FOR SOAKING THE BEANS

1½ cups dried kidney beans or navy beans
2 tablespoons canola oil
3 medium onions, finely chopped (about 3 cups)
2 stalks celery, finely chopped
5 cloves garlic, minced
1 tablespoon minced fresh ginger (optional)
¼ cup finely chopped parsley (preferably flat-leaf)
2 tablespoons sweet paprika
1 cup pearl barley
Salt and freshly ground black pepper
1½ pounds brisket

6 ounces beef salami, cut into 1-inch chunks (optional)
4 potatoes (6 to 8 ounces each), scrubbed and cut in quarters
4 carrots, peeled and cut into 2-inch pieces
2 cups tomato juice
6 to 8 cups beef, chicken, or vegetable broth or water, or as needed
1 bay leaf
¼ cup toasted bread crumbs (optional)
2 teaspoons olive oil (optional)

1. Spread out the beans on a baking sheet and pick through them, discarding any twigs or stones. Rinse the beans in a colander under cold water and place in a large bowl with water to cover by 2 inches. Soak the beans for at least 6 hours, preferably overnight. Or use the quick-soak method: place the beans in a large pot with 3 inches water to cover. Boil the beans for 10 minutes. Remove the pan from the heat and let the beans soak for 1 hour.

2. Preheat the oven to 275 degrees.

3. Heat the oil in a large, deep, heavy casserole. (A Dutch oven works great.) Add the onions, celery, garlic, ginger (if using), and 3 tablespoons parsley and cook over medium heat until the vegetables are nicely

browned, 5 to 8 minutes, stirring with a wooden spoon. Stir in the paprika and barley. Drain the beans and stir them in, too. Add salt and pepper: you'll need at least 1 tablespoon of the former and 1 teaspoon of the latter.

4. Cut the brisket across the grain into 2 or 3 pieces. Season the pieces with salt and pepper and bury among the beans and barley. Bury the salami (if using), potatoes, and carrots the same way. Add the tomato juice, broth, and bay leaf. (You'll need enough liquid to cover the beans and barley by 2 to 3 inches. Add more if needed.) Bring the mixture to a boil on the stove. Tightly cover the casserole and place it in the oven.

5. Bake the cholent until the beans and meat are tender, 5 to 6 hours. The broth should be absorbed, but the mixture should remain moist. (Add water or broth if you need to.) If you'd like to put a crust on your cholent, uncover the pot the last 30 minutes, sprinkle the bread crumbs over the top, and drizzle with the 2 teaspoons olive oil. Finish baking the cholent uncovered until top is crusty and brown. Sprinkle the remaining parsley on top and serve. (To facilitate serving, fish out the chunks of brisket and cut them into slices.) Discard the bay leaf.

Cholent is delectable hot out of the oven and leftovers are great rewarmed.

Serves 8

496 CALORIES PER SERVING; 32 G PROTEIN; 10 G FAT; 3 G SATURATED FAT; 69 G CARBOHYDRATE; 333 MG SODIUM; 53 MG CHOLESTEROL

Vegetarian Dishes

❧❧◆❧❧

🍴 Ratner's Vegetable Cutlets with Tomato Mushroom Gravy 🍴

Ratner's is a legendary kosher restaurant on Manhattan's Lower East Side. These vegetarian cutlets, chock-full of fresh vegetables and served with a tangy tomato mushroom gravy, are a long-standing specialty of this venerable restaurant. They're popular among the vegetarian members of my family and are even loved by my highly carnivorous stepson and son-in-law.

PREPARATION TIME: 40 MINUTES, PLUS 1 HOUR FOR CHILLING   COOKING TIME: 45 MINUTES

6 medium potatoes, scrubbed
Salt
1 pound carrots, peeled and cut into ¼-inch dice
1 pound green beans, trimmed and cut in ¼-inch pieces
1 pound frozen peas
1½ tablespoons olive oil
2 medium onions, finely chopped
6 white mushrooms, trimmed, wiped clean, and finely chopped

3 tablespoons finely chopped fresh parsley, plus 8 whole sprigs for garnish
¾ cup egg substitute or 2 eggs plus 2 whites, beaten with a fork
Approximately 2 cups matzo meal
Freshly ground black pepper
Spray oil
Tomato mushroom gravy (see page 109)

1. Place the potatoes in a large pot with cold, lightly salted water to cover by 2 inches. Bring the potatoes to a boil. Reduce the heat and simmer the potatoes until tender, about 20 minutes. (When cooked, a metal skewer will pierce the spuds easily.) Drain the potatoes in a colander, rinse under cold water until cool, and slip off the skins. Cut the cooked potatoes in quarters and mash in a large bowl with a potato masher or pestle. (Do not puree the potatoes in the food processor.)

2. Meanwhile, bring 2 quarts lightly salted water to a boil in a large saucepan. Cook the carrots, green beans, and peas until just tender, about 2 minutes. Drain these vegetables in a colander, refresh (rinse) under cold running water, drain well, and blot dry with paper towels.

3. Heat the oil in a large nonstick skillet. Cook the onions, mushrooms, and chopped parsley over medium-high heat until lightly browned, 5 minutes, stirring often.

4. Stir the onion-mushroom mixture, carrots, green beans, and peas into the mashed potatoes. Stir in ½ cup egg substitute and enough matzo meal to obtain a stiff but pliable mixture that you can form into patties. Add salt and pepper to taste. The mixture should be highly seasoned.

5. Shape the mixture into 12 flat patties and arrange on a platter lined with plastic wrap. Chill for 1 hour.

6. Place a nonstick baking sheet in the oven and preheat to 350 degrees.

7. Paint the tops of the cutlets with half the remaining egg substitute. Remove the preheated baking sheet from the oven and lightly spray it with oil.

Ratner's vegetable cutlets with tomato mushroom gravy.

Arrange the cutlets, egg glaze side down, on the baking sheet. Brush the tops of the cutlets with the remaining egg glaze. Bake the cutlets until firm and lightly browned, about 45 minutes.

8. Arrange the cutlets on a platter or plates. Garnish each with a sprig of parsley and serve with the following tomato mushroom gravy on the side.

Makes 12 cutlets, which will serve 6 as a main course

475 CALORIES PER SERVING; 17 G PROTEIN; 5.3 G FAT; .8 G SATURATED FAT; 92 G CARBOHYDRATE; 166 MG SODIUM; .3 MG CHOLESTEROL

⚱ Tomato Mushroom Gravy ⚱

This rich, colorful "gravy" (actually, it's more a tomato sauce) owes its complex flavor to the addition of mushroom powder. The latter, made from ground dried mushrooms, can be found at gourmet shops and natural food stores. (One good mail order source is Marché aux Délices, P. O. Box 1164, New York, N.Y. 10028; telephone 888-547-5471.) If unavailable, you can make your own mushroom powder by pulverizing dried porcini or Chinese black mushrooms in a spice mill.

PREPARATION TIME: 10 MINUTES   COOKING TIME: 15 MINUTES

1½ tablespoons olive oil
1 medium onion, finely chopped
1 carrot, peeled and finely chopped
2 stalks celery, finely chopped
1 green bell pepper, finely chopped
1 clove garlic, minced

2 tablespoons finely chopped parsley
3 tablespoons matzo meal
2 (16-ounce) cans peeled tomatoes
1 tablespoon mushroom powder
1 teaspoon hot or sweet paprika
Salt and freshly ground pepper

1. Heat the oil in a large nonstick skillet. Cook the onion, carrot, celery, pepper, garlic, and parsley over medium heat until soft but not brown, 4 minutes, stirring with a wooden spoon. Stir in the matzo meal and cook for 1 minute.

2. Drain the tomatoes, reserving the juices. Coarsely chop the tomatoes in the food processor or by hand. Stir the tomatoes with their juices, the mushroom powder, paprika, and 1 cup water into the vegetable mixture and bring to a boil. Reduce the heat and simmer the sauce until thick and richly flavored, about 10 minutes. Correct the seasoning, adding salt and pepper to taste. The sauce should be highly seasoned.

Note: This gravy is designed to be served with vegetable cutlets, but it's also fantastic ladled over pasta or poached chicken.

Makes 5 cups, which will serve 6 to 8

108 CALORIES PER 6 SERVINGS; 3 G PROTEIN; 4 G FAT; .5 G SATURATED FAT; 16 G CARBOHYDRATE; 304 MG SODIUM; 0 MG CHOLESTEROL

⚔ Passover Spanekopita ⚔
(Greek Spinach Pie)

When it comes to adapting the recipes of their adopted homelands to their time-honored religious beliefs, Jews have been dazzlingly ingenious. Consider this Passover version of Greek spanekopita (spinach pie). Traditional spanekopita, of course, would be made with filo dough. Greek Jews achieved something of the buttery crispness of the pastry by sandwiching the filling between buttered or oiled sheets of matzo. I like the sourish tang provided by grated feta cheese, but you could also use milder Parmesan (freshly grated, please!), or omit the cheese entirely. Also, I've called for fresh spinach here, but you could certainly use frozen. Finally, I've opted for a firm, cakey spanekopita. For a lighter pie, beat the egg whites to firm peaks and fold them into the spinach mixture.

PREPARATION TIME: 10 MINUTES   COOKING TIME: 35 MINUTES

20 ounces fresh spinach (2 packages) or 2 (10-ounce) packages frozen
Salt
1 bunch of scallions, finely chopped
1 bunch of fresh dill (about ¼ cup chopped)
½ cup matzo meal
1 egg plus 6 egg whites or 1 cup egg substitute

⅓ cup fresh lemon juice, or to taste
½ cup finely grated feta or Parmesan cheese
Freshly ground black pepper
4 sheets matzo
1½ tablespoons extra-virgin olive oil or melted butter

1. Preheat the oven to 350 degrees.

2. If using fresh spinach, wash and stem. Bring 2 cups salted water to a boil in a large pot. Add the spinach and cook until wilted, about 2 minutes, stirring often. Drain the spinach in a colander, rinse with cold water, and drain again. When cool enough to handle, grab handfuls of spinach and squeeze between your fingers to wring out the water. Coarsely chop the spinach in a food processor or by hand. If using frozen spinach, cook according to the instructions on the package. Drain and wring as described above.

3. Place the spinach in a mixing bowl and stir in the scallions, dill, matzo meal, egg and egg whites,

lemon juice, cheese, and pepper. Correct the seasoning, adding salt, pepper, or lemon juice to taste. The filling should be highly seasoned.

4. Lightly brush 2 sheets of matzo with olive oil and place in a lightly oiled 8 by 14-inch baking dish. Spread the spinach filling evenly on top. Brush the remaining 2 sheets of matzo with oil and arrange on top. Lightly sprinkle the top of the spanekopita with salt.

5. Bake the spanekopita until the top crust is crisp and golden brown and the filling is set, about 30 minutes. Remove the spanekopita from the oven and let set for 3 minutes, then cut into squares for serving.

Serves 8

169 CALORIES PER SERVING; 9.2 G PROTEIN; 6 G FAT; 2 G SATURATED FAT; 21 G CARBOHYDRATE; 240 MG SODIUM; 35 MG CHOLESTEROL

✄ Rice-and-Pine-Nut-Stuffed Cabbage Rolls ✄

Whenever I make a meat dish in our household, I try to prepare a vegetarian version. This plays well with the non-meat-eaters of the family and it generally also serves as a good way to trim the fat. The following cabbage rolls were created for my wife, Barbara, who loves the nutty crunch of the pine nuts and earthy flavor provided by the mushrooms and chickpeas. **Note:** *This recipe calls for the boiling method for separating the cabbage leaves—useful when you want to prepare the recipe from start to finish in a couple of hours. On page 94 you'll find the freezing method for separating the leaves. It's less work, but you need to start the day before.*

PREPARATION TIME: 30 MINUTES   COOKING TIME: 2 HOURS

Salt
1 medium green cabbage

FOR THE FILLING:
1¼ cups uncooked rice
¼ cup currants or raisins
2 tablespoons pine nuts
1 tablespoon extra-virgin olive oil
1 medium onion, finely chopped
1 carrot, finely chopped
1 stalk celery, finely chopped

2 cloves garlic, minced
½ pound mushrooms, trimmed, wiped clean with a damp cloth, and thinly sliced
3 tablespoons chopped flat-leaf parsley
½ cup cooked chickpeas
Freshly ground black pepper

TO FINISH THE STUFFED CABBAGE:
1 small onion, thinly sliced
Sweet and sour tomato sauce (page 95)
1 lemon, thinly sliced widthwise

1. Bring 4 quarts salted water to a boil in a large pot. Cut the core out of the cabbage (remove it in a cone-shaped plug), using a sharp paring knife. Boil the cabbage until the outside leaves are soft and pliable enough to pull off whole, 5 to 10 minutes. Pull these leaves off, rinse under cold water in a colander, and drain. Continue cooking the cabbage until you have 12 large whole leaves.

2. Prepare the filling. Bring 1½ cups water to a boil in a large saucepan. Add the rice and currants and bring to a boil. Cover the pan, reduce the heat to a gentle simmer, and cook the rice until tender, 18 to 20 minutes. Remove the pan from the heat and let stand for 5 minutes. Fluff the rice with a fork.

3. Heat a nonstick skillet over medium heat. Add the pine nuts and toast until lightly browned, shaking the pan to ensure even browning, 2 minutes. Add the pine nuts to the rice.

4. Heat the oil in the pan. Add the onion, carrot, celery, and garlic and cook over medium heat until the onion is soft but not brown, 3 minutes. Add the

mushrooms and parsley, increase the heat to medium-high and cook until the vegetable mixture is lightly browned and the mushroom liquid has evaporated, 5 minutes. Stir the mushroom mixture and chickpeas into the rice. Add salt and pepper to taste. The filling should be highly seasoned.

5. Preheat the oven to 325 degrees.

6. Peel off and discard any tough, dark green, exterior leaves from the cabbage. Peel off a leaf and lay it flat on your work surface, cupped side up. Using the side of a cleaver or a scaloppine pounder, flatten the stem to make the leaf pliable. Place 3 tablespoons rice mixture in the center of the leaf toward the bottom (the stem end). Roll the leaf up one third of the way to encase the filling, fold in the sides, and continue rolling to obtain a neat bundle. (The cabbage is rolled the same way you'd fold a crepe to make a blintz.) Repeat until all the filling is used up. You should wind up with 12 cabbage rolls.

7. Thinly slice a little of the cabbage core (the part left over) and arrange the slices over the bottom of a 9

by 12-inch baking dish. Arrange the sliced onion on top. Arrange the stuffed cabbage rolls, seam side down, on top. Pour the sweet and sour tomato sauce over the cabbage. Arrange the lemon slices on top. Cover the dish with foil. The recipe can be prepared several hours ahead to this stage and refrigerated.

8. Bake the cabbage for 1 hour covered. Remove the foil and continue baking uncovered until the cabbage rolls are tender and the sauce is thick and flavorful, 1 hour longer.

Makes 12 cabbage rolls, which will serve 4 to 6

656 CALORIES PER 4 SERVINGS; 15 G PROTEIN; 9 G FAT; 1.2 G SATURATED FAT; 138 G CARBOHYDRATE; 1,132 MG SODIUM; 0 MG CHOLESTEROL

✂ Portobello Paprikash ✂

I've always thought of chicken paprikash as Jewish—in part because I used to enjoy it at the home of my Hungarian aunt, Judy Raichlen. But to make paprikash kosher (you can't combine meat and dairy products), you had to use nondairy "sour cream," which always seemed like cheating. Instead, I decided to keep the traditional sour cream sauce, but eliminate the meat, so I now make paprikash with portobello mushrooms. This goes over well with the vegetarians in the family, and it also makes a satisfying side dish. In the interest of convenience, I've called for sautéing the mushrooms, but for a richer, meatier flavor, I would grill or roast them first. (See instructions at the end of the recipe.) For an even more extravagant paprikash, use fresh porcini mushrooms or shiitakes.

PREPARATION TIME: 10 MINUTES   COOKING TIME: 15 MINUTES

1½ pounds portobello or large button mushrooms
1½ tablespoons olive oil
1 medium onion, thinly sliced
1 green bell pepper, cored and thinly sliced
3 cloves garlic, thinly sliced
2 tablespoons finely chopped flat-leaf parsley, plus 1 tablespoon for garnish
1 ripe red juicy tomato, cut into ½-inch dice, with juices

1 tablespoon sweet Hungarian paprika
1 tablespoon hot Hungarian paprika (for more sweet)
1 cup chicken, vegetable broth
1 cup no-fat sour cream
Salt and freshly ground black pepper

1. Trim the ends off the mushroom stems and wipe the caps clean with a damp paper towel. Cut each cap into ½-inch-thick slices.

2. Heat the oil in a large nonstick frying pan. Add the onion, pepper, and garlic and cook over medium heat until just beginning to brown, about 4 minutes, stirring as needed with a wooden spoon.

3. Increase the heat to high and stir in the mushrooms and 2 tablespoons parsley. Cook until the vegetables are lightly browned, about 2 minutes. Stir in the tomatoes and cook until the mushrooms are tender and most of the mushroom and tomato juices have evaporated, 3 to 5 minutes. Stir in the paprikas and cook for 1 minute.

4. Stir in the broth and sour cream and bring to a boil. Briskly simmer the paprikash until the sauce is thick and flavorful, 5 to 8 minutes. Don't let the sauce cook down too much, or it will be pasty. (If it does cook down too much, add a little more broth.) Season the paprikash with salt and pepper to taste. Sprinkle the remaining parsley on top and serve at once. I like to serve the paprikash over noodles or spaetzle.

Note: To roast mushrooms, stem and wipe clean with a damp paper towel. Lightly brush or spray with oil and bake in a nonstick roasting pan in a 450-degree oven until lightly browned and tender, about 10 minutes. Alternatively, cook on a barbecue grill preheated to medium-high. Omit slicing the mushrooms in step 1 (you may want to quarter them) and sautéing the mushrooms for 2 minutes in step 3. Otherwise, the recipe remains the same. Roasting or grilling the mushrooms gives you a richer, meatier flavor, but it also adds an extra step.

Serves 4

215 CALORIES PER SERVING; 11 G PROTEIN; 5.5 G FAT; .7 G SATURATED FAT; 29 G CARBOHYDRATE; 77 MG SODIUM; 0 MG CHOLESTEROL

🎝 Jewish Polenta 🎝
(Mamaliga)

What's in a name? mused Shakespeare. Describe mamaliga as cornmeal mush and you won't whet many appetites. But call it Jewish polenta and people will be clamoring for a seat at your table. Mamaliga is Roumanian soul food: cornmeal boiled to a rib-sticking mush, enriched with cottage cheese or sometimes gribenes (chicken cracklings). Some people serve the cheese on top of the mamaliga; others cook it right in the mush. I prefer the latter, for it gives the mamaliga a richness, a creaminess, a delicate piquancy that makes polenta pale in comparison. Below is a simple recipe for mamaliga that you can serve savory-style (with green onions and garlic) or sweet (sprinkled with cinnamon-sugar). If you're feeling innovative, chill the mamaliga in a baking dish, cut it into squares, and cook it on the barbecue grill. Polenta never tasted so good!

PREPARATION TIME: 5 MINUTES   COOKING TIME: 15 TO 20 MINUTES

1 cup cornmeal
3 cups cold water
1 teaspoon salt
Freshly ground black pepper to taste
1 cup low- or no-fat cottage cheese

FOR GARNISH:
4 scallions, finely chopped
1 clove garlic, minced
or
2 tablespoons sugar
2 teaspoons cinnamon

1. Combine the cornmeal, water, salt, and pepper in a large, heavy saucepan (preferably nonstick). Stirring steadily with a wooden spoon, bring the mixture to a boil over high heat; it will thicken.

2. Reduce the heat to medium-low (the mixture should bubble slowly) and cook the mamaliga until thick and flavorful. The mixture should come away smoothly from the side of the pan. This will take 10 to 15 minutes. You don't need to stir constantly, but do stir every few minutes to prevent scorching.

3. Stir in the cottage cheese and scallions and garlic if using. Briskly simmer the mamaliga until the cottage cheese is melted, 3 to 5 minutes. (Don't worry if a few white bits of cheese remain.) Serve the mamaliga at once in bowls or on plates. If serving the sweet garnish, combine the sugar and cinnamon in a bowl and sprinkle the mixture over the mamaliga.

Note: To grill mamaliga, spoon the cooked mush into an oiled baking dish. Refrigerate until firm, 1 to 2 hours. Cut the mamaliga in squares, brush or spray with oil, and grill over a high flame until golden brown, 3 to 5 minutes per side.

Serves 4

151 CALORIES PER SERVING; 10 G PROTEIN; 1.1 G FAT; .16 G SATURATED FAT; 27 G CARBOHYDRATE; 804 MG SODIUM; 0 MG CHOLESTEROL

⚱ Malai ⚱
(Cornmeal Pudding with Buttermilk and Cheese)

"I have another recipe for you," my friend Shirley says with excitement. Since learning about this book, Shirley has appointed herself my resident authority on Polish-Jewish cooking. Her expertise comes from a lifetime spent with relatives from Kozienice, Poland, who survived the Holocaust and settled in Israel and the United States. This dish comes from Shirley's friend Franya Rubinek and it's unlike anything I've ever tasted. Think of a cross between spoonbread and cheesecake (with overtones of kugel) and you start to get an idea of malai. The farmer cheese and buttermilk lend a piquancy that's particularly delicious. To trim the fat, I've reduced the amount of butter and cheese, using egg substitute in place of eggs and low-fat buttermilk. Even with these adjustments, you'll find malai one of the most pleasing and comforting dishes you've ever had the pleasure to sink a fork into.

PREPARATION TIME: 5 MINUTES   COOKING TIME: 1 HOUR

½ cup sugar
½ cup egg substitute
5 tablespoons unbleached white flour
¼ cup yellow cornmeal
1 teaspoon baking powder
Pinch of salt
1 cup low- or no-fat buttermilk

1 pound low- or no-fat farmer cheese or small curd cottage cheese
Spray oil
1 tablespoon melted butter (preferably salted) or margarine
1½ cups no-fat sour cream for serving (optional)

1. Preheat the oven to 350 degrees.
2. In a large mixing bowl, combine the sugar and egg substitute, and whisk to mix. Whisk in the flour, cornmeal, baking powder, and salt. Whisk in the buttermilk, followed by the cheese. Spoon the mixture into a 9-inch square baking dish generously sprayed with oil. Drizzle the butter on top.

3. Bake the malai until puffed, set, and lightly browned, 40 to 50 minutes. Turn off the heat and leave the malai in the oven for 10 minutes more. Cut the malai into rectangles and serve with dollops of sour cream on the side if desired.

Serves 6 as a side dish,
4 as a light main course for a dairy brunch

379 CALORIES PER 6 SERVINGS; 37 G PROTEIN; 5.7 G FAT; 3 G SATURATED FAT; 44 G CARBOHYDRATE; 176 MG SODIUM; 22 MG CHOLESTEROL

Vegetable Dishes

❧❦◆❧❦

✄ Tropical Tsimmis ✄

"Don't make such a big tsimmis about it," our friend Charlie Cinnamon says, whenever there's a momentary crisis. How did something as easy to make as this delicious sweet vegetable and fruit stew become slang for a problem, fuss, or vexation? Perhaps it's because traditional tsimmis was a production to make, requiring the stewing of a brisket prior to adding the fruits and vegetables— a 3-hour process in all. As North American Jews have lightened up their diets, they've tended to eliminate the meat from tsimmis. This slashes not only the fat, but the cooking time, making the preparation of tsimmis no big tsimmis at all. Tsimmis is traditionally served at Rosh Hashanah: the carrot slices symbolize coins and, by extension, prosperity for the New Year. But in my family, we have tsimmis at any big family gathering. When I moved to Miami, my tsimmis took on a tropical accent, featuring ginger and fresh ripe pineapple. Feel free to customize the following recipe with any fresh or dried fruits you may prefer.

PREPARATION TIME: 15 MINUTES   COOKING TIME: 20 TO 30 MINUTES

1 cup apple cider or apple juice
1 cup water
¾ cup pineapple juice (1 6-ounce can)
2 cups pitted prunes
½ cup raisins
1 pound large carrots, peeled and cut into ½-inch rounds
1 pound sweet potatoes (2 potatoes), peeled and cut into ½-inch rounds

2 cups diced fresh pineapple
1 tablespoon minced fresh or candied ginger
3 strips lemon zest
3 tablespoons fresh lemon juice
2 cinnamon sticks
¼ cup honey
¼ cup brown sugar, or to taste
¼ teaspoon salt

1. Combine the cider, water, and pineapple juice in a large, heavy saucepan and bring to a boil. Remove the pan from the heat and add the prunes and raisins. Let steep for 15 minutes.

2. Stir in the carrots, sweet potatoes, pineapple, ginger, lemon zest and juice, cinnamon sticks, honey, brown sugar, and salt and bring to a boil over high heat. Reduce the heat to medium and simmer the tsimmis, covered, for 10 minutes.

3. Uncover the tsimmis and continue cooking un-til the carrots and sweet potatoes are tender and the pan juices have reduced to a thick, rich-flavored sauce, 10 to 20 minutes longer. Discard the cinnamon sticks. Correct the seasoning, adding sugar or lemon juice to taste. The tsimmis should be somewhat sweet (but not sugary), with just a hint of tartness. Serve hot or at room temperature. In the unlikely event you have leftovers, know that tsimmis just gets better each day you rewarm it.

Serves 8 to 10

309 CALORIES PER 8 SERVINGS; 3 G PROTEIN; .7 G FAT; .11 G SATURATED FAT; 75 G CARBOHYDRATE; 104 MG SODIUM; 0 MG CHOLESTEROL

Tropical tsimmis.

✥ Amazing Low-Fat Latkes ✥

Hanukkah without latkes would be like, well, Christmas without a tree. Jews the world over eat fried foods at Hanukkah to commemorate the miracle of the oil (that a one-day supply of oil for the holy lamp burned for eight straight days until more could be obtained). In Eastern Europe and North America, the quintessential Hanukkah food is fried potato pancakes. (For Sephardic Hanukkah dishes, see the zvingous recipe on page 158.)

Deep-frying may be symbolic, but it's not particularly healthy. Some years ago, I began bake-frying my latkes in a hot oven to reduce the fat. (You "fry" them on a preheated oiled baking sheet in a superhot oven.) Bake-frying has another advantage: it makes a lot less mess in your kitchen. If possible, use Yukon gold potatoes. Their buttery flavor makes the bake-fried latkes taste almost as rich as the real thing. **Note:** *I like to make cocktail-size, "mini" latkes that measure 2 to 2½ inches across. (I find they cook better.) You can certainly make the latkes larger. To further trim the fat, you could use spray oil to grease the baking sheets, omitting the 2 to 3 tablespoons of canola oil.*

PREPARATION TIME: 10 MINUTES COOKING TIME: 15 MINUTES

3 pounds potatoes (preferably Yukon golds)
1 medium onion
⅓ cup matzo meal or flour
½ teaspoon baking powder
1 cup egg substitute or 2 eggs and 4 whites

3 tablespoons chopped parsley
Salt and freshly ground black pepper
2 to 3 tablespoons canola oil
No- or low-fat sour cream for serving
Applesauce (page 147) for serving

1. Place a large nonstick baking sheet in the oven and preheat to 450 degrees.

2. Peel the potatoes and onion and coarsely grate in a food processor fitted with a shredding disk or on a box grater. Grab handfuls of the grated vegetables and squeeze tightly between your fingers to wring out as much liquid as possible.

3. Transfer the grated vegetables to a mixing bowl and stir in the matzo meal, baking powder, egg substitute, parsley, and plenty of salt and pepper. The latkes should be highly seasoned.

4. Pour the oil on the hot baking sheet, spreading it around with the back of a wooden spoon. (**Note:** If working with small baking sheets, hold back half the oil, so you can "fry" the latkes in 2 batches.) Spoon small mounds of potato mixture onto the baking sheet to form 2½-inch pancakes, leaving 1 inch between each.

5. Bake the latkes until golden brown, 6 to 8 minutes per side, turning once with a spatula. (When you turn the latkes, try to flip them onto spots on the baking sheet that still have oil.) Transfer to plates or a platter and serve at once with sour cream and/or applesauce.

*Makes 50 to 60 2-inch latkes,
which will serve 8 to 10*

246 CALORIES PER 8 SERVINGS; 7.4 G PROTEIN; 6.3 G FAT; .6 G SATURATED FAT; 40 G CARBOHYDRATE; 66 MG SODIUM; .3 MG CHOLESTEROL

✄ Sweet Potato Latkes ✄

Here's a switch on traditional latkes: handsome orange Hanukkah pancakes made from grated sweet potatoes.
As in the preceding recipe, we "bake-fry" the latkes on an oiled baking sheet in the oven, which dramatically
slashes the fat. To keep the latkes crisp (sweet potatoes tend to soften when baked), I recommend making small
pancakes, which are quick to crisp. The cinnamon and nutmeg add a sweet note: I've made them optional.
Note: *To further trim the fat, you could grease the baking sheets with spray oil, omitting the 2 tablespoons olive oil.*

PREPARATION TIME: 10 MINUTES   COOKING TIME: 15 MINUTES

1½ pounds sweet potatoes, peeled
1 small onion
⅓ cup egg substitute or 3 egg whites
2 tablespoons finely chopped parsley
¼ cup matzo meal or flour

½ teaspoon baking powder
½ teaspoon cinnamon (optional)
¼ teaspoon freshly grated nutmeg (optional)
Salt and freshly ground black pepper
2 tablespoons olive oil or canola oil

1. Place a large nonstick baking sheet in the oven and preheat to 450 degrees.

2. Coarsely grate the sweet potatoes and onion into a mixing bowl, using a food processor or box grater. Stir in the egg substitute, parsley, matzo meal, baking powder, cinnamon, nutmeg, and salt and pepper to taste.

3. Pour the oil on the hot baking sheet, spreading it around with the back of a metal spatula. Spoon small mounds of sweet potato mixture onto the bak-ing sheet to form 2-inch pancakes, leaving an inch or so between each.

4. Bake the latkes until golden brown, 6 to 8 minutes per side, turning once with a spatula. (When you turn the latkes, try to flip them onto spots on the baking sheet that still have oil.) Do not overcook, or the latkes will become too soft or too dark. Transfer to plates or a platter and serve at once.

Makes 24 2-inch latkes,
which will serve 4 to 6

359 CALORIES PER 4 SERVINGS; 7.2 G PROTEIN; 8 G FAT; .8 G SATURATED FAT; 64 G CARBOHYDRATE; 102 MG SODIUM; .2 MG CHOLESTEROL

✂ Garlic Creamed Spinach ✂

There's nothing traditionally Jewish about this recipe: it just happened to be a standby at the great Jewish restaurants in Miami in the 1950s. But Jews have revered its principal flavoring since the dawn of our religion. Mindful of its energizing properties, the pharaohs fed the Hebrew slaves garlic during the construction of the pyramids. Mindful of its aphrodisiac powers, the Jewish sage Rabbi Ezra urged eating garlic on Friday nights "to promote love and arouse desire." Here's a creamed spinach that's bursting with garlicky richness. Note the use of evaporated skim milk in place of heavy cream to create a rich, creamy consistency without fat.

PREPARATION TIME: 10 MINUTES   COOKING TIME: 10 MINUTES

10 ounces fresh spinach or 10 ounces frozen
Salt
1 tablespoon olive oil
1 small onion, minced
3 cloves garlic, minced

1½ tablespoons flour or matzo meal
1 cup evaporated skim milk
Freshly ground white pepper
Freshly grated nutmeg

1. If using fresh spinach, wash and stem. Bring 2 cups salted water to a boil in a large pot. Add the spinach and cook until wilted, about 2 minutes, stirring often. Drain the spinach in a colander, rinse with cold water, and drain again. When cool enough to handle, grab handfuls of spinach and squeeze between your fingers to wring out the water. Finely chop the spinach in a food processor or by hand. If using frozen spinach, cook according to the instructions on the package. Drain and dry as described above.

2. Heat the oil in a heavy saucepan. Add the onion and garlic and cook over medium heat until soft but not brown, about 3 minutes. Whisk in the flour and cook for 1 minute. Off the heat, whisk in the evaporated skim milk. Return the pan to a medium heat and simmer until thick and flavorful, about 3 minutes, whisking steadily.

3. Whisk in the spinach and simmer for 1 minute. Whisk in salt, pepper, and just a hint of nutmeg. The spinach should be highly seasoned. Serve at once.

Serves 4

116 CALORIES PER SERVING; 8 G PROTEIN; 4 G FAT; .5 G SATURATED FAT; 14 G CARBOHYDRATE; 159 MG SODIUM; 2.2 MG CHOLESTEROL

🐟 Basil-Marinated Zucchini in the Style of Roman Jews 🐟

Concia, marinated zucchini, was a specialty of the Jews in the Roman ghetto. I learned of the dish in Edda Servi Machlin's fine book,
The Classic Cuisine of the Italian Jews (Giro Press, 1981). The original was deep-fried in prodigious quantities of olive oil. I had
the idea to grill the zucchini, which boosts flavor without a lot of fat, reserving the olive oil for the marinade. I also added some
grilled onion to hint at the sweetness achieved by deep-frying. Authentic? Not strictly speaking. But you'd have to search hard
and long to find a tastier way to prepare zucchini. **Note:** *Sometimes I make this dish with fresh mint in place of the basil.*

PREPARATION TIME: 15 MINUTES   COOKING TIME: 10 MINUTES

4 medium zucchini (1¾ to 2 pounds)
1 sweet onion
Spray oil
Salt and freshly ground black pepper
12 basil leaves, thinly slivered

1 to 2 cloves garlic, minced
½ teaspoon hot pepper flakes
2 tablespoons extra-virgin olive oil
1 to 2 tablespoons balsamic vinegar

1. Light a hot fire in your barbecue grill.

2. Cut the zucchini lengthwise into ¼-inch slices. Cut the onion widthwise into ¼-inch slices. Lightly spray the vegetables on both sides with oil and season with salt and pepper. Grill the vegetables until nicely browned on both sides, 4 to 6 minutes per side. Transfer the vegetables to a platter.

3. Arrange a layer of zucchini slices in the bottom of a 6 by 8-inch serving dish. Break the onion slices into rings and arrange a few on top. Sprinkle this layer of vegetables with slivered basil, minced garlic, hot

pepper flakes, and drizzles of olive oil and balsamic vinegar. Season with salt and pepper.

4. Make another layer of zucchini and onion, sprinkling with more basil, garlic, hot pepper flakes, oil, vinegar, salt, and pepper. Continue layering the ingredients until all are used up.

5. Let the zucchini cool to room temperature. You can serve it now, but it will be even more flavorful if you refrigerate it for several hours or even overnight.

Serves 6

72 CALORIES PER SERVING; 2 G PROTEIN; 5 G FAT; .6 G SATURATED FAT; 7 G CARBOHYDRATE; 5.1 MG SODIUM; 0 MG CHOLESTEROL

⚘ Mashed Potatoes with Fried Onions ⚘

This dish may not have religious significance, but eating it can be a religious experience. The combination of flavors—earthy potatoes and sweet caramelized onions—are common currency in Jewish cooking and are often used as a filling for blintzes and knishes. So why not serve them American-style, as mashed potatoes? Chicken stock and skim milk stand in for such fattening ingredients as butter and cream. When serving these mashed potatoes with a milchig meal, substitute vegetable broth or more skim milk for the chicken broth and use oil instead of schmaltz.

PREPARATION TIME: 10 MINUTES   COOKING TIME: 30 MINUTES

1 tablespoon canola oil, schmaltz, or mock schmaltz
1 medium-large onion, thinly sliced or finely chopped
2 large baking potatoes (1½ pounds), peeled and cut into 1-inch pieces

Salt
¼ cup skim milk
¼ cup low- or no-fat sour cream
¼ cup chicken stock
Freshly ground black pepper

1. Heat the oil in a nonstick frying pan. Add the onions and cook until caramelized (a deep golden brown). You'll need to start the onions on medium heat, reducing the flame to medium-low, then low, as the onions darken. Do not let the onions burn. The whole process takes 10 to 15 minutes.

2. Place the potatoes and 1 teaspoon salt in a large saucepan with water to cover by 2 inches. Slowly bring the potatoes to a boil. Reduce the heat to a simmer and cook the potatoes until very tender, 8 to 10 minutes. Drain the potatoes in a colander, then return them to the pan. Cook over medium heat, stirring with a wooden spoon, to evaporate any excess liquid and dry out the potatoes, 2 minutes.

3. Using a potato masher or handheld mixer, mash the potatoes. (Do not use a food processor, or the potatoes will be gummy.) Beat in the onions, milk, sour cream, chicken stock, and salt and pepper to taste. The potatoes should be highly seasoned.

Serves 4

214 CALORIES PER SERVING; 5 G PROTEIN; 4 G FAT; .3 G SATURATED FAT; 41 G CARBOHYDRATE; 30 MG SODIUM; .3 MG CHOLESTEROL

✂ Almond-Stuffed Prunes and Apricots ✂

This unusual side dish comes from a Jewish friend from Morocco. The serving of prunes and apricots as a "vegetable" may remind you of the tsimmises of Eastern Europe. And while the notion of prunes may turn some people off, this is one of the most delicious recipes in creation. Almond-stuffed prunes and apricots would go particularly well with any of the tagines or couscous dishes in this book, not to mention European-style entrées, too.

PREPARATION TIME: 15 MINUTES   COOKING TIME: 10 TO 15 MINUTES

8 ounces pitted prunes
8 ounces apricots
⅓ cup slivered almonds
2 tablespoons sugar
1 tablespoon vegetable oil

2 cloves
2 strips lemon zest
1 cinnamon stick
4 cardamom pods

1. Soak the prunes and apricots in a bowl with 2 quarts hot water until soft, about 30 minutes.

2. Meanwhile, roast the almonds in a dry skillet over medium heat until lightly browned and very fragrant, 3 minutes, shaking the pan to ensure even browning. Let cool.

3. Drain the prunes and apricots well and blot dry with paper towels. Insert a few slivered almonds into each prune and apricot. You should have about 3 tablespoons slivered almonds left over. Combine these with the sugar in a food processor or blender and grind to a coarse powder.

4. Heat the oil in a nonstick frying pan. Add the apricots and prunes and cook over medium heat until the apricots are lightly browned, about 3 minutes. Stick the cloves in the strip of lemon zest and add them to the fruit with the cinnamon stick and cardamom. Add 1 cup water.

5. Simmer the fruit, uncovered, over medium heat until soft and until most of the water has evaporated and the pan juices are thick and syrupy, 10 to 15 minutes. Transfer the fruit to a serving dish and sprinkle with the almond sugar. Serve at once.

Serves 6

137 CALORIES PER SERVING; 2.4 G PROTEIN; 6 G FAT; .6 G SATURATED FAT; 20 G CARBOHYDRATE; 2 MG SODIUM; 0 MG CHOLESTEROL

Grain Dishes

❧❧❧❀❧❧❧

🔔 Red Rice 🔔

To taste this Greek-Jewish rice dish—with its alluring ocher color and tangy tomatoey taste—you'd never guess how utterly simple and quick it is to make. The addition of the broth and tomato juice transforms rice from a forgettable starch to a memorable side dish.

PREPARATION TIME: 5 MINUTES   COOKING TIME: 25 MINUTES

1 tablespoon extra-virgin olive oil
1 medium onion, finely chopped
3 tablespoons finely chopped parsley
1 cup long-grain white rice

1 cup chicken broth
½ cup tomato juice
Salt (about 1 teaspoon) and freshly ground black
  pepper to taste

1. Heat the oil in a sauté pan or shallow saucepan. Add the onion and 2 tablespoons parsley and cook over medium heat until just beginning to brown, about 4 minutes. Add the rice and sauté until the grains are aromatic and shiny, 1 minute. Stir in the chicken broth, tomato juice, salt, and pepper and bring to a boil.

2. Reduce the heat to low, tightly cover the pan, and gently simmer the rice for 18 to 20 minutes, or until the individual grains are tender and the liquid is completely absorbed. Remove the pan from the heat and let the rice stand for 3 minutes. Fluff the rice with a fork, correcting the seasoning, and sprinkle with the remaining 1 tablespoon parsley before serving.

Serves 4

220 CALORIES PER SERVING; 4 G PROTEIN; 4 G FAT; .5 G SATURATED FAT; 42 G CARBOHYDRATE; 115 MG SODIUM; 0 MG CHOLESTEROL

Kasha varniskas.

✣ Bulghur Pilaf ✣

Bulghur (cracked wheat) has a soulful, earthy, nutty flavor, which makes it popular throughout the Middle and Near East as an ingredient in salads, casseroles, and meat dishes. In this recipe, the bulghur is prepared pilaf-style. Try it with lamb or as a light vegetarian entrée.

PREPARATION TIME: 20 MINUTES   COOKING TIME: 20 MINUTES

1 tablespoon olive oil
1 medium onion, finely chopped
1 clove garlic, minced
2 tablespoons pine nuts
¼ cup finely chopped parsley (preferably flat-leaf)
1 cup bulghur, rinsed in a strainer and drained
½ cup cooked chickpeas
2 cups vegetable broth (page 191) or chicken broth (page 189)
Salt and freshly ground black pepper

1. Heat the oil in a nonstick sauté pan. Add the onion and cook over medium heat for 3 minutes. Add the garlic, pine nuts, and 3 tablespoons parsley and continue cooking until the onion and nuts are lightly browned, 2 to 3 minutes more. Stir in the bulghur and cook until the grains are shiny, 1 minute.

2. Add the chickpeas, broth, salt, and pepper and bring to a boil. Reduce the heat to low, cover the pot, and cook the bulghur until tender, about 20 minutes.

The broth should be completely absorbed. If it isn't, cook the pilaf uncovered for a few minutes.

3. Remove the pan from the heat, uncover, drape the pan with a dish towel, re-cover the pan, and let the bulghur stand for 5 minutes to steam.

4. Fluff the bulghur with a fork, adding salt and pepper to taste. Transfer it to an attractive serving dish and sprinkle with the remaining parsley.

Serves 4

225 CALORIES PER SERVING; 8 G PROTEIN; 7 G FAT; .9 G SATURATED FAT; 37 G CARBOHYDRATE; 11 MG SODIUM; 0 MG CHOLESTEROL

✄ Basic Kasha ✄

Kasha isn't exactly what you'd call mainstream among North American Jews, but in shtetls across Eastern Europe our ancestors ate buckwheat groats for breakfast, lunch, and dinner. And with good reason! This buff-colored, grainlike staple grows in cool, damp climates where wheat won't. (Despite its grainlike appearance, kasha is actually a fruit.) Its rich, earthy, nutty flavor lends itself both to savory and sweet dishes. Kasha is also good for you: a ¾-cup serving contains 6 grams of protein, 20 percent of the RDA for phosphorus, and useful amounts of the B vitamins and iron. When buying kasha, look for medium or coarse cut and always buy it roasted. (This is how it's usually sold and is what gives kasha its nutty flavor.) One good common supermarket brand is Wolff's. Kasha is usually sautéed with beaten egg prior to boiling or braising. This produces light, fluffy grains.

PREPARATION TIME: 3 MINUTES   COOKING TIME: 15 MINUTES

1 cup kasha
1 egg white
2 cups hot chicken broth or vegetable broth or
water

1 tablespoon butter or olive oil (optional)
Salt and freshly ground black pepper

1. Place the kasha in a mixing bowl with the egg white. Stir until all the grains are coated with egg and shiny.

2. Transfer the kasha to a large nonstick frying pan over medium heat and cook, stirring with a wooden spoon. First the kasha grains will stick together; then the egg will dry and the kasha will separate into individual grains. The whole process will take 2 to 3 minutes.

3. Stir in the broth, butter if using, and salt and pepper to taste. (I use a scant 1 teaspoon of the salt and ¼ teaspoon of the pepper.) When the mixture boils, reduce the heat to low and tightly cover the pan. Cook the kasha until tender and all the liquid has been absorbed, 8 to 10 minutes. Remove the pan from the heat and fluff the kasha with a fork. Serve as a side dish, just as you would bulghur or rice.

Makes about 4 cups, enough to serve 4 to 6

146 CALORIES PER 4 SERVINGS; 5.6 G PROTEIN; 1.1 G FAT; .2 G SATURATED FAT; 30 G CARBOHYDRATE; 18 MG SODIUM; 0 MG CHOLESTEROL

VARIATION—SWEET KASHA

This version of kasha makes a great breakfast cereal or light dairy supper. Fat-free half-and-half is manufactured by the Land O' Lakes Company and can be found at most supermarkets.

PREPARATION TIME: 3 MINUTES   COOKING TIME: 15 MINUTES

1 cup kasha
1 egg white
2 cups hot water
1 tablespoon butter (optional)
¼ teaspoon salt

3 tablespoons sugar
2 teaspoons cinnamon
¾ cup fat-free half-and-half

1. Prepare the kasha as described above.
2. In a small bowl, mix together the sugar and cinnamon.
3. Serve the kasha in bowls, pouring half-and-half over each serving and sprinkling with cinnamon-sugar.

Serves 4

213 CALORIES PER 4 SERVINGS; 6 G PROTEIN; 1.1 G FAT; .25 G SATURATED FAT; 47 G CARBOHYDRATE; 164 MG SODIUM; 0 MG CHOLESTEROL

Kasha Varniskas
(with Bow Tie Pasta and Mushrooms)

Kasha with bow ties is a Russian/Polish Jewish classic. Your great-grandmother would have made the noodles by hand.
You can do this if you're feeling ambitious, but store-bought bow ties work just fine. You can use just
about any type of fresh mushroom for the recipe: button mushrooms, shiitakes, porcini (boletus).

PREPARATION TIME: 10 MINUTES   COOKING TIME: 30 MINUTES

1 cup kasha (buckwheat groats)
1 cup small bow tie noodles
Salt
1 tablespoon extra-virgin olive oil
1 medium onion, finely chopped

1½ cups thinly sliced button mushrooms,
  shiitakes, or fresh porcini
1 egg white
2 cups boiling beef or chicken broth or water
Freshly ground black pepper

1. Wash the kasha under cold water, drain well, and blot dry. Cook the bow ties in boiling salted water until al dente, 6 to 8 minutes. Drain in a colander, refresh under cold water, and drain.

2. Heat the oil in a large, heavy saucepan (preferably nonstick). Add the onions and mushrooms and cook over medium heat until the onions are golden brown and the mushrooms have lost most of their liquid, 5 to 7 minutes. Transfer the onions and mushrooms to a bowl and let the pan cool.

3. Add the kasha and egg white to the pan and stir well. Cook over high heat, stirring steadily, for 1 to 2 minutes, or until the individual kasha grains are dry. Stir in the onion, mushrooms, broth, salt, and pepper. Simmer the kasha, covered, until tender and all the liquid has been absorbed, about 15 minutes. Add the bow ties the last 3 minutes. Correct the seasoning, adding salt and pepper to taste.

Serves 4 to 6

289 CALORIES PER 4 SERVINGS; 10 G PROTEIN; 5 G FAT; 0 G SATURATED FAT; 53 G CARBOHYDRATE; 174 MG SODIUM; 0 MG CHOLESTEROL

✂ Farfel with Israeli Spices ✂

East meets West in this recipe, a sort of pilaf made with farfel. The latter is a European Jewish delicacy—tiny pellets or pieces of toasted noodle dough. (One theory on their origin holds that Jews first learned to make farfel by grating noodle dough.) In this recipe, the farfel are flavored with a turmeric, cumin, black pepper mixture modeled on the Yemenite seasoning hawaij. Packaged farfel is available at Jewish grocery stores and some supermarkets. If you're very ambitious, you could make your own by grating homemade noodle dough on the coarse side of a box grater.
Note: *To make this recipe for Passover, use matzo farfel—which is available at Jewish markets.*

PREPARATION TIME: 10 MINUTES   COOKING TIME: 15 TO 20 MINUTES

1½ tablespoons extra-virgin olive oil
1 large onion, finely chopped
2 stalks celery, finely chopped
2 cloves garlic, minced
1 teaspoon turmeric
1 teaspoon ground cumin

1 teaspoon black pepper
¼ teaspoon ground cardamom
2 cups farfel
3 tablespoons chopped fresh parsley
4 cups chicken or vegetable broth
1 teaspoon salt, or to taste

1. Heat the olive oil in a large saucepan. Add the onion and celery and cook over medium heat for 3 minutes. Add the garlic and spices and continue cooking until the onion is lightly browned, 2 minutes. Stir in the farfel and parsley and cook for 2 minutes.

2. Stir in the broth and bring to a boil. Reduce the heat and gently simmer the farfel until it is tender and the stock is absorbed, 10 to 15 minutes, stirring occasionally. Correct the seasoning, adding salt or pepper to taste.

Serves 6 to 8

210 CALORIES PER 6 SERVINGS; 5 G PROTEIN; 4 G FAT; .5 G SATURATED FAT; 39 G CARBOHYDRATE; 407 MG SODIUM; 0 MG CHOLESTEROL

⚑ Israeli Couscous with Mushrooms ⚑

These tiny pearls of pasta are newcomers to the American food scene and, oddly, chefs seem to know more about them than civilians. Which is a shame, because Israeli couscous has a deliciously chewy texture and the ability to absorb flavors readily. And it's quick and easy to cook. Look for it in gourmet shops, ethnic markets, and many supermarkets. **Note:** *Sometimes, for a really exotic flavor, I'll use 8 Chinese dried black mushrooms in place of the fresh mushrooms. I soak them in the broth for 1 hour to soften, then stem and thinly slice them.*

PREPARATION TIME: 10 MINUTES   COOKING TIME: 20 MINUTES

8 ounces fresh shiitake mushrooms or button
  mushrooms
1½ tablespoons olive oil
1 medium onion, finely chopped
2 cloves garlic, minced

3 tablespoons finely chopped parsley
2 cups Israeli couscous
4 cups chicken or vegetable broth or water
Salt and freshly ground black pepper

1. Trim the mushrooms (if using shiitakes, remove the whole stem) and wipe the caps with a damp paper towel. Cut the mushrooms into ¼-inch slices.

2. Heat the oil in a nonstick sauté pan. Add the onion and cook over medium heat for 2 minutes. Add the garlic, mushrooms, and parsley and cook until the onions are lightly browned, 2 to 3 minutes more. Add the couscous and cook for 1 minute.

3. Add the broth and salt and pepper and bring to a boil. Reduce the heat and simmer the couscous, uncovered, until tender, 12 to 15 minutes. Remove the pan from the heat and let stand for a few minutes, so that any excess broth is absorbed by the couscous. Correct the seasoning, adding salt and pepper to taste.

Serves 6 to 8

282 CALORIES PER 6 SERVINGS; 9 G PROTEIN; 4 G FAT; .5 G SATURATED FAT; 52 G CARBOHYDRATE; 10 MG SODIUM; 0 MG CHOLESTEROL

Kugels

✄ Carrot Apple Kugel ✄

*This recipe, indeed, this whole chapter, is dedicated to the memory of my friend, Bob Ginn. Bob was what today would be called a Jew-Bu (Jewish Buddhist) and his zeal for life was infectious. When Bob cooked a holiday dinner, one kugel wasn't enough, no, nor two, nor even a half dozen. I remember a Rosh Hashanah dinner Bob prepared in the 1970s, when he served seven different kugels! Bob died too young (he was only forty-nine), but his memory lives on vividly in everyone who had the good fortune to know him. This kugel is particularly good for Rosh Hashanah—the apples, honey, and carrots being foods that symbolize prosperity and happiness for the New Year. **Note:** For ease in measuring and mixing, warm the honey jar in a bowl of hot water before pouring.*

PREPARATION TIME: 15 MINUTES   COOKING TIME: 1 HOUR

½ cup raisins
½ cup warm apple juice or apple cider
1½ tablespoons olive oil or schmaltz
1 medium onion, finely chopped
2 cloves garlic, minced
1 teaspoon minced or grated fresh ginger
½ teaspoon ground cinnamon
¼ teaspoon ground nutmeg
1 pound carrots, peeled

1 apple, peeled
¾ cup egg substitute
½ cup bread crumbs or matzo meal
3 tablespoons chopped fresh parsley (preferably flat-leaf)
1 tablespoon honey, or to taste
Salt and freshly ground black pepper
Spray oil

1. Soak the raisins in the apple juice for 30 minutes. Drain well. (You can drink or reuse any remaining apple juice.)

2. Preheat the oven to 350 degrees.

3. Heat 1 tablespoon oil in a nonstick skillet. Add the onion, garlic, ginger, cinnamon, and nutmeg and cook over medium heat until the onion is lightly browned, 4 to 5 minutes. Set aside.

4. Shred the carrots and apple on the julienne disk of a food processor or on the large-holed side of a box grater. Transfer the carrots and apple to a mixing bowl and stir in the sautéed onion mixture, raisins, egg substitute, bread crumbs, parsley, and honey. Add salt and pepper to taste. Spoon the mixture into a 10-inch oval baking dish, lightly greased with spray oil. Drizzle the top with the remaining ½ tablespoon oil.

5. Bake the kugel until golden brown and cooked through, 50 to 60 minutes. Cut into squares or wedges for serving.

Serves 6

207 CALORIES PER SERVING; 6.5 G PROTEIN; 5 G FAT; .8 G SATURATED FAT; 36 G CARBOHYDRATE; 164 MG SODIUM; .3 MG CHOLESTEROL

Three kugels (from left to right: zucchini, carrot apple, sweet noodle with apples).

✎ Sweet Noodle Kugel with Apples ✎

Lokshen (noodle) kugel is the most famous of all Jewish puddings—a satisfying casserole of noodles and cottage cheese,
lightly sweetened with sugar, tart with sour cream, perfumed with vanilla, and graced with grated apples.
I've drastically slashed the butter from the recipe I grew up on and yet I think you'll find this kugel
brimming with richness and flavor. Serve it as a light dairy entrée, side dish, or even dessert.

PREPARATION TIME: 20 MINUTES   COOKING TIME: 1 HOUR

1 cup golden raisins
1 cup apple juice
8 ounces flat egg noodles
Salt
2 firm sweet apples, like Galas
2 cups no- or low-fat sour cream
¾ cup egg substitute or 1 egg plus 4 whites
2 teaspoons vanilla extract
½ teaspoon almond extract
1 teaspoon ground cinnamon
1 teaspoon grated lemon zest

2 cups low-fat cottage cheese (large curd)
⅓ to ½ cup light brown sugar or regular sugar

Spray oil for the pan

FOR THE TOPPING:
½ cup cinnamon graham cracker crumbs or
  regular graham cracker crumbs or bread crumbs
2 tablespoons white sugar
1 tablespoon butter (optional)

1. Soak the raisins in the apple juice for 30 minutes to soften them. Drain well. (Save the apple juice for drinking.)

2. Preheat the oven to 350 degrees.

3. Cook the noodles in 4 quarts rapidly boiling salted water until a little shy of al dente, about 6 minutes. Drain the noodles in a colander, rinse with cold water, and drain again.

4. Wash, core, and coarsely grate the apples (on the large-holed side of a grater). I don't generally bother to peel the apples. Squeeze the grated apples between your fingers to wring out the excess liquid.

5. In a mixing bowl, combine the sour cream, egg substitute, vanilla and almond extracts, cinnamon, and lemon zest and whisk until smooth. Stir in the cottage cheese, brown sugar, noodles, raisins, and grated apples. Correct the seasoning, adding sugar or cinnamon to taste.

6. Spoon the noodle mixture into an 8 by 12-inch baking dish lightly oiled with spray oil. Sprinkle the top with the graham cracker crumbs and sugar and dot with butter (if using).

7. Bake the kugel until set and golden brown, about 50 minutes. Let the kugel cool for 5 minutes, then cut into squares for serving.

Serves 8

362 CALORIES PER SERVING; 17 G PROTEIN; 3 G FAT; 1 G SATURATED FAT; 65 G CARBOHYDRATE; 435 MG SODIUM; 54 MG CHOLESTEROL

✄ Zucchini Kugel ✄

I first tasted this offbeat kugel at the home of my friend Shirley Drevich in Miami. (Shirley learned it from her Polish-born cousin, Hannah Kuperstock.) I like to think of it as Jewish zucchini bread. The mint isn't strictly traditional, but I love the way it electrifies the flavor of the zucchini. If you happen to grow zucchini in your garden, you'll really appreciate this recipe as a way to use up extra vegetables.

PREPARATION TIME: 10 MINUTES   COOKING TIME: 1 HOUR

2 pounds medium zucchini
Salt
1½ tablespoons olive oil
1 large onion, finely chopped
2 cloves garlic, minced
¾ cup egg substitute or 1 egg plus 4 whites

2 tablespoons chopped fresh parsley
2 tablespoons chopped fresh mint or ½ teaspoon dried
½ cup matzo meal
Freshly ground black pepper

1. Preheat the oven to 375 degrees.

2. Trim the zucchini and cut on the diagonal into ¼-inch-thick slices. Bring 2 quarts salted water to a rapid boil. Boil the zucchini until tender, about 2 minutes. Drain the zucchini in a colander, rinse under cold water, and drain again. Blot dry with paper towels. Place the zucchini slices in a mixing bowl.

3. Meanwhile, heat the olive oil in a large nonstick skillet. Add the onion and garlic and cook over medium heat until soft but not brown, about 4 minutes. Add the onion mixture to the zucchini.

4. Stir the egg substitute and herbs into the zucchini mixture. Stir in the matzo meal and salt and pepper to taste. (Go easy on the salt, as the zucchini will be salty from boiling.) Transfer the mixture to an 8 by 8-inch baking dish, lightly greased with spray oil. Bake until the kugel is set and the top is golden brown, about 45 minutes. Cut into squares for serving.

Serves 6

130 CALORIES PER SERVING; 7 G PROTEIN; 5 G FAT; .7 G SATURATED FAT; 16 G CARBOHYDRATE; 63 MG SODIUM; .3 MG CHOLESTEROL

⚡ Yukon Gold Potato Kugel ⚡

Is there anything more comforting than a slab of potato kugel? Dense and substantial, succulent and soft, this is Jewish soul food at its best. In the old days, kugel would be made moist and palatable by the addition of schmaltz and gribenes (chicken fat and cracklings). These days, I take advantage of the creamy texture and naturally buttery flavor of the Yukon gold potato to make a kugel that's loaded with flavor, not fat. (Okay, sometimes I use a little schmaltz—just a little—for frying the onions.) Yukon golds are available at specialty greengrocers and most supermarkets.

PREPARATION TIME: 10 MINUTES   COOKING TIME: 50 MINUTES

2 tablespoons olive oil or schmaltz
1 large onion, finely chopped (about 2 cups)
1 clove garlic, finely chopped
3 pounds Yukon gold potatoes, peeled
3 tablespoons finely chopped parsley (preferably flat-leaf)
2 tablespoons finely chopped celery leaves (optional)

½ cup matzo meal or flour
1 tablespoon sweet paprika (optional)
1 teaspoon baking powder
¾ cup egg substitute or 1 egg and 4 whites
Salt and freshly ground black pepper

1. Preheat the oven to 350 degrees.

2. Heat 1½ tablespoons oil in a large nonstick skillet. Add the onion and garlic and cook over medium heat until the onion is lightly browned, 5 to 8 minutes.

3. Meanwhile, coarsely grate the potatoes in a food processor fitted with a shredding disk or on a box grater. Grab handfuls of the grated potato and squeeze tightly between your fingers to wring out as much liquid as possible.

4. Transfer the potatoes to a mixing bowl and stir in sautéed onions, parsley, celery leaves (if using), matzo meal, paprika, and baking powder. Add the egg substitute and stir to mix. Add salt and pepper to taste (I'd use 1½ teaspoons of salt, ½ teaspoon of pepper). The kugel should be highly seasoned. Spoon the kugel mixture into a 7 by 12-inch ovenproof baking dish, lightly sprayed with oil, and drizzle the top with the remaining ½ tablespoon olive oil.

5. Bake the kugel until the top is lightly browned and the filling is cooked through, 30 to 40 minutes. (To test for doneness, insert a metal skewer: it should enter the kugel easily and come out very hot to the touch.) Cut the kugel into rectangles or squares for serving.

Serves 8

243 CALORIES PER SERVING; 7 G PROTEIN; 4.4 G FAT; .6 G SATURATED FAT; 44 G CARBOHYDRATE; 54 MG SODIUM; .2 MG CHOLESTEROL

Mushroom Matzo Kugel

I love the earthy flavors of this kugel, the pungency of the mushrooms, the comforting richness of onions and celery. The kugel is great made with commonplace button mushrooms and even better if you use exotic mushrooms, like porcinis or shiitakes. You could make the kugel even richer by adding dried porcini mushrooms, which are available in Italian markets and gourmet shops (see note below). But even with button mushrooms, this kugel is the sort of dish you'll want to highlight for the holidays, serve at everyday dinners, and munch on cold for breakfast or lunch. The use of matzo farfel might make this seem strictly a Passover dish, but my family eats it year-round.

PREPARATION TIME: 10 MINUTES   COOKING TIME: 25 MINUTES

1 pound mushrooms (button or exotic)
2 tablespoons extra-virgin olive oil or schmaltz
1 medium onion, finely chopped
1 stalk celery, finely chopped
2 cups matzo farfel
2 cups hot chicken broth, beef broth, vegetable broth, or water

3 tablespoons finely chopped parsley
2 scallions, finely chopped
1 tablespoon chopped parsley leaves
¾ cup egg substitute or 1 egg plus 4 whites
Salt and freshly ground black pepper
Spray oil

1. Preheat the oven to 400 degrees. Trim the ends off the mushroom stems and wipe the caps clean with a damp paper towel. Thinly slice the mushrooms.

2. Heat 1½ tablespoons oil in a nonstick frying pan. Add the onion and celery and cook until lightly browned, about 5 minutes, stirring often. Increase the heat to high and add the mushrooms. Cook until most of the mushroom juices are evaporated and the mushrooms are browned, about 5 minutes, stirring often. Remove the pan from the heat.

3. Meanwhile, place the farfel in a mixing bowl and stir in the hot broth. Let stand until the farfel is soft, about 5 minutes. Drain off any excess broth. Stir in the mushroom mixture and the parsley, scallions, celery leaves (if using), and egg substitute. Add plenty of salt and pepper. The kugel should be highly seasoned. Spoon the matzo mixture into an 8 by 8-inch baking dish you've lightly greased with spray oil. Drizzle the remaining ½ tablespoon oil on top.

4. Bake the kugel until cooked through and the top is lightly browned, 10 to 15 minutes. Cut into squares or rectangles for serving.

Note: For an even richer kugel, soak 1 ounce dried porcini mushrooms in 1 cup of the warm broth. Transfer the mushrooms to a bowl with cold water and agitate with your fingers to wash off any grit. Mince the porcini and sauté them with the onion, and celery. Strain the broth through a cheesecloth or coffee filter, if gritty, and use as directed above.

Serves 6 to 8

262 CALORIES PER 6 SERVINGS; 11 G PROTEIN; 7.2 G FAT; 1 G SATURATED FAT; 41 G CARBOHYDRATE; 72 MG SODIUM; .3 MG CHOLESTEROL

Pickles and Relishes

Majorly Garlicky Dill Pickles

*The Rascal House is Miami's ultimate kosher-style restaurant—a sprawling deli that serves more than twenty-five hundred meals each day. Talk about early bird specials—this North Miami Beach landmark is actually busier at 5:00 P.M. than at 8:30! One of my favorite things about the Rascal House is the complimentary pickle spread that accompanies each meal—a mouth-puckering smorgasbord of pickled tomatoes, peppers, cabbage, and, of course, dill pickles. The Rascal House would never disclose a recipe, no, but here's how I imagine they make their dill pickles. **Note:** One of the endearing things about this recipe is how quick it is to prepare. You can eat the pickles the day after they're made. Naturally, if you have the patience to wait the full week, they'll taste even better.*

PREPARATION TIME: 15 MINUTES   COOKING TIME: 5 MINUTES, PLUS 1 TO 5 DAYS FOR PICKLING

12 pickling cucumbers (each about 3 inches long)
4 cloves garlic, peeled
3 heads or sprigs of fresh dill
1 to 3 hot dried peppers
6 coriander seeds
6 black peppercorns
2 allspice berries
1/8 teaspoon mustard seeds

FOR THE BRINE:
1 quart water
1/4 cup salt
2/3 cup distilled vinegar

1. Rinse out a 2-quart jar and its lid with boiling water. Lightly scrub the cucumbers with a sponge or vegetable brush. Arrange the cucumbers in the jar, adding the garlic, dill, peppers, and spices.

2. Combine the water, salt, and vinegar in a saucepan and bring to a boil. Let cool slightly, then pour this mixture into the jar over the pickles. Seal the jar.

3. Let the cucumbers pickle at room temperature for at least 24 hours, at which point they'll be half pickled, or as long as 1 week, at which point they'll be real pickles.

Makes 12 pickles

★★ CALORIES PER PICKLE; ★★ G PROTEIN; ★★ G FAT; ★★ G SATURATED FAT; ★★ G CARBOHYDRATE; ★★ MG SODIUM; 0 MG CHOLESTEROL

(Clockwise starting at the left): pickled tomatoes, majorly garlicky dill pickles, pickled peppers.

⤬ Pickled Tomatoes ⤬

Is there anything more sensual than biting into a pickled tomato? The firm, squeaky, crisp shell gives way to a soft, gooey interior that literally squirts when you take a bite. You expect something of the sweetness of a tomato (which is, after all, a fruit). Instead, you're rewarded with a powerful blast of garlic and spices. A pickled tomato should be tart and garlicky enough to send you lunging for a sip of Cel-Ray soda, yet not so sour that you forget you're eating a tomato. A pastrami sandwich would be a pitiful thing without it. Here's a simple recipe for home-pickled tomatoes that takes about 5 minutes' actual preparation time and a week to 10 days for the actual pickling.

PREPARATION TIME: 10 MINUTES   COOKING TIME: NONE, BUT ALLOW 7 TO 10 DAYS FOR PICKLING

8 firm green tomatoes (without the least blush of pink)
7½ cups water
1¼ cups distilled vinegar
½ cup kosher salt

6 cloves garlic, peeled
4 dried hot red chilies
2 teaspoons coriander seeds
2 teaspoons black peppercorns
2 teaspoons dill seed

1. Wash the tomatoes and blot dry. Prick each tomato 12 times with a fork.

2. You can use a clean 4-quart earthenware crock or glass jar for the pickles. Place the water, vinegar, and salt in the container you've chosen and whisk until the salt crystals are dissolved. Add the tomatoes, garlic, chilies, and spices. Place a small bowl, jar, or water-filled Ziploc bag on top of the tomatoes to keep any that float submerged. Loosely cover the crock with plastic wrap and place in a cool spot in your kitchen.

3. Let the tomatoes pickle at room temperature until tart but still quite firm, 7 to 10 days. Inspect the tomatoes periodically to make sure no scum or foam has risen to the surface. If it has, skim it off with a spoon or ladle. Make sure the tomatoes remain submerged. Once pickled, the tomatoes should be stored in the refrigerator.

Makes 8 tomatoes, which will serve 8

51 CALORIES PER TOMATO; 2.2 G PROTEIN; .5 G FAT; .05 G SATURATED FAT; 12 G CARBOHYDRATE; 6,995 MG SODIUM; 0 MG CHOLESTEROL

🔏 Pickled Onions 🔏

Here's the third of our quartet of pickles designed to bring excitement to any deli spread. My favorite onion for this pickle would be a white pearl onion. But yellow or red onions can be pickled the same way. **Note:** *I like my pickled onions bracingly tart, so I never add sugar. Mrs. Raichlen likes a sweeter pickled onion: you can certainly add sugar if you desire.*

PREPARATION TIME: 10 MINUTES
COOKING TIME: NONE, BUT YOU'LL NEED 3 TO 4 DAYS FOR THE ONIONS TO PICKLE

24 pearl onions (each about 1 inch in diameter)
3 cups distilled white vinegar
3 tablespoons salt
1 to 3 teaspoons sugar (optional)

1 jalapeño pepper, cut in half lengthwise
1 tablespoon pickling spice
10 black peppercorns

1. Peel the onions and set aside.

2. Wash and dry a 2-quart crock or jar. Place the vinegar, salt, and sugar (if using) in the crock and whisk until the salt crystals are dissolved. (If using a jar, tightly cover and shake until salt is dissolved.) Add the onions, jalapeño, pickling spice, and pepper-corns. Cover the crock with plastic wrap (do so even if using a jar with a lid) and place in a cool spot in your kitchen.

3. Let the onions pickle at room temperature until tart but still firm, 3 to 4 days. Store in the refrigerator.

Makes 24

12 CALORIES PER ONION; .3 G PROTEIN; .1 G FAT; .02 G SATURATED FAT; 3 G CARBOHYDRATE; 875 MG SODIUM; 0 MG CHOLESTEROL

🖾 Pickled Peppers 🖾

"Peter Piper picked a peck of pickled peppers" goes the old tongue twister. Which peppers? I'd certainly pick these delectable sweet-sour pickled peppers! Broiling or grilling the peppers imparts an unexpected smoke flavor that, while not traditional, adds great complexity to this seemingly simple dish. These peppers go exceedingly well with deli platters or dairy spreads.

PREPARATION TIME: 10 MINUTES
COOKING TIME: NONE, BUT YOU'LL NEED 24 HOURS FOR THE PEPPERS TO PICKLE

4 green bell peppers
2 cups distilled white vinegar
2 cups water
2½ tablespoons salt

½ cup sugar
3 sprigs fresh dill
3 cloves garlic, peeled
2 dried hot chili peppers

1. Preheat your broiler to high. Broil the peppers until the skins are nicely browned and blistered, 2 to 3 minutes per side. Transfer the peppers to a plate and let cool.

2. Cut each pepper in quarters, discarding the stem, veins, and seeds.

3. Wash and dry a 2-quart crock or jar. Place the vinegar, water, salt, and sugar in the crock and whisk until the salt crystals are dissolved. (If using a jar, tightly cover and shake until salt is dissolved.) Taste for seasoning, adding sugar or salt as desired. Add the peppers, dill, garlic, and chilies. Cover the crock with plastic wrap (do so even if using a jar with a lid).

4. Let the peppers pickle in the refrigerator for 24 hours. Store in the refrigerator until serving.

Serves 4 to 6

98 CALORIES PER 4 SERVINGS; 1.4 G PROTEIN; .25 G FAT; .03 G SATURATED FAT; 24 G CARBOHYDRATE; 2,914 MG SODIUM; 0 MG CHOLESTEROL

✄ Miami-Style Coleslaw ✄

To most Americans, coleslaw means shredded cabbage in a creamy mayonnaise sauce. Here in Miami at the great Jewish-style restaurants—the Rascal House, the Pub, the late Wolfie's, and the late Famous—coleslaw was a simpler and healthier affair, a naturally low-fat salad of shredded cabbage and carrots lightly pickled in sweetened vinegar. Serve this slaw as part of a pickle spread or on any occasion you'd serve traditional coleslaw.

PREPARATION TIME: 10 MINUTES   COOKING TIME: 1 TO 24 HOURS FOR PICKLING

½ cup cider vinegar
3 tablespoons sugar, or to taste
1 teaspoon salt, or to taste
½ teaspoon freshly ground black pepper

½ teaspoon celery seeds
1 small head green cabbage (about 1 pound—6 cups shredded)
2 large carrots

1. Combine the vinegar, sugar, salt, pepper, and celery seed in a large jar, crock, or mixing bowl and whisk or shake until the salt and sugar crystals are dissolved.

2. Cut the cabbage in half lengthwise. Cut out the core. Cut the cabbage widthwise into the thinnest possible slices. Toss with your fingers to break the slices into shreds. You should have about 6 cups. Alternatively, use the slicing disk of a food processor for shredding the cabbage. Stir the cabbage into the vinegar mixture.

3. Coarsely shred the carrots, using a grater or food processor fitted with a shredding disk, and stir them into the cabbage.

4. Allow the slaw to pickle for at least 1 hour or as long as overnight. Correct the seasoning. Refrigerate until serving.

Serves 6

62 CALORIES PER SERVING; 1.4 G PROTEIN; .3 G FAT; .04 G SATURATED FAT; 15 G CARBOHYDRATE; 415 MG SODIUM; 0 MG CHOLESTEROL

⚡ Haroset—Passover Apple, Nut, and Honey Relish ⚡

Like most Jewish holidays, Passover celebrates a bittersweet experience in the history of the Jewish people. The misery of the Israelites' slavery in Egypt, followed by the sweetness of liberation from bondage. True to form, there's a Passover dish that symbolizes this dichotomy, one of the most distinctive and delectable dishes in the holiday tradition: haroset. Part relish, part pâté, haroset symbolizes the mortar used by the Hebrew slaves to build pharaoh's pyramids, but the honey, wine, and apples represent the sweetness of the Jews' eventual freedom. Here's an Ashkenazi haroset, followed by an offbeat rhubarb haroset from Colorado.

PREPARATION TIME: 10 MINUTES

3 tablespoons slivered almonds
3 tablespoons chopped walnuts
3 tablespoons sunflower seeds
2 sweet apples, like Galas
Finely grated zest and juice of 1 lemon

8 pitted dates, finely chopped
¼ cup honey, or to taste
¼ cup red wine
1 teaspoon ground cinnamon
3 to 4 tablespoons matzo meal

1. Roast the nuts and sunflower seeds in a dry skillet over medium heat until fragrant and lightly browned, 2 to 3 minutes. Transfer to a mixing bowl.

2. Peel, core, and coarsely grate the apples. Stir them into the nut mixture with the lemon zest and juice, dates, honey, wine, cinnamon, and 3 tablespoons matzo meal. Adjust the seasoning, adding lemon juice for tartness or honey for sweetness; if the mixture seems too wet, add a little more matzo meal. Alternatively, the apples can be chopped and the haroset can be mixed in the food processor.

Makes about 2½ to 3 cups; serves 10 to 12

124 CALORIES PER 10 SERVINGS; 2 G PROTEIN; 4 G FAT; .4 G SATURATED FAT; 21 G CARBOHYDRATE; 2 MG SODIUM; 0 MG CHOLESTEROL

⚘ Rhubarb Haroset ⚘

Haroset is an essential at a Passover seder, but beside the requirement that it be mortarlike in its consistency (it symbolizes the mortar the Hebrews used to build pharaoh's pyramids), anything goes. One of the more offbeat versions is this tangy rhubarb haroset made by my friend, Rocky Mountain News food editor Marty Meitus. Rhubarb provides the piquancy; jícama the crunch. This is a perfect way to take advantage of the first of the season's rhubarb.

PREPARATION TIME: 10 MINUTES   COOKING TIME: 10 MINUTES

2 cloves
1 strip lemon zest
1 cup Riesling or other semisweet white wine
1 cinnamon stick
1 cup sugar, or as needed

1 cup water
1 cup diced rhubarb (cut into ½-inch dice)
1 cup diced jícama (cut into ½-inch dice)
¼ cup toasted pecans

1. Stick the cloves in the strip of lemon zest. Combine the Riesling, lemon zest, cloves, and cinnamon stick in a large, heavy saucepan and bring to a boil. Boil until reduced to ¼ cup.

2. Add the sugar and water and bring to a boil. Reduce the heat and simmer until clear and syrupy, about 3 minutes. Stir in the rhubarb and simmer until crispy-tender, 1 to 2 minutes. Transfer rhubarb with a slotted spoon to a food processor and let cool. Remove the pan from the heat and let the cooking liquid cool to room temperature. Discard the cinnamon stick, lemon zest, and cloves.

3. Add the jícama, pecans, and rhubarb cooking liquid to the food processor. Run the machine in short bursts to coarsely chop the ingredients: the haroset should remain chunky. Taste for sweetness, adding sugar to taste.

Note: Toasting heightens the flavor of the pecans, so you can use less. To toast the pecans, place them on a piece of foil in a 350-degree oven or toaster oven. Roast until lightly browned and aromatic.

Makes 1½ cups, which will serve 6 to 8

195.1 CALORIES PER 6 SERVINGS; .78 G PROTEIN; 3.1 G FAT; .25 G SATURATED FAT; 36.5 G CARBOHYDRATE; 5.4 MG SODIUM; 0 MG CHOLESTEROL

Sauces and Spice Mixes

❧❧❧❧❧

✖ Made-from-Scratch Applesauce ✖

Applesauce or sour cream? That is the question. At least it is in my family when it comes to serving latkes. Pair latkes with sour cream and you emphasize the earthy qualities of the potatoes. Serve applesauce and you blur the traditional distinction between vegetable dish and dessert. The best applesauce for latkes I ever tasted was made not by a Jew, but by my Cuban friend Elida Proenza, who cooks with a Jewish heart and soul. Her secret? A splash of wine and a piece of fresh vanilla bean, which add a haunting perfumed flavor to the sauce. Latkes will never be the same!

PREPARATION TIME: 10 MINUTES   COOKING TIME: 30 MINUTES

3 pounds fragrant apples, like Galas or McIntoshes
  (4 to 6 apples)
1 cinnamon stick or 1 teaspoon ground cinnamon
2-inch piece of vanilla bean, cut in half lengthwise
2 strips lemon zest

1½ tablespoons fresh lemon juice, or to taste
¼ cup sugar, or to taste
2 tablespoons dry white wine
2¼ cups water, or as needed

1. Wash the apples and cut each in half. Remove the stems and cores with a melon baller, but leave the skins intact. Place the apples in a large, heavy pot with the cinnamon, vanilla, lemon zest and juice, sugar, wine, and water. Bring to a boil.

2. Reduce the heat and simmer the apples, covered, until soft, 20 to 30 minutes. Remove the pan from the heat and let cool slightly. Discard the cinnamon stick and vanilla bean.

3. Puree the apples and pan juices in a blender or food processor: the former will give you a silky smooth puree; the latter a chunkier applesauce. Serve this applesauce with latkes or blintzes. Or eat it out of the bowl with a spoon.

Makes about 4 cups, which will serve 8

94 CALORIES PER 6 SERVINGS; .25 G PROTEIN; .4 G FAT; .07 G SATURATED FAT; 24 G CARBOHYDRATE; .4 MG SODIUM; 0 MG CHOLESTEROL

Two sauces: volcanic horseradish and zehug.

✄ Volcanic Horseradish Sauce ✄

"Gefilte fish without horseradish sauce," runs a Yiddish saying, "is punishment enough!" How curious that something so tongue-torturing as freshly grated horseradish sauce should be so near and dear to the Jewish heart. In my family, contests were held every Passover to see who could consume the most horseradish sauce with his gefilte fish. My aunt Annette made the sauce from freshly grated horseradish and, let me tell you, it hurt! (Horseradish owes its bite to sulfuric acid, which is formed when the root comes in contact with air in the process of grating.) Jewish-style horseradish sauce comes both white and red (the latter colored with beets). If you're used to bottled horseradish sauce, this recipe will make you bolt upright and take notice.

PREPARATION TIME: 5 MINUTES

1 pound fresh horseradish root (enough to make 2 cups grated)
⅔ cup distilled vinegar

3 tablespoons dry white wine
2 teaspoons sugar
1 teaspoon salt, or to taste

1. Peel the horseradish with a paring knife and cut into ½-inch slices. Finely chop the horseradish in a food processor fitted with a metal blade. Work in the vinegar, wine, sugar, and salt to taste. Process to make a creamy puree.

If working by hand, grate the horseradish on the fine side of a box grater. Transfer it to a bowl and stir in vinegar, wine, sugar, and salt.

2. Store the horseradish sauce in a glass jar in the refrigerator. Try to serve it the same day or within a week. (Its bite will fade with time.) Place a piece of plastic wrap under the lid of the jar, as the fumes will eventually corrode the metal of most jar lids.

Note: To make red horseradish sauce, add ¼ cup grated cooked beets.

Makes 2 cups, which will serve 12 to 16

39 CALORIES PER SERVING (BASED ON 12 SERVINGS); 1.2 G PROTEIN; .11 G FAT; .02 G SATURATED FAT; 9 G CARBOHYDRATE; 3.3 MG SODIUM; 0 MG CHOLESTEROL

⚰ Tahini Sauce ⚰

Tahini sauce could be thought of as the "mayonnaise" of the Middle East—a creamy, beige sauce that owes its richness to pureed sesame seeds and piquancy to fresh lemon juice. You can buy tahini (sesame seed paste) in Middle Eastern markets and most supermarkets. Stir the contents of the can well before using: the oil has a tendency to separate. This sauce can be served by itself as a dip for pita bread (it's a traditional part of a meze platter). It's also delicious spooned over grilled chicken or fish.

PREPARATION TIME: 5 MINUTES

2 cloves garlic, minced
½ teaspoon salt
¼ teaspoon finely ground white pepper
⅓ cup tahini

½ cup water
¼ cup fresh lemon juice, or to taste
3 tablespoons minced fresh parsley
Cayenne pepper or hot paprika

1. Mash the garlic, salt, and pepper to a smooth paste in the bottom of a mixing bowl. Stir in the tahini. Add the water and stir or whisk until smooth. (Just so you know, the sauce will first thin, then thicken—the result of the emulsification of the sesame oils and water.)

2. Stir in the lemon juice, parsley, and a pinch of cayenne. Correct the seasoning, adding salt or lemon juice to taste. Transfer the sauce to a serving bowl and lightly sprinkle the top with cayenne.

Makes 1¼ cups, which serves 6

79.3 CALORIES PER SERVING; 2.3 G PROTEIN; 6.7 G FAT; .9 G SATURATED FAT; 4 G CARBOHYDRATE; 209.5 MG SODIUM; 0 MG CHOLESTEROL

✄ Mushroom Gravy ✄

*Kasha without mushroom gravy is like, well, gefilte fish without horseradish. For truly sublime gravy, you'd use fresh Steinpilze (aka porcini/boletus mushrooms), which are available at gourmet shops and specialty greengrocers. The following recipe achieves a similar woodsy richness by using a combination of commonplace fresh button mushrooms and dried mushrooms. The last time I made the gravy, I used Chinese black mushrooms for dried—they're not traditional, of course, but their flavor is haunting, and they don't need the kind of scrubbing that dried porcini do. To make gravy for milchig meals, use vegetable broth. For fleischig meals, use beef or chicken broth and omit the sour cream. **Note:** I like a rib-sticking gravy, so I call for a flour roux in the following recipe. My wife prefers a thinner gravy (more like a jus): she thickens her gravy with ½ teaspoon potato starch (stirred into the sour cream and added at the end) in place of the flour.*

PREPARATION TIME: 5 MINUTES, PLUS 30 TO 60 MINUTES FOR SOAKING THE MUSHROOMS
COOKING TIME: 10 MINUTES

4 dried Chinese black mushrooms or 1 ounce dried porcini
2 cups hot vegetable broth (page 191), beef broth (page 190), or chicken broth (page 189)
1 tablespoon olive oil
8 ounces fresh portobello or button mushrooms (or fresh porcini if you're feeling flush)
3 cloves garlic, finely chopped
2 tablespoons flour
¼ cup no-fat sour cream
Salt and freshly ground black pepper

1. Place the dried mushrooms in a large bowl with the hot broth. Let soak until soft, 1 hour.

2. Drain the dried mushrooms, reserving the broth. If using Chinese black mushrooms, remove and discard the stems. Thinly slice the caps. If using dried porcini, you'll need to transfer them to another bowl with hot water to cover and agitate briskly with your fingers to remove any grit. (You may need to repeat this process several times.) Here, too, reserve the broth, but you'll need to strain it through cheesecloth or a coffee filter to remove the grit.

3. Trim the ends off the fresh mushroom stems. Wipe the caps clean with a damp paper towel. Thinly slice the mushrooms or cut into ½-inch dice.

4. Heat the olive oil in a saucepan. Add the fresh and dried mushrooms and garlic and, stirring with a wooden spoon, cook over medium-high heat until the mushrooms are lightly browned and most of the mushroom juices have evaporated, 4 minutes. Stir in the flour and cook for 1 minute.

5. Whisk in the broth off the heat. Return the sauce to the heat and simmer until thickened and richly flavored, 5 minutes, whisking often. Whisk in the sour cream and boil for 2 minutes. Add salt and pepper to taste. The gravy should be highly seasoned. Serve mushroom gravy over kasha or with the vegetable cutlets on page 107.

Makes 2 cups, which will serve 4 to 6

106 CALORIES PER 4 SERVINGS; 4.5 G PROTEIN; 3.5 G FAT; .5 G SATURATED FAT; 13 G CARBOHYDRATE; 21 MG SODIUM; 0 MG CHOLESTEROL

⚡ Zehug ⚡
(Yemenite Hot Sauce)

This fiery condiment is Israel's answer to salsa. Its popularity extends way beyond the Yemenite community.
It's enjoyed with a wide variety of dishes, from grilled chicken and seafood to breads. The recipe
below gives you a green zehug. To make a red zehug, you'd use red jalapeños or Thai chilies.

PREPARATION TIME: 5 MINUTES

6 jalapeño peppers, stemmed and seeded (for a
    spicier zehug, leave the seeds in)
6 cloves garlic, peeled
½ cup chopped cilantro or parsley

2 tablespoons fresh lemon juice
2 tablespoons water, as needed
1 teaspoon ground cumin
½ teaspoon each salt and black pepper, or to taste

1. In a food processor, finely chop the chilies, garlic, and cilantro. Add the lemon juice, water, cumin, salt, and pepper and grind to a smooth puree. (Add water as needed to obtain a pourable sauce.) Store the zehug in a glass jar, placing a piece of plastic wrap under the lid.

Makes 1 cup, which will serve 6 to 8

4 CALORIES PER SERVING; 0 G PROTEIN; 0 G FAT; 0 G SATURATED FAT; 1 G CARBOHYDRATE; 1 MG SODIUM; 0 MG CHOLESTEROL

✥ Harissa ✥
(North African Hot Sauce)

What would couscous be without this fiery red condiment? Or tagine or other North African Jewish dishes? Harissa plays the same role among the Sephardic Jews of North Africa that horseradish does among the Ashkenazim. While you can buy canned harissa, it's easy to make from scratch and the results are far superior. Below are two versions: one with fresh chilies, one with dried.
Note: *Sometimes I add a tablespoon or two of chopped cilantro, which has a nice way of rounding out the flavor.*

PREPARATION TIME: 10 MINUTES

Fresh Harissa

12 red jalapeño chilies or 20 red serranos, stemmed
3 cloves garlic, coarsely chopped
2 teaspoons salt
1 teaspoon ground cumin

½ teaspoon black pepper
3 tablespoons olive oil
2 tablespoons distilled white vinegar, or to taste
2 to 4 tablespoons water

1. Seed, and devein the chilies. (It's a good idea to wear rubber or plastic gloves when handling chilies.) For a really hot harissa, you could leave some or all of the seeds in.

2. Combine the chilies, garlic, salt, cumin, and pepper in a blender and puree to a smooth paste. Gradually work in the oil and vinegar. Add enough water to make the sauce pourable and mellow the flavor.

3. Transfer the harissa to a clean jar and store in the refrigerator. (It's a good idea to put a sheet of plastic wrap between the top of the jar and the lid: this keeps the lid from corroding.) The harissa will keep in the refrigerator for several weeks. Stir before using.

Makes 1¼ cups, which will serve 12 to 16

38 CALORIES PER SERVING (1½ TABLESPOONS); .35 G PROTEIN; 3.5 G FAT; .5 G SATURATED FAT; 2 G CARBOHYDRATE; 194 MG SODIUM; 0 MG CHOLESTEROL

Dried Pepper Harissa

You can use any number of dried red chilies for this recipe: Chinese red chili peppers, cayenne peppers, or even Mexican chiles de árbol. For a hotter harissa, leave some or all of the seeds intact.

PREPARATION TIME: 10 MINUTES

1 ounce dried red chilies, stemmed
2 cups boiling water
3 cloves garlic, coarsely chopped
2 teaspoons salt

1 teaspoon ground cumin
½ teaspoon black pepper
3 tablespoons olive oil
2 tablespoons distilled vinegar

1. Place the chilies in a heatproof bowl and pour the water over them. Let soak for 1 hour. Drain the chilies, reserving the soaking liquid.

2. Seed and devein the chilies. (It's a good idea to wear rubber or plastic gloves when handling chilies.)

3. Combine the chilies, garlic, salt, cumin, and pepper in a blender and puree to a smooth paste. Gradually work in the oil and vinegar. Add enough chili soaking liquid (about ½ cup) to obtain thick but pourable sauce.

4. Transfer the harissa to a clean jar and store in the refrigerator. (It's a good idea to put a sheet of plastic wrap between the top of the jar and the lid: this keeps the lid from corroding.) The harissa will keep in the refrigerator for several weeks. Stir before using.

Makes about 1 cup, which will serve 16

29 CALORIES PER SERVING (1 TABLESPOON); .4 G PROTEIN; 3 G FAT; .3 G SATURATED FAT;
1.1 G CARBOHYDRATE; 291 MG SODIUM; 0 MG CHOLESTEROL

🖎 Zataar 🖎
(Israeli Herb Rub)

Let the French have their herbes de Provence; the Chinese, their five-spice powder. I raise my plate for zataar. This intensely aromatic mixture of dried herbs, sesame seeds, and sumac looms large on Israel's culinary landscape; indeed, it's enjoyed throughout the Middle and Near East. The herbs in zataar can include oregano, thyme, summer savory, and one or more of a half dozen local herbs that have no equivalents in the West. You can buy zataar ready-made at Israeli and Middle East markets. Here's a homemade version that's very tasty stirred into dips, sprinkled on pita bread, or used as a seasoning for grilled meats.
Note: *Sumac is a lemony purple spice made from a tart Middle East berry. Look for it in the sources mentioned above.*

PREPARATION TIME: 5 MINUTES

¼ cup dried oregano
¼ cup dried summer savory
3 tablespoons dried thyme

3 tablespoons lightly toasted sesame seeds
3 tablespoons ground sumac

Combine the ingredients in a mixing bowl and toss to mix, crumbling the herbs with your fingertips.

Store the zataar in an airtight jar. It will keep for several months.

Makes 1 cup, which will serve 16

⌘ Hawaij ⌘
(Yemenite Spice Rub)

This aromatic spice mix plays pinball on your tastebuds, delivering turmeric and cumin for pungency, plenty of black pepper for bite, and cardamom and cloves for a touch of sweetness. Hawaij came to Israel with the Yemenite Jews, but today Israelis of all ethnic persuasions rub it on meats and seafood for grilling and add it to soups and stews. There's even a sweet hawaij for adding to coffee. Note: For a quicker, more convenient, but slightly less flavorful hawaij, you can use preground spices and omit the roasting and grinding in steps 1 and 2.

PREPARATION TIME: 5 MINUTES   COOKING TIME: 5 MINUTES

⅓ cup black peppercorns
⅓ cup cumin seeds
1 teaspoon cloves

1 tablespoon cardamom pods
3 tablespoons ground turmeric

1. Combine the peppercorns, cumin, cloves, and cardamom in a dry skillet. Cook over medium heat until toasted and fragrant, about 3 minutes. Transfer the spices to a bowl and let cool.

2. Grind the roasted spices and turmeric to a fine powder in a spice mill or blender. Store in a sealed glass jar away from heat and light.

To use, rub 1 to 3 teaspoons hawaij on each pound of poultry, meat, or fish. Don't forget to season with salt as well.

Makes 1 cup, which will serve 16

Desserts

❧❧❧❀❧❧

✄ Apricot Mousse ✄

This tangy mousse belongs to a large family of Jewish desserts that includes the fruit jellies of Eastern Europe and the fruit leathers of the Near East. Serve the mousses in wine or martini glasses and you have a quick, easy, regal dessert.

PREPARATION TIME: 20 MINUTES, PLUS 30 MINUTES FOR SOAKING THE APRICOTS   COOKING TIME: 15 MINUTES

8 ounces dried apricots
1 package unflavored gelatin
2 cups fresh orange juice
¼ cup sugar, or to taste, plus 3 tablespoons for the
   egg whites
2 cloves

1 strip lemon zest (½ by 2 inches)
1 cinnamon stick
2 tablespoons fresh lime juice
3 egg whites
½ teaspoon cream of tartar
6 sprigs fresh mint for garnish

1. Soak the apricots in warm water to cover for 30 minutes. Drain well.

2. Sprinkle the gelatin over ¼ cup cool water in a metal measuring cup. Let sit until spongy, 10 minutes.

3. Combine the apricots, orange juice, ½ cup water, and ¼ cup sugar in a saucepan. Stick the cloves in the strip of lemon zest and add it to the apricots with the cinnamon stick and lime juice. Gently simmer the apricots until very soft, about 10 minutes. Remove the pan from the heat and remove and discard the lemon zest, cloves, and cinnamon stick. Puree the apricot mixture in a blender, then transfer to a metal mixing bowl.

4. Place the measuring cup with the gelatin in a shallow pan of simmering water and cook until the gelatin melts. Whisk the gelatin into the apricot mixture. Place the apricot bowl over a bowl of ice and chill until the mixture is on the verge of setting. Stir with a rubber spatula to ensure even gelling.

5. Meanwhile, beat the egg whites and cream of tartar to soft peaks in a mixer, starting on low speed, gradually increasing the speed to medium, then high. Sprinkle in the remaining 3 tablespoons sugar as the whites stiffen. Beat until firm and glossy but not dry. The whole process will take about 8 minutes.

6. Fold the egg whites into the gelling apricot mixture. Spoon the mixture into 6 wine or martini glasses. Chill until set, 4 hours. Garnish each mousse with a sprig of fresh mint before serving.

Serves 6

217 CALORIES PER SERVING; 16 G PROTEIN; .4 G FAT; .04 G SATURATED FAT; 41 G CARBOHYDRATE; 60 MG SODIUM; 0 MG CHOLESTEROL

Apricot mousse.

⚒ Zvingous ⚒
(Greek Hanukkah "Fritters" with Honeyed Syrup)

As we saw in the latke recipe on page 118, Jews traditionally eat fried foods for Hanukkah. (The oil symbolizes the Miracle of the Lights: that a one-day supply of Holy Oil burned for eight days, until a messenger could arrive with a fresh supply.) Greek Jews celebrate Hanukkah by eating zvingous, small puffs of fried dough drizzled with honey syrup and cinnamon. In reading traditional recipes, I realized that the dough was a sort of choux pastry that could be baked instead of deep-fried. (The puffs don't rise quite as dramatically when baked, but the results are still impressive.) Baking brings the fat levels within acceptable limits while maintaining the pleasing contrast of savory and sweet, of crisp and syrupy, of spice and sweetness that makes zvingous such a beloved Hanukkah dessert in Greece. For the best results, try to find Greek honey, which has a delicate thyme flavor.

PREPARATION TIME: 20 MINUTES   COOKING TIME: 50 MINUTES

FOR THE SYRUP:
1 cup sugar
¼ cup honey (preferably Greek)
1¼ cups water
1 cinnamon stick
4 cloves
2 strips lemon zest
2 strips orange zest
2 tablespoons cognac or brandy

FOR THE PASTRY:
1 cup water
¼ cup olive oil
½ teaspoon salt
½ teaspoon sugar
1 cup unbleached white flour
1 teaspoon grated lemon zest
1 cup egg substitute or 2 large eggs plus 4 whites

1 tablespoon egg substitute or 1 egg white beaten with a little salt, for glaze
Cinnamon in a sifter for sprinkling

1. Prepare the syrup. Combine the sugar, honey, water, cinnamon, cloves, and lemon and orange zest in a saucepan and boil until thick and syrupy, about 4 minutes. Strain the syrup into a bowl and let cool to room temperature. Add the cognac and refrigerate until cold. The syrup can be prepared up to a day ahead to this stage.

2. Preheat the oven to 400 degrees.

3. Place the water, oil, salt, and sugar in a heavy saucepan. Bring the mixture to a boil over a high heat. Remove the pan from the heat and sift in the flour. Stir well with a wooden spoon to make a thick paste. Return the pan to a high heat and cook until the dough is thick enough to come away from the sides of the pan in a smooth ball, 2 to 4 minutes.

4. Beat in the lemon zest. Add the egg substitute in 4 batches, beating vigorously with a wooden spoon

until the mixture is smooth before adding the next batch. The final mixture should be the consistency of soft ice cream.

5. Lightly spray a nonstick baking sheet with oil. Transfer the dough to a piping bag fitted with a ⅜-inch round tip. Pipe 1-inch balls of dough onto the baking sheet, leaving 2 inches between each. (If you don't have a piping bag, use 2 spoons to drop balls of dough on the baking sheet.) Dip a fork in a bowl of cold water and use the back of the tines to smooth the top of each ball. Lightly brush the balls with the egg glaze, taking care not to drip glaze on the baking sheet. Sprinkle the baking sheet with a few drops of water.

6. Bake the dough balls until puffed, firm, and nicely browned, 40 to 50 minutes. If the puffs brown too much before they're completely dried out, reduce

the heat. Remove the baking sheet from the oven and let cool for 3 minutes.

7. Using a spatula, transfer the hot puffs to a serving bowl or deep platter. Pour the cold syrup over them. Let soak for 3 minutes, spooning the syrup over the puffs. Serve the puffs with syrup in bowls or deep dessert plates. Sprinkle with cinnamon and serve at once.

Makes 32 to 40 puffs, which will serve 8 to 10

280 CALORIES PER 8 SERVINGS; 5 G PROTEIN; 8 G FAT; 1.3 G SATURATED FAT; 45 G CARBOHYDRATE; 190 MG SODIUM; 53 MG CHOLESTEROL

✂ My Mother's Lemon Fruit Compote ✂

My mother was a ballet dancer and her rigorous training prevented her from indulging in the cakes and pastries that crowned our holiday dinners. But, oh, how she loved this compote. Knowing my mother's fondness for lemons, my aunt Annette would load the compote with this mouth-puckering fruit, so this is one compote that won't strike you as too sweet.

PREPARATION TIME: 10 MINUTES   COOKING TIME: 20 MINUTES

1 or 2 lemons
4 cloves
2 cups Concord wine
2 cups apple juice
1 cup water
1 pound prunes

½ pound dried apricots
½ pound dried figs
½ pound golden raisins
2 cinnamon sticks
¼ cup sugar, or to taste

1. Using a vegetable peeler, remove 3 strips of lemon zest (the oil-rich outer rind) and set aside. Stick the cloves in the strips of lemon zest. (This facilitates their removal later.)

2. Using a paring knife, cut the rinds off the lemon(s), leaving only the juicy flesh. Cut the lemons crosswise into ¼-inch slices, removing any seeds you may find with a fork.

3. Combine the wine, apple juice, water, lemon slices, prunes, apricots, figs, raisins, and cinnamon sticks in a large, heavy saucepan. Cover the pan and gently simmer the compote until the fruits are swollen and soft, about 20 minutes. (Add water as needed to keep the compote moist.) Taste the compote for sweetness, adding sugar to taste. Serve the compote chilled or at room temperature. Discard the cinnamon sticks and strips of lemon zest with the cloves before serving.

Serves 8

308 CALORIES PER SERVING; 0 G PROTEIN; 1 G FAT; 0 G SATURATED FAT; 74 G CARBOHYDRATE; 13 MG SODIUM; 0 MG CHOLESTEROL

🐾 Miriam's Delight 🐾
(Blueberry Banana Parfait)

Grandchildren everywhere are highly proprietary about the culinary specialties of their grandmothers. Especially when it comes to desserts. Thus, in my family, my father and aunt and uncle grew up eating Grammie Ethel's cookies and fudge, but I was the one who raised them to the level of cult foods. My wife grew up on the following dessert, but her children act as though their grandmother Miriam Seldin created it especially for them. I call for bananas and blueberries in the following recipe, but you could easily substitute other fruits, like strawberries or peaches.

PREPARATION TIME: 10 MINUTES

1 pint fresh blueberries
2 ripe bananas
1½ cups no-fat sour cream

6 to 8 tablespoons brown sugar
4 sprigs fresh mint

1. Stem and wash the blueberries, discarding any that are shriveled or moldy. Peel and thinly slice the bananas. Arrange some blueberries and banana slices in the bottoms of four parfait or wine glasses. Top with sour cream and brown sugar.

2. Add two more layers of fruit, sour cream, and sugar. Garnish each parfait with a sprig of fresh mint.

Serves 4

251 CALORIES PER SERVING; 7 G PROTEIN; .6 G FAT; .13 G SATURATED FAT; 55 G CARBOHYDRATE; 85 MG SODIUM; 0 MG CHOLESTEROL

✑ Sephardic Pumpkin Strudels ✑
(Rodanchas de la Calabaza)

*These coiled pumpkin strudels are a popular Greek-Jewish dessert. They're traditionally served at Rosh Hashanah and Sukkot: their spiral shape symbolizes the cycle of life and the ascent of the soul into heaven. There's a more practical reason for serving rodanchas in the fall: this is when calabazas (the squash used for making rodanchas) are harvested. This recipe comes from my great-aunt Lily Modiano, who found when she moved to America that canned pumpkin could be substituted for calabaza. To reduce the fat, I use spray oil and sprinkle finely chopped nuts and bread crumbs between the layers of filo dough. **Note:** The easiest way to chop the nuts is in the food processor.*

PREPARATION TIME: 30 MINUTES   COOKING TIME: 1 HOUR

FOR THE FILLING:
2 (15-ounce) cans pureed pumpkin
½ cup sugar
1 teaspoon cinnamon
¼ teaspoon ground cloves

TO FINISH THE RODANCHAS:
⅓ cup toasted unflavored bread crumbs

⅓ cup sugar
3 tablespoons very finely chopped toasted walnuts, plus 1 tablespoon for garnish
½ teaspoon cinnamon
16 large sheets filo dough
Spray oil or 3 tablespoons melted butter

1. Prepare the filling. Combine the pumpkin, sugar, cinnamon, and cloves in a large, heavy saucepan, and cook over medium heat until thick and pasty, 15 to 20 minutes, stirring often with a wooden spoon. (The mixture should be thick enough to leave clean traces on the bottom of the pan when stirred with a wooden spoon.) Let the filling cool to room temperature, then refrigerate until cold.

2. Combine the bread crumbs, sugar, 3 tablespoons walnuts, and cinnamon in a mixing bowl and toss to mix. Preheat the oven to 375 degrees.

3. Open the package of filo, unfold the dough, and keep covered with a damp cloth. Spread a single sheet of filo on the work surface, narrow side facing you. Spray the filo with oil (or brush with melted butter), then lightly sprinkle with the bread crumb mixture. Place another sheet of filo on top, spray with oil, and sprinkle with bread crumbs. Fold up the bottom quarter of the filo rectangle, as though you were folding a business letter.

4. Spoon one eighth of the pumpkin mixture in a cigar shape along the bottom of the filo dough, not quite to the edges. (You'll need 2 spoons to do this. If you're handy with a pastry bag, you could pipe the pumpkin mixture through a ½-inch tip.) Starting at the bottom, roll up the filo and filling into a tube.

5. Starting at the end on the left and working gently so as not to tear the filo (it may tear a little anyway—don't worry if it does), loosely coil the filo tube into a spiral. Set it on a nonstick baking sheet you've lightly sprayed with oil. Make the remaining rodanchas the same way.

6. Spray the tops of the rodanchas with oil (or brush with butter) and sprinkle with remaining chopped walnuts and any remaining bread crumb mixture. Bake until golden brown and crisp, 30 to 40 minutes. Serve the rodanchas warm.

Serves 8

264 CALORIES PER SERVING; 5 G PROTEIN; 4.5 G FAT; .9 G SATURATED FAT; 53 G CARBOHYDRATE; 228 MG SODIUM; 0 MG CHOLESTEROL

✄ Aunt Annette's Apple Strudel ✄

My aunt Annette's strudel was legendary—not only in our family, but also up and down the eastern seaboard. People would come from as far away as Washington and Philadelphia to enjoy it. What made the strudel so great was the homemade dough and a fresh apple filling lavishly enriched with raisins, nuts, and even cherry preserves. There's no way to completely eliminate the fat in Aunt Annette's recipe. (Thank goodness!) But with a couple of tricks, the fat can be reduced dramatically. First, I cook the apples by poaching instead of sautéing. Then I use filo dough instead of homemade strudel dough and I sprinkle ground nuts and sugar between the layers to create extra crunch and lift with less fat. Finally, I spray the filo with oil, rather than brushing it with melted butter. The result is packed with flavor, but mercifully short on fat. And I'm pretty sure Aunt Annette would like it!

PREPARATION TIME: 40 MINUTES   COOKING TIME: 30 MINUTES

FOR THE FILLING:
2 pounds firm, tart apples
Juice and grated zest of 1 lemon
3 cups cider or apple juice
1 cinnamon stick
½ vanilla bean, split
⅛ teaspoon ground cloves
¼ cup brown sugar, or to taste
1 cup raisins

1 tablespoon cornstarch
1 tablespoon brandy
¾ cup cherry or apricot preserves

¼ cup chopped walnuts
¼ cup granulated sugar
8 large sheets filo dough
Spray oil (if desired, use butter-flavored spray oil)
Confectioners' sugar in a sifter for dusting

1. Peel and core the apples and cut into ½-inch dice. Toss the apple pieces with lemon juice to prevent discoloring. Combine the lemon zest, cider, spices, and ¼ cup brown sugar in a large saucepan and bring to a boil. Reduce the heat, add the apples and raisins, and gently simmer for 4 to 6 minutes, or until the apples are tender, but not too soft.

2. Remove the apples and raisins with a slotted spoon and transfer to a bowl. Meanwhile, boil the cider mixture until reduced to a thick syrupy glaze. Remove the lemon zest, cinnamon stick, and vanilla bean. Stir the apples and raisins into the reduced cider. Dissolve the cornstarch in the brandy and stir it into the apple mixture with the cherry preserves. Bring to a boil: the mixture should thicken. Taste the mixture for seasoning, adding sugar or lemon juice as necessary. Return this mixture to the bowl, place over ice, and stir until cold. **Note:** The apple mixture should be fairly dry. If too wet, add a tablespoon or two of toasted bread crumbs.

3. Assemble the strudels. Grind the walnuts and sugar to a coarse powder in a food processor. Unwrap

8 sheets of filo dough and keep covered with a damp dishcloth. Preheat the oven to 400 degrees.

4. Lay one sheet of filo dough on another dishcloth on a work surface, long edge toward you. Lightly spray it with oil and sprinkle a spoonful of nut-sugar mixture on top. Lay another sheet of filo on top, spray with oil, and sprinkle with nut mixture. Repeat with a third and fourth sheet of filo.

5. Mound half the apple filling along the long edge of the filo closest to you. Roll the filo rectangle up lengthwise, halfway, using the dishtowel to help with rolling. Tuck in the side ends and continue rolling the strudel. Carefully transfer it to a nonstick baking sheet. Assemble the second strudel the same way. Lightly spray the tops of the strudels with oil and sprinkle with the remaining nut mixture. Lightly score the tops of the strudels with a sharp knife.

6. Bake the strudels until nicely browned, about 30 minutes. Let cool for 5 minutes. Cut each strudel into diagonal slices. Dust with confectioners' sugar and serve at once.

Makes 2 strudels, which will serve 8 to 10

Cakes

❧ Bisteeya ❧
(Moroccan "Napoleon")

Bisteeya is one of the High Holies of Moroccan confectionary—a napoleonlike cake made by layering warka (a Moroccan dough similar to filo) with almonds, sugar, and an exquisitely creamy custard perfumed with orange-flower water. Like all good Moroccan desserts, it shatters into a million buttery flakes when you take a bite. To trim the fat, I make the custard with skim milk and use a mixture of butter and oil for brushing the pastry. Because it contains milk and butter, you'd serve this showy dessert at a dairy meal, where it makes a spectacular finale. Bisteeya looks difficult to make and it tastes as rich as sin. This version is, in fact, quick and easy and remarkably low in fat.

PREPARATION TIME: 30 MINUTES   COOKING TIME: 15 MINUTES

FOR THE FILLING:
1½ cups skim milk
1 cinnamon stick
3 strips orange zest (remove it with a vegetable peeler)
6 tablespoons sugar
7 teaspoons (2 tablespoons plus 1 teaspoon) cornstarch
1 or 2 eggs
2 teaspoons orange-flower water or rose water, or to taste
1 teaspoon vanilla extract

FOR THE PASTRY:
½ cup sugar
¼ cup toasted almonds
1 tablespoon canola oil
1 tablespoon melted butter or more oil
12 sheets filo dough

Spray oil

FOR THE GARNISH:
2 to 3 tablespoons confectioners' sugar for sifting
Ground cinnamon for sifting

1. Prepare the filling. Combine the milk, cinnamon stick, orange zest, and 2 tablespoons sugar in a saucepan and gradually bring to a boil, stirring steadily. (Stirring prevents the milk from scorching.) Meanwhile, in a mixing bowl, whisk together the remaining 4 tablespoons sugar and cornstarch. Whisk in the egg(s).

2. Strain the scalded milk into the egg mixture in a thin stream, whisking steadily. Return the mixture to the pan and bring to a boil, whisking steadily. Reduce the heat and cook until thick and creamy, about 3 minutes. Remove the pan from the heat, transfer the filling to a bowl, and let cool to room temperature. Whisk in the orange-flower water and vanilla extract. The filling can be prepared the day before and refrigerated.

3. Preheat the oven to 375 degrees.

4. Prepare the pastry. Grind the sugar and almonds

Lemon poppyseed Passover sponge cake.

165

to a very coarse powder in the food processor. (Run the machine in spurts.) Combine the oil and butter. Lay the 12 sheets of filo dough in a stack on a cutting board. Using a sharp knife and a pot lid as a guide, cut out 10-inch circles. (The filo scraps can be used for making small pastries.)

5. Transfer one of the circles to a nonstick baking sheet you've lightly sprayed with oil. Lightly brush the circle with the oil-butter mixture and sprinkle with 1 tablespoon sugar-almond mixture. Place a second filo circle on top, brush with more butter mixture and sprinkle with more sugar mixture. Cut out a third filo circle, place on top, and top with butter and sugar. Make a second stack of filo in this fashion, then a third

and fourth. Bake the filo circles until crisp and golden brown, about 5 minutes. Transfer the circles to cake racks to cool. The bisteeya can be prepared up to several hours ahead to this stage.

6. Not more than 10 minutes before serving, place the first-baked filo circle on a platter. Gently spread one third of the orange-flower water cream on top. Place a second circle on top and spread with half the remaining cream. Place a third circle on top and spread with the remaining cream. Place the fourth pastry circle on top. Dust the top of the bisteeya with confectioners' sugar and sprinkle with cinnamon. Present the bisteeya whole, then cut it into wedges for serving.

Serves 10

264 CALORIES PER SERVING; 5 G PROTEIN; 8 G FAT; 1.9 G SATURATED FAT; 43 G CARBOHYDRATE; 185 MG SODIUM; 31 MG CHOLESTEROL

✎ Irene Roth's Honey Cake ✎

Why are Jews so passionate about food? One reason, I believe, is the profound symbolism associated with so many Jewish dishes. Tsimmis (page 117) is a symbol of prosperity, for example, the round slices of carrots representing gold shekels. The salt water served with parsley at the Passover Seder symbolizes the tears shed by the enslaved Hebrews. Lehkach (honey cake) is a traditional European Jewish dessert served for the Sabbath and especially for Rosh Hashanah, and its symbolism is particularly poignant for a people that has endured so much suffering. The honey represents the hope for sweetness in the coming week and in the New Year. The best honey cake I ever tasted was made by a wonderful Czech cook and concentration camp survivor named Irene Roth, who lives in Corpus Christi, Texas. By beating the egg whites and yolks separately, she achieves an airy lightness more akin to a sponge cake than a traditional honey cake. To trim the fat, I've omitted a few egg yolks (the traditional recipe calls for 8), but otherwise left the recipe as Irene makes it.

PREPARATION TIME: 25 MINUTES   COOKING TIME: 1 HOUR

4 teaspoons baking soda
¼ cup rum
1 cup honey
2 tablespoons strong coffee
2 tablespoons canola oil
1 tablespoon fresh lemon juice
2 teaspoons grated lemon zest

5 egg yolks
⅓ cup sugar

8 egg whites
½ teaspoon cream of tartar
⅓ cup sugar

2 cups unbleached white flour
3 tablespoons walnut halves or pieces
3 tablespoons confectioners' sugar in a sifter for sprinkling (optional)

1. Preheat the oven to 300 degrees.
2. Dissolve the baking soda in the rum in a small saucepan. Add the honey, coffee, oil, lemon juice, and zest and warm until the honey is melted, stirring with a wooden spoon to mix. Prepare a 10-inch springform pan by spraying it with oil and dusting it with flour.
3. In a stand mixer (or using a handheld mixer), beat the egg yolks and ⅓ cup sugar until the mixture is pale yellow and forms a thick, silky ribbon when dropped from a raised beater. This will take 6 to 8 minutes mixing at high speed.
4. Combine the egg whites and cream of tartar in another mixer bowl, and, using clean beaters, beat to soft peaks, starting on low speed, gradually increasing the speed to medium, then high. This will take about 8 minutes. Add the ⅓ cup sugar in a thin stream and beat until whites are firm and glossy but not dry, 1 to 2 minutes.

5. Using a rubber spatula, fold the honey mixture into the yolk mixture. Fold the yolk mixture into the egg whites. Sift the flour into the honey-egg mixture in 4 batches, gently folding after each addition. Spoon the cake mixture into the prepared mold and decorate the top with walnuts. Tap the pan on the counter a few times to knock out any air bubbles.
6. Bake the honey cake until puffed, browned, and cooked through, 40 to 60 minutes. (When cooked, an inserted skewer will come out clean.) If the top of the cake browns too much before the cake is cooked through, cover it with a sheet of foil.
7. Remove the cake from the oven and let cool to room temperature, then unmold and invert. If you like, dust the top with confectioners' sugar. Cut into wedges for serving.

Serves 12

282 CALORIES PER SERVING; 6 G PROTEIN; 6 G FAT; .9 G SATURATED FAT; 50 G CARBOHYDRATE; 461 MG SODIUM; 88 MG CHOLESTEROL

⚄ My Great-grandmother's Chocolate Roll ⚄

*Do you have a grandmother or great-grandmother who has a long-beloved family specialty? A recipe inherited from her mother or grandmother? Run, don't walk, to the kitchen and beg her to show you how to make it. My great-grandmother Bertha Fribush made a chocolate roll that was so buttery and cakey, so chocolaty and crumbly, you could hear the angels sing when you took a bite. "Come, watch me make it while I still can," she would tell her daughter, and my grandmother would say, "Oh, Mother, you'll live forever." Well, Grandma Fribush died at the age of ninety-four and no one did learn to make her chocolate roll, but everyone in my family can remember how great it tasted and how much we enjoyed it. Over the years, I've reconstructed the recipe: the cocoa-and-sugar filling came from a bakery in the Meah Sharim in Jerusalem; the dough, from a Czech baker in Texas. But good as it is, it will never be quite like Grandma Fribush's chocolate roll. I dedicate this recipe to her memory. **Note:** Just for the record, Grandma Fribush would have used whole milk, not skim, and ½ cup butter, not the mixture of oil and butter in the reduced-fat, but eminently tasty, recipe below. This recipe makes 2 loaves, so it's great for a crowd.*

PREPARATION TIME: 30 MINUTES
COOKING TIME: ABOUT 40 MINUTES, PLUS 2 HOURS TO LET THE DOUGH RISE

FOR THE PASTRY:
½ cup warm water
¼ cup sugar
1 package dried yeast
3 cups flour, or as needed
½ teaspoon salt
4 tablespoons unsalted butter, cut into ½-inch
　pieces
¼ cup canola oil
½ cup warm skim milk
1 egg, lightly beaten with a fork
A little oil for oiling the bowl and baking sheet

FOR THE FILLING:
½ cup unsweetened cocoa powder
½ cup sugar
3 tablespoons golden raisins

FOR THE TOPPING:
2 tablespoons skim milk
2 tablespoons sugar

1. Combine ¼ cup water, the sugar, and the yeast in a small bowl and stir to mix. Let stand until foamy, about 10 minutes. Meanwhile, combine the flour, salt, and butter in a food processor and pulse to cut in the butter. (The mixture should feel coarse and crumbly, like cornmeal.) If you don't have a food processor, cut the butter into the flour and salt, using 2 knives.

2. Add the yeast mixture to the flour, along with the oil, milk, egg, and remaining ¼ cup water. Pulse the processor (or mix with your fingers) to obtain a soft, pliable dough. (The dough should be soft but not wet. If too sticky, add a little more flour.) Transfer the dough to a lightly oiled bowl, cover with plas-

tic wrap, and let rise until doubled in bulk, 1 to 1½ hours.

3. Meanwhile, make the filling. Combine the cocoa powder, sugar, and raisins in a mixing bowl and stir with your fingers to mix.

4. Punch down the dough and cut in half. Lightly flour your work surface and roll out half the dough to form a rectangle 10 inches long and 7 inches wide. Sprinkle half the cocoa mixture on top. Starting at one long end, roll the dough rectangle into a fat tube. Transfer it to a lightly oiled baking sheet. Prepare the other chocolate roll the same way.

5. Brush the top and sides of the roll with the 2 ta-

blespoons skim milk and sprinkle with the 2 table-spoons sugar. Loosely cover with plastic wrap and let the dough rise again until puffy and soft, about 30 minutes. Preheat the oven to 350 degrees.

6. Bake the chocolate roll until golden brown and cooked through, 30 to 40 minutes. Let cool to room temperature, then cut on the diagonal into 1-inch slices for serving.

Makes 2 rolls, which will serve 16

196 CALORIES PER SERVING; 3.7 G PROTEIN; 6.3 G FAT; 1.8 G SATURATED FAT; 31.4 G CARBOHYDRATE; 110.9 MG SODIUM; 19.8 MG CHOLESTEROL

New York–Style Cheesecake

My mother wasn't much of a dessert eater (actually, she didn't eat much of anything—her ballet dancer diet wouldn't allow it), but she did have a weakness for cheesecake. Not just any cheesecake: the dense, rich, silky, creamy, cheesy cheesecake served at her favorite New York hangout, the Stage Deli. New York–style cheesecake may seem like an unlikely dish for a heart-healthy makeover, but by using pureed cottage cheese, reduced-fat cream cheese, and plenty of lemon juice, you can make a cake that tastes as tangy and rich as the real thing. I dedicate this recipe to the memory of my mother, who often hungered for the life that most of us take for granted. You can certainly use no-fat cream cheese and cottage cheese for this recipe, but if your fat budget allows it, use low-fat dairy products. The resulting cheesecake will taste much richer, but will still contain only 12 grams of fat per serving.

PREPARATION TIME: 15 MINUTES   COOKING TIME: 1 HOUR

1 pound low-fat (1 percent) cottage cheese
1 pound low-fat cream cheese, at room temperature
1¼ cups sugar
2 eggs plus 4 egg whites (or 1 cup Eggbeaters)
¼ cup fresh lemon juice
1 tablespoon grated lemon zest

1 tablespoon vanilla extract
Pinch of salt

FOR THE TOPPING:
2 cups no-fat sour cream
⅓ cup sugar

1. Preheat the oven to 350 degrees. (The rack should be set in the lower third of the oven.) Lightly spray an 8-inch springform pan with oil. Bring 1 quart of water to a boil. Wrap a piece of foil around the bottom and sides of the springform pan. (This prevents water from leaking in.)

2. Puree the cottage cheese in the food processor, scraping down the sides. This will take 2 to 3 minutes. Add the cream cheese and puree until smooth. Add the sugar and puree. Add the eggs, egg whites, lemon juice, lemon zest, vanilla, and salt and puree. Pour the mixture into the prepared pan. Tap the pan a few times on the counter to knock out any bubbles.

3. Set the springform pan in a roasting pan in the oven. Add 1 inch boiling water to the pan and bake the cheesecake for 30 minutes.

4. Meanwhile, in a large mixing bowl, whisk together the sour cream and sugar. Spoon this mixture on top of the cheesecake. Continue baking the cheesecake until set, 10 to 20 minutes longer. To test for doneness, gently poke the side—when the top no longer jiggles, the cheesecake is cooked. Another test: An inserted skewer will come out clean when the cheesecake is cooked. Do not overcook or the cheesecake will become watery.

5. Transfer the cheesecake to a cake rack to cool to room temperature, then refrigerate until cold. To serve, run the tip of a small knife around the inside of the pan. Unfasten the sides. **Note:** Many people like to serve cheesecake with strawberry sauce (page 171).

Serves 10 to 12

287 CALORIES PER 10 SERVINGS; 13 G PROTEIN; 9.5 G FAT; 5.6 G SATURATED FAT;
36.7 G CARBOHYDRATE; 362 MG SODIUM; 70 MG CHOLESTEROL

Strawberry Sauce

1 quart fresh strawberries, washed, hulled, and
   thinly sliced
¼ cup sugar or to taste

½ cup fresh orange juice
2 teaspoons cornstarch dissolved in 1 tablespoon
   water

To make the sauce, combine the strawberries with ¼ cup sugar and the orange juice. Gently simmer for 4 to 6 minutes, or until the strawberries are soft but not mushy. Add more sugar to taste. Stir the dissolved cornstarch into the sauce and bring it to a boil. Remove the pan from the heat and let the mixture cool.

Serves 10 to 12

45.3 CALORIES PER 10 SERVINGS; .5 G PROTEIN; .3 G FAT; 0 G SATURATED FAT; 10.9 G CARBOHYDRATE; 1 G SODIUM; 0 G CHOLESTEROL

✎ Lemon Poppy Seed Passover Sponge Cake ✎

*This tangy sponge cake is one of my favorite Passover desserts. At first glance, lemon and poppy seed couldn't seem like less likely flavoring companions, the former high-pitched and bracingly tart, the latter muted and earthy. But put them together and you get one of the most pleasing contrasts of texture and flavor ever to pep up a sponge cake. The key to making a light sponge cake is to beat as much air as possible into the egg yolks and whites. Don't overbeat the latter, however, or the cake will collapse. (**Note:** If you can't find matzo meal cake flour, simply place matzo meal in a blender and grind to a fine powder.)*

PREPARATION TIME: 30 MINUTES   COOKING TIME: 1 HOUR

5 egg yolks
1½ cups sugar
Grated zest of 2 lemons (about 1 tablespoon)
½ cup fresh lemon juice
½ cup poppy seeds
1 cup matzo meal cake flour
3 tablespoons potato starch

10 egg whites
1 teaspoon cream of tartar
⅛ teaspoon salt

1 cup confectioners' sugar or lemon glaze (see below)

1. Preheat oven to 325 degrees.
2. Combine the egg yolks and 1 cup sugar in the bowl of an electric mixer and beat until thick, moussey, and pale yellow, about 8 minutes. (Start the mixer on low speed and gradually increase it to medium, then high. When the mixture is the proper consistency, it will fall from a raised whisk in a thick ribbon.) Beat in the lemon zest, lemon juice, and poppy seeds.
3. Sift the matzo meal cake flour and potato starch over the yolk mixture and gently whisk to mix.
4. Place the egg whites in another clean mixer bowl. Beat at low speed, until frothy, 2 minutes. Add the cream of tartar and salt. Increase the mixer speed to medium and beat for 2 minutes. Increase the speed to high and continue beating the whites until firm and glossy, but not dry, about 4 minutes more, 8 minutes in all. Gradually sprinkle the remaining ½ cup sugar into the whites as they stiffen.

5. Gently fold the whites into the yolk mixture and spoon the batter into an ungreased 10-inch angel food cake pan.
6. Bake the sponge cake until the top is browned and springy and the cake is cooked through (test it by inserting a slender skewer—it should come out clean), 50 to 60 minutes. Invert the pan and let the cake cool completely before unmolding. Unmold the sponge cake onto a round platter. (You may need to loosen the edges of the cake with the tip of a paring knife. Give the mold a firm shake: the cake should slide out.)
7. Sift the confectioners' sugar over the cake. Or spoon the lemon glaze over it, if using. Cut the sponge cake into wedges for serving, using a serrated knife.

Serves 12

305 CALORIES PER SERVING; 6 G PROTEIN; 5 G FAT; .9 G SATURATED FAT; 61 G CARBOHYDRATE; 76 MG SODIUM; 88 MG CHOLESTEROL

⚡ Lemon Glaze ⚡

The fresh lemon juice and zest in this simple glaze reinforces the lemon flavor of the cake.

PREPARATION TIME: 5 MINUTES

3 cups confectioners' sugar
7 tablespoons (½ cup minus 1 tablespoon) fresh
lemon juice

2 teaspoons finely grated lemon zest

Sift the confectioners' sugar into a mixing bowl. Add the lemon juice and zest and whisk to mix. The glaze should be thick but pourable. (Add lemon juice if the glaze is too thick, confectioners' sugar if too thin.) Spoon the glaze over the sponge cake and serve at once.

Serves 12

100 CALORIES PER SERVING; .04 G PROTEIN; .03 G FAT; .005 G SATURATED FAT; 25 G CARBOHYDRATE; .4 MG SODIUM; 0 MG CHOLESTEROL

Cookies and Candies

❧❦❧❦◆❦❧❦❧

✒ Traditional Mandelbrot ✒

Mandelbrot are Jewish biscotti. These long, flat cookies are sweet enough to enjoy for dessert, yet not so sweet that you wouldn't have them for breakfast. They're softer than biscotti, so you can munch them straight, but they're also great dipped in coffee or tea. Here's a recipe for traditional mandelbrot—flavored with almonds and almond extract. (Mandel is the Yiddish word for "almond"; brot for "bread.") **Note:** *This dough is wetter than most (a wet dough produces a light mandelbrot), so our friend Hannah Kuperstock makes it the night before she plans to roll it out. This firms up the dough to the point where you can shape it.*

PREPARATION TIME: 15 MINUTES   COOKING TIME: 30 MINUTES

1 egg plus 2 egg whites (or ½ cup egg substitute)
1 cup sugar
⅓ cup vegetable oil
2 teaspoons vanilla extract
½ teaspoon almond extract
2½ cups flour

2 teaspoons baking powder
Pinch of salt
3 ounces sliced almonds (with skins on)

Spray oil

1. Combine the egg, egg whites, and sugar in the bowl of a mixer and mix at high speed until pale yellow, thick, and mousselike, 8 minutes. Reduce the speed to low and mix in the oil, vanilla extract, and almond extract. Sift the flour, baking powder, salt, and the almonds into the egg mixture. Beat just to mix. Transfer the dough to the refrigerator and chill for at least 6 hours, preferably overnight.

2. Preheat the oven to 350 degrees.

3. Wet your hands. Lightly spray a nonstick baking sheet with oil. Turn the dough onto it and pat the dough into a rectangle that's about 18 inches long, 3 inches wide, and ½ inch tall. Using a sharp knife (dip the blade in cold water), make a series of parallel widthwise cuts through the top of the rectangle, each about ¼ inch deep.

4. Bake the mandelbrot until lightly browned, 20 to 30 minutes. Remove the baking sheet and transfer the loaf to a cutting board. Cut it crosswise into ½-inch-wide slices, following the cut marks you made earlier. Separate the slices so that each stands up ½ inch apart from its neighbor. Continue baking the mandelbrot until firm and lightly browned, 5 to 10 minutes. Remove the baking sheet from the oven and let the mandelbrot cool to room temperature. Store in airtight containers (but only once the mandelbrot have cooled completely) until serving. The mandelbrot are delicious eaten straight and even better dipped in coffee or tea!

Makes about 36

69 CALORIES PER PIECE; 1.7 G PROTEIN; 3.4 G FAT; .36 G SATURATED FAT; 7.5 G CARBOHYDRATE; 5.2 MG SODIUM; 5.9 MG CHOLESTEROL

Traditional mandelbrot.

✎ Cinnamon Snaps ✎
(Panlevi)

These crisp, wafer-thin cookies are common currency in the Jewish community of Curaçao in the Dutch West Indies—crunchy, not overly sweet flatcakes dispensed at holiday dinners, brought to sick friends as a get-well wish, or served with hot chocolate after a brith (circumcision ceremony). The cookies are remarkable in their lack of fat: they contain no butter, oil, or shortening. So the 3 eggs used in the batter don't unduly tip the scale in fat grams. This recipe was inspired by the panlevi found in a charming cookbook by the sisterhood of the temple Mikve Israel-Emanuel in Willemstad: Recipes from the Jewish Kitchens of Curaçao.

PREPARATION TIME: 10 MINUTES   COOKING TIME: 15 MINUTES

Spray oil
3 large eggs
⅔ cup sugar
⅛ teaspoon salt
1 teaspoon ground cinnamon
½ teaspoon ground ginger

¼ teaspoon ground cloves
1 teaspoon grated lemon zest
1 teaspoon vanilla extract
1 tablespoon Curaçao or other orange liqueur
¾ cup unbleached all-purpose white flour
½ teaspoon baking powder

1. Preheat the oven to 325 degrees. Lightly spray 2 nonstick baking sheets with oil. (For ease in cleaning the baking sheets, line them with parchment paper before spraying.)

2. Beat the eggs, sugar, salt, and spices in a mixer or in a bowl with a whisk until light and frothy, 3 minutes. Beat in the lemon zest, vanilla extract, and Curaçao. Sift in the flour and baking powder and fold to mix with a rubber spatula. Whisk the mixture for 30 seconds.

3. Spoon heaping tablespoons of batter onto the prepared baking sheets to form 2-inch cookies, leaving 3 inches between each blob. Tap the baking sheet on the work surface to knock out any stray air bubbles. Bake the cookies until golden brown, 15 to 18 minutes. Using a spatula, transfer the cookies to a cake rack and let cool completely: the cookies will crisp on cooling. Serve at once or store in an airtight container.

Makes 30 to 36 2-inch cookies, which will serve 6

186.1 CALORIES PER SERVING; 4.7 G PROTEIN; 2.7 G FAT; .8 G SATURATED FAT; 34.7 G CARBOHYDRATE; 279 MG SODIUM; 106.2 MG CHOLESTEROL

⚙ My Aunt Linda's Poppy Seed Crisps ⚙

My aunt Linda learned to make these cookies when she was pregnant with my cousin Andy. They've been a Millison family favorite ever since. Poppy seeds are much beloved by Eastern European Jews and their descendants; their pungent, earthy flavor makes a welcome addition not just to these cookies but to many Jewish desserts.

PREPARATION TIME: 10 MINUTES   COOKING TIME: 20 MINUTES

Spray oil
1 cup flour
½ cup sugar
1 teaspoon baking powder
⅛ teapoon salt
2 eggs, lightly beaten

¼ cup canola oil
½ cup ice water
1 teaspoon vanilla extract
1 teaspoon almond extract
½ teaspoon grated lemon zest
⅓ cup poppy seeds

1. Preheat the oven to 325 degrees. Lightly spray 2 nonstick baking sheets with spray oil or line them with parchment paper and spray with oil.

2. Sift the flour, sugar, baking powder, and salt into a mixing bowl. Make a depression in the center. Add the eggs, oil, water, vanilla and almond extracts, and lemon zest and stir to obtain a thick but pourable batter. Stir in the poppy seeds.

3. Drop spoonfuls of the batter onto the baking sheets (about 2 teaspoons batter in each drop), leaving 2 inches between each cookie. Lightly bang the baking sheets on the work surface to knock out any air bubbles.

4. Bake the cookies until golden brown, 15 to 20 minutes. Using a spatula, transfer the cookies to a platter or cake rack to cool. Once cooled completely, store cookies in an airtight container until serving.

Make 24 cookies, which will serve 6 to 8

72 CALORIES PER COOKIE; 1.4 G PROTEIN; 3.6 G FAT; .4 G SATURATED FAT; 8.6 G CARBOHYDRATE; 18 MG SODIUM; 17 MG CHOLESTEROL

⤫ Greek Almond Meringues ⤫
(Asuplados)

These nutty meringues are traditional holiday treats among the Jews of Rhodes in Greece. Many cooks place whole blanched almonds atop the meringues. I like the craggy look of slivered almonds. For extra flavor, I like to add cinnamon (again, not traditional) and a bit of turbinado sugar (also known as sugar in the raw). To make chocolate asuplados, add 2 tablespoons cocoa powder.

PREPARATION TIME: 15 MINUTES   COOKING TIME: 2 HOURS

Spray oil
Flour for dusting
4 egg whites
½ **teaspoon cream of tartar**

⅔ **cup granulated sugar**
⅓ **cup turbinado sugar or more granulated sugar**
½ **teaspoon ground cinnamon (optional)**
⅓ **cup slivered almonds**

1. Preheat the oven to 200 degrees. Line a baking sheet with parchment paper, spray with oil, and lightly dust with flour.

2. Combine the egg whites and cream of tartar in the bowl of a mixer and beat to soft peaks, starting on low speed, gradually increasing the speed to medium, then high. This will take about 8 minutes. Add the sugars and cinnamon (if using) in a thin steam and beat until whites are firm and glossy but not dry, 1 to 2 minutes.

3. Using a piping bag fitted with a large star or round tip, pipe 1½-inch rosettes. (They should look like Hershey's Kisses.) Alternatively, use 2 teaspoons to make small mounds. Sprinkle slivered almonds on top of each.

4. Place the asuplados in the oven and bake until firm, 1½ to 2 hours. Turn off the heat and let the asuplados cool in the oven. Remove the asuplados from the oven and pry off the baking sheet with a spatula.

Makes about 36 asuplados, which will serve 9 to 12

29.4 CALORIES PER ASUPLADO; .6 G PROTEIN; .6 G FAT; 0 G SATURATED FAT; 5.6 G CARBOHYDRATE; 6.2 MG SODIUM; 0 MG CHOLESTEROL

✄ Rose Hip Kisses ✄

There's a book that's unique in the literature of the Holocaust, the most unlikely book you'd ever expect to find coming from this reign of hunger, deprivation, and death: a cookbook. Yet that's precisely what Mina Pachter and her friends wrote to pass the time (and remember pleasanter times) while they were interned at the Theresienstadt Concentration Camp. Twenty-five years after her death in the camp, Mina's manuscript reached her daughter, Anny Stern, who arranged for the handwritten manuscript to be translated and published as In Memory's Kitchen *(Aronson, 1998). The recipes are terse—even telegraphic—but by reading between the lines, you can imagine the dishes these poor women must have remembered with so much longing. One that caught my eye was "Cheap Rose Hip Kisses," a sort of meringue candy flavored with rose hip jam. Here's a modern adaptation.* **Note:** *Rose hip jam can be found in gourmet shops or markets catering to an Eastern European clientele. I've also made the kisses using apple butter or plum butter.*

PREPARATION TIME: 20 MINUTES   COOKING TIME: 2 HOURS

½ cup hazelnuts

Spray oil
Flour for dusting

1 cup sugar
4 large egg whites

½ teaspoon cream of tartar
1 teaspoon lemon juice
2 tablespoons cornstarch or potato starch
3 tablespoons rose hip jam

1. Preheat the oven to 350 degrees. Place the hazelnuts in a roasting pan and bake until toasted and fragrant, about 10 minutes. Remove the pan from the oven and let the nuts cool for 5 minutes. Line 2 non-stick baking sheets with parchment paper or spray with oil and dust with flour.

2. Rub the hazelnuts between the palms of your hands to remove the skins (don't worry if you don't get every last bit of skin). Let the nuts cool to room temperature. Place them in a food processor with ¼ cup sugar. Grind to a fine powder. (Do not overgrind, or the nuts will become pasty.) Lower the oven temperature to 250 degrees.

3. Combine the egg whites and cream of tartar in the bowl of a mixer and beat to soft peaks, starting on low speed, gradually increasing the speed to medium, then high. This will take about 8 minutes. Add the remaining ¾ cup sugar in a thin steam and beat until whites are firm and glossy but not dry, 1 minute.

4. Sift the cornstarch over the egg whites. Sprinkle in the hazelnut mixture and gently fold to mix. Gently fold in the rose hip jam. Using a piping bag or 2 spoons, make 1-inch domes or rosettes of meringue mixture on the baking sheets, leaving 2 inches between each.

5. Bake the kisses until firm and lightly browned, 1½ to 2 hours. Remove the baking sheets from the oven and let the kisses cool. Gently pry them off the baking sheet with a spatula.

Makes 24 to 30

58.9 CALORIES PER KISS; 1 G PROTEIN; 1.5 G FAT; .1 G SATURATED FAT; 10.8 G CARBOHYDRATE; 10.3 MG SODIUM; 0 MG CHOLESTEROL

Drinks

❧❀❧

✍ Egg Cream ✍

Question: What contains neither eggs nor cream? Answer: An egg cream. The drink that made New York soda fountains famous contains neither of its namesakes, although its refreshing richness and frothy head suggest the presence of both ingredients. Legend credits a Jewish immigrant, one Louis Auster, with the invention of the egg cream. The New York candy store owner had the idea to combine seltzer, milk, and homemade chocolate syrup to make a refreshing drink he dubbed "egg cream." (Back in those days, eggs and cream were luxuries.) Tradition calls for egg creams to be made with a chocolaty syrup called Fox's U-Bet. I'm about to suggest a heresy. While Fox's U-Bet will give you a respectable egg cream, you'll achieve a far richer flavor by using Hershey's chocolate syrup. There. I've said it. The hit men will probably be on my doorstep by nightfall. For the best results, use whole milk (if you have any in your refrigerator). Skim milk or evaporated skim milk will give you fine results, too.

PREPARATION TIME: 5 MINUTES

1½ tablespoons cold chocolate syrup
1½ tablespoons cold whole or skim milk or
evaporated skim milk

8 ounces cold seltzer water or club soda

1. Place the chocolate syrup and milk in a tall glass (preferably a fountain glass you've chilled in the freezer) and stir with a long-handled spoon.
2. Add a little of the seltzer and stir until foamy.

Continue adding seltzer and stirring to obtain a frothy head.

Serves 1

69 CALORIES PER SERVING; 1.3 G PROTEIN; .3 G FAT; .2 G SATURATED FAT; 18 G CARBOHYDRATE; 88 MG SODIUM; .4 MG CHOLESTEROL

Egg creams.

⚰ Guggel-Muggel ⚰
(Grandmother's Soporific)

Sometimes, the people you think you know the best surprise you the most. Not once in forty-six years did I see my grandparents take a sip of hard liquor. One day, I happened to mention to my grandmother that I was having trouble sleeping. "Whenever your grandfather couldn't sleep, I'd make him a guggel-muggel," said Grammie. Guggel-muggel turns out to be a sort of hot eggnog laced with rum or brandy. (So that's what those liquor bottles were doing hidden in the coat closet!) I can attest to its soporific qualities—not to mention the way it soothes your throat when you're coming down with a cold.

PREPARATION TIME: 5 MINUTES   COOKING TIME: 5 MINUTES

1 egg
3 tablespoons light brown sugar or granulated
 sugar
½ teaspoon ground cinnamon
¼ teaspoon ground nutmeg, plus nutmeg for
 sprinkling

⅛ teaspoon ground cloves
1 cup skim milk
1 cup evaporated skim milk or more skim milk
3 tablespoons rum or brandy
1 teaspoon vanilla extract

1. In a heatproof mixing bowl, combine the egg, sugar, cinnamon, nutmeg, and cloves and whisk to mix.

2. Scald the milks in a heavy saucepan. Whisk them in a thin stream into the egg mixture. Return the mixture to the pan and cook over medium heat until it thickens, about 2 minutes, stirring with a wooden spoon. Do not let the mixture boil, or the egg will scramble. Remove the pan from the heat and stir in the rum and vanilla extract.

3. Pour the guggel-muggel into mugs. Sprinkle each with a little nutmeg and serve at once.

Serves 2

295 CALORIES PER SERVING; 17 G PROTEIN; 3.1 G FAT; 1.1 G SATURATED FAT; 35 G CARBOHYDRATE; 247 MG SODIUM; 113 MG CHOLESTEROL

❧ Curaçaoan Hot Chocolate ❧

Hot chocolate certainly wasn't part of my family's Jewish tradition, but for the Jews of the Dutch West Indian island of Curaçao, a brith (circumcision ceremony) simply wouldn't be complete without it. Steaming cups of hot chocolate are traditionally served with crisp, flat cinnamon cookies called panlevi (page 176). Traditionally, the chocolate would be thickened with egg. To trim the fat, I use a little cornstarch.

PREPARATION TIME: 5 MINUTES   COOKING TIME: 5 MINUTES

⅓ cup cocoa powder
⅓ cup sugar, or to taste
1½ teaspoons cornstarch
⅛ teaspoon salt

1 (12-ounce) can evaporated skim milk
2½ cups skim milk
1 teaspoon vanilla extract

1. Combine the cocoa, sugar, cornstarch, and salt in a heavy saucepan and whisk to mix. Gradually whisk in the milks. Slowly bring the mixture to a boil, whisking steadily.

2. Remove the pan from the heat and whisk in the vanilla extract. Taste for sweetness, adding sugar if desired.

Serves 4

205 CALORIES PER SERVING; 14 G PROTEIN; 1.6 G FAT; .3 G SATURATED FAT; 34 G CARBOHYDRATE; 254 MG SODIUM; 6 MG CHOLESTEROL

🐟 Break-Fast Sangría 🐟

To most North Americans, sangría means a Spanish-style spiced wine punch. It usually contains fruit and it's always served cold. For centuries, Jews in the Dutch West Indies have enjoyed hot sangría on returning home from synagogue to break the fast after Yom Kippur. If the notion of hot sangría seems strange to you, try calling it by its North American name: hot mulled wine.

PREPARATION TIME: 10 MINUTES
COOKING TIME: 5 MINUTES, PLUS 4 HOURS TO LET THE WINE STEEP

1 bottle dry red wine
1 cup water
½ cup sugar, or as needed
2 cinnamon sticks
4 cloves
4 allspice berries

1 whole nutmeg
2 strips lime zest
2 strips orange zest
¼ cup fresh lime juice
¼ cup fresh orange juice

1. Combine the wine, water, sugar, cinnamon, cloves, allspice, nutmeg, lime and orange zest, and lime and orange juices in a large saucepan and bring to a boil. Reduce the heat to medium and gently simmer the sangría for 5 minutes. Remove the pan from the heat and let the mixture steep for 4 hours.

2. Strain the sangría into another saucepan. Taste for sweetness, adding sugar as desired. Heat the sangría until piping hot and serve at once. You could even spoon a dollop of egg mousse (page 187) on top of each serving.

Serves 4

245 CALORIES PER SERVING; .6 G PROTEIN; .2 G FAT; .025 G SATURATED FAT; 32 G CARBOHYDRATE; 12 MG SODIUM; 0 MG CHOLESTEROL

✖ Greek Coffee ✖
(aka Turkish Coffee, Arabic Coffee)

A meal at my aunt Rosa Miller's was always an adventure. Rosa was born in Salonika, Greece, of Italian parents, whose ancestors were exiled Jews from Spain. She and my uncle Sheldon, a hospital administrator for the navy, lived in countries as diverse as Iran, Brazil, and Ecuador. Whenever I dined with the Millers, Rosa would bring out her brass ibriki (a tiny hour-glass-shaped pot) and brew me a cup of Greek coffee. She combined the sugar, water, and coffee, which was ground as fine as flour, in the ibriki, heated the mixture to the verge of boiling over three times, then poured it into a tiny cup with an eighth of an inch of cold water in the bottom. (The cold water helped precipitate out the grounds.) A similar preparation is popular in Turkey, of course, and Israel, where it's served Arab-style, with a pinch of cardamom. Serve this coffee to a Jew from one of these countries and he'll feel instantly at home.

PREPARATION TIME: 5 MINUTES   COOKING TIME: 5 MINUTES

1 cup cold water
3 tablespoons Greek or Turkish coffee (which is ground as fine as flour)

½ teaspoon ground cardamom (for Israeli-style coffee)
3 tablespoons sugar

1. Pour 1 tablespoon cold water into each of 2 demitasse cups. Combine the remaining ingredients in an ibriki (available in a Middle East grocery store) or tall, narrow pot.

2. Bring the coffee to a boil on the stove three times, removing the pot from the heat just before it threatens to boil over. Pour the coffee into the cups and serve at once.

Serves 2

102.2 CALORIES PER SERVING; .9 G PROTEIN; .7 G FAT; 0 G SATURATED FAT; 23.7 G CARBOHYDRATE; 32.7 MG SODIUM; 0 MG CHOLESTEROL

⚛ Mint Tea ⚛

Tea figures prominently in the Jewish gastronomic landscape, from samovar-brewed tea of Russian Jews to the "glass" of tea sipped through a sugar cube by our Yiddish-speaking ancestors on the Lower East Side to the fragrant mint tea enjoyed by Jews of North Africa (especially Morocco) and the Middle East. North Africa tea masters make a great ceremony out of serving mint tea, pouring it from dizzying heights into tiny, gold-rimmed glasses.

PREPARATION TIME: 5 MINUTES   COOKING TIME: 5 MINUTES

1 bunch of fresh mint, washed and shaken dry
1 tablespoon black tea, such as Russian caravan or

English breakfast
3 tablespoons sugar or honey, or to taste

1. Twist the bunch of mint a few times between your fingers to bruise the leaves. (This releases the aromatic oils.) Prepare a 5-cup teapot by rinsing it with boiling water to warm it. Place the mint in the teapot with the black tea and sugar. Fill the teapot with 4 cups boiling water and let steep for 5 minutes.

2. Serve the tea in small glasses or cups, with a dollop of egg mousse (see opposite) if desired.

Serves 4 to 6

41 CALORIES PER 4 SERVINGS; .1 G PROTEIN; .1 G FAT; 0 G SATURATED FAT; 10 G CARBOHYDRATE; 2.2 MG SODIUM; 0 MG CHOLESTEROL

⚰ Egg Mousse for Coffee or Tea ⚰

This egg mousse is traditionally served with coffee or tea at a Yom Kippur break-fast in Sephardic communities and I've found it in countries as diverse as the Dutch West Indies and Morocco. The idea behind it is that the eggs and sugar give you strength after fasting. Traditionally, the mousse is made with egg yolks, but whites will mousse nicely with considerably less fat.

PREPARATION TIME: 10 MINUTES

2 large egg whites
½ cup sugar
1 teaspoon brandy (optional)

½ teaspoon cinnamon
⅛ teaspoon ground cloves

1. Combine the ingredients in a mixer and beat until thick and moussey, about 8 minutes. (Start the mixer on slow, gradually increasing the speed to medium, then high.) The mixture should fall from the raised whisk in a thick ribbon. Transfer the mousse to a serving bowl. Have your guests place dollops in their coffee or tea.

Serves 8

51 CALORIES PER 8 SERVINGS; .9 G PROTEIN; 0 G FAT; 0 G SATURATED FAT; 12.2 G CARBOHYDRATE; 13.9 MG SODIUM; 0 MG CHOLESTEROL

Basic Recipes

❧❧❀❧❧

❧ Chicken Broth ❧

Chicken broth is the very lifeblood of Jewish cooking—a golden elixir that soothes your soul when you're feeling blue or perks you up when you're under the weather. Without a good homemade broth, chicken soup is merely aspirin, not Jewish penicillin. Broth has another advantage for the high-flavor, low-fat cook: you can use it as a flavorful substitute for oil, cream, and butter. And the boiled chicken makes a great stuffing for pirogi (page 11), knishes (page 70), or kreplach (page 3).

PREPARATION TIME: 10 MINUTES   COOKING TIME: 1 HOUR

1 (3½-pound) chicken or 2 pounds chicken parts
  (such as backs, necks, or wings)
1 medium onion, quartered
1 large carrot, cut into 1-inch pieces
2 stalks celery, cut into 1-inch pieces
1 small parsnip, cut into 1-inch pieces (optional)
2 cloves garlic, cut in half

1 piece parsley root (optional)
5 sprigs of fresh parsley
5 black peppercorns
1 bay leaf
1 clove
10 to 12 cups cold water, or as needed

1. Remove the skin and any visible fat from the chicken and wash the bird inside and out. Place the chicken, onion, carrot, celery, parsnip (if using), garlic, and parsley root (if using) in a large pot and add water to cover by 2 inches. Tie the parsley, peppercorns, bay leaf, and clove in a piece of cheesecloth—or wrap in foil and pierce with a fork—and add to the pot.

2. Bring the broth to a boil over high heat. Skim off any fat or foam that rises to the surface. Lower the heat and gently simmer the broth until the bird is cooked, about 1 hour, adding cold water as needed to keep the chicken covered. Skim the broth often with a ladle to remove any fat or impurities that rise to the surface. (The best time to skim is after an addition of cold water—the water brings the fat to the surface.)

3. Line a strainer with paper towels and place it over a large bowl. Transfer the chicken to a plate to cool. Pour or ladle the broth through the strainer. Let the strained broth cool to room temperature, then refrigerate until cold. Skim off any congealed fat that rises to the surface. I like to freeze chicken broth in 1- or 2-cup containers, so I always have a premeasured amount on hand.

4. Meanwhile, pull the chicken meat off the bones and cut or tear it into pieces. Use the meat in any recipe calling for cooked chicken.

Makes about 8 cups

Chicken and beef broth.

Aunt Annette's Rich Beef Broth

When I think about the extraordinary food I grew up on—and how primitive the kitchens were where it was cooked—I can only marvel at the ingenuity of women like my aunt Annette and Bubbe Marks. They had no food processors, immersion blenders, or microwave ovens. They didn't know from extra-virgin olive oil, balsamic vinegar, or shiitake mushrooms. Yet their food possessed a depth of flavor and character that would be the envy of most chefs today. One of their secrets was broth—meat-laden, slow-simmered, with plenty of marrow bones for richness. The sort of broth you could stand a spoon in or make a meal of by itself. Here's a beef broth that will make an instant masterpiece of almost any dish you add it to. And you can use it to provide richness in place of butter, oil, or chicken fat. Save the boiled meat for the kreplach and knishes on pages 3 and 70.

PREPARATION TIME: 15 MINUTES   COOKING TIME: 1½ HOURS

1 onion, cut into quarters
2 carrots, cut into 1-inch pieces
2 stalks celery, cut into 1-inch pieces
1 small parsnip, cut into 1-inch pieces (optional)
2 pounds brisket or flanken
2 pounds marrow bones or beef bones
1 pound chicken backs, skin removed

4 cloves garlic, cut in half
1 piece parsley root (optional)
5 sprigs of fresh parsley
5 black peppercorns
1 bay leaf
1 clove
12 to 16 cups cold water, or as needed

1. Preheat the broiler. Place the onion quarters, carrots, celery, and parsnip (if using) on a baking sheet and broil until a dark golden brown, 5 to 10 minutes. You can even char the onion black. (The charring will help give the broth a dark, rich color.)

2. Trim any visible fat off the meat, wash it, and blot dry. Place the brisket, marrow bones, chicken, onion, carrot, celery, parsnip (if using), garlic, and parsley root (if using) in a large pot and add water to cover by 2 inches. Tie the parsley, peppercorns, bay leaf, and clove in a piece of cheesecloth—or wrap in foil and pierce with a fork—and add to the pot.

3. Bring the broth to a boil over high heat. Skim off any fat or foam that rises to the surface. Lower the heat and gently simmer the broth until the beef is tender, 1½ to 2 hours, adding cold water as needed to keep the ingredients covered. Skim the broth often with a ladle to remove any fat or impurities that rise to the surface. (The best time to skim is after an addition of cold water—the water brings the fat to the surface.)

4. Line a strainer with paper towels and place it over a large bowl. Using a slotted spoon or tongs, transfer the beef to a plate to cool. Pour or ladle the broth through the strainer. Let the strained broth cool to room temperature, then refrigerate until cold. Skim off any congealed fat that rises to the surface. I like to freeze beef broth in 1- or 2-cup containers so I always have a premeasured amount on hand.

5. Meanwhile, cut or tear the beef into pieces. Use the meat in any recipe calling for cooked beef.

Makes about 3 quarts

⚛ Basic Vegetable Broth ⚛

Vegetable broth was not part of my family's culinary heritage, although my grandmother's vegetable soup was the stuff of legends.
Perhaps it was because we wouldn't have a vegetarian in the family until the birth of my cousin Martha Millison in 1970.
We do have vegetarians now—lots of them—and here's how I make vegetable broth when cooking for them. The roasting of the
vegetables adds a dark color and rich smoky flavor: you won't miss the meat for a minute. Feel free to substitute other vegetables
for the ones called for below: corn, squash, fennel, green beans, and turnips make good candidates. Go easy on strong-
tasting vegetables, such as rutabagas. Avoid beets, which will turn a stock red, and artichokes, which will make it bitter.

PREPARATION TIME: 20 MINUTES   COOKING TIME: 2 HOURS

1 large onion, skin on, quartered
1 leek, trimmed, washed, and cut into 1-inch
  pieces
3 tomatoes, cut in half
3 carrots, cut into 1-inch pieces
3 stalks celery, cut into 1-inch pieces
3 zucchini, cut into 1-inch pieces
1 small cabbage, cut into quarters
1 parsnip, cut into 1-inch pieces
8 ounces mushrooms, trimmed
1 head garlic, cut in half
1 tablespoon olive oil
Sea salt and freshly ground black pepper, to taste

FOR THE SPICE BUNDLE:
6 sprigs of fresh parsley
2 bay leaves
2 sprigs of thyme or ½ teaspoon dried
10 peppercorns
2 cloves

2 tablespoons tomato paste
2 tablespoons soy sauce
3 quarts water

1. Preheat the oven to 400 degrees.

2. Arrange the onion, leek, tomatoes, carrots, celery, zucchini, cabbage, parsnip, mushrooms, and garlic in a nonstick roasting pan and toss with the oil, salt, and pepper. Roast the vegetables until dark brown, 40 to 60 minutes, turning occasionally with a spoon to ensure even browning.

3. Meanwhile, tie the herbs and spices in a piece of cheesecloth or wrap in foil and pierce with a fork.

4. Combine the roasted vegetables, herb bundle, and remaining ingredients in a stockpot and bring to a boil. Reduce the heat and simmer the broth, uncovered, until richly flavored, about 1 hour. Add water as necessary to keep the vegetables covered. (A certain amount of evaporation will take place—this helps concentrate the flavor.) Skim the broth once or twice and season with salt and pepper at the end.

5. Strain the broth, pressing with the back of a spoon to extract as much liquid as possible from the vegetables. Cool the broth to room temperature, then refrigerate or freeze. For a thicker, richer broth, force the liquid and vegetables through a vegetable mill or puree in a blender, then strain.

Note: I like to freeze 1-cup portions of vegetable broth, so I always have the right amount on hand.

Makes 2½ to 3 quarts
(Yield will vary, depending on the vegetables used, the
size of the pot, and the length of the cooking time)

❧ Schmaltz ❧
(Rendered Chicken Fat)

No book on Jewish food would be complete without schmaltz (rendered chicken fat). This golden fat is the very soul of Jewish cooking—used for frying onions, flavoring chopped liver, or even for smearing on a slice of bread. Rendered chicken fat may seem like an unlikely ingredient to find in a low-fat Jewish cookbook, but there are many recipes that simply won't taste Jewish without it.

Now here's the shocker. Schmaltz is actually better for you than butter. Tablespoon for tablespoon, schmaltz contains one third the amount of cholesterol (11 mg vs. 31 mg) and half the amount of saturated fat (3.8 g vs. 7.1 g) found in butter. A tablespoon of schmaltz actually contains less overall fat than an equal amount of olive oil. (The reason for this is that schmaltz contains water.)

That's not to say schmaltz is a health food—far from it—and you definitely use this golden elixir in moderation. But a spoonful of schmaltz here and there can add that Old World flavor that will make even healthy Jewish cooking taste authentic.

So here are instructions for making this Jewish staple. **Note:** *Whenever I prepare chicken, I save the pale yellow lumps of fat in the cavity and any extra skin, collecting them in a plastic bag in the freezer. When I have 2 cups, I make schmaltz.*

PREPARATION TIME: 5 MINUTES   COOKING TIME: 30 MINUTES

2 cups raw chicken fat and skins, thawed
1 medium onion, finely chopped

Salt

1. Wash the chicken fat and skins and blot dry. Place them in a nonstick frying pan. Cook over medium-low heat until the fat starts to render, 10 to 15 minutes. When there's enough fat on the bottom of the pan, add the onion and cook until the onion is a deep golden brown and all the fat is rendered, 10 to 15 minutes more. Add salt to taste.

2. Strain the schmaltz into a clean jar: you should have about ½ cup. The crisp bits of skin and fat and onions that remain are called gribenes and these are the most delicious food in the world. In my family, we fought over the gribenes, brothers turning against sisters, fathers against sons. We always ate them straight (with a pinch of salt), but you can also add them to chopped liver and egg dishes.

Makes ½ cup; suggested serving, 1 teaspoon

156 CALORIES PER SERVING; .07 G PROTEIN; 17 G FAT; 5 G SATURATED FAT; .6 G CARBOHYDRATE; .2 MG SODIUM; 14 MG CHOLESTEROL

🐾 Mock Schmaltz 🐾

Mock schmaltz started turning up in Jewish kitchens in the 1970s—the result of a dual desire to reduce the cholesterol found in regular schmaltz and to create a flavorful cooking fat you could use in a fleischig meal. By frying onions in a mixture of margarine and canola oil, we create a schmaltzlike fat rich with flavor of browned onions that contains no cholesterol and only 1.5 g saturated fat per tablespoon (compared with 5 g in an equal amount of butter).

PREPARATION TIME: 5 MINUTES   COOKING TIME: 15 MINUTES

½ **cup canola oil**
½ **cup (1 stick) margarine**

1 **medium onion, finely chopped**

1. Heat the oil and margarine in a nonstick skillet over medium heat until the margarine melts. Add the onion. Cook the onion until dark brown, 10 to 15 minutes, stirring as needed to ensure even browning. You'll need to lower the heat to medium-low, then low, to keep the onion from burning.

2. Strain the mock schmaltz into a clean jar and refrigerate until using. (The mixture will keep for several weeks.) Reserve the fried onions: these are the vegetarian equivalent of gribenes (cracklings) and they're great sprinkled over potatoes and kugels, not to mention nibbled in small quantities as a snack!

Makes 1 cup

114 CALORIES PER TABLESPOON; .15 G PROTEIN; 12 G FAT; 1.5 G SATURATED FAT; .8 G CARBOHYDRATE; .4 MG SODIUM; 0 MG CHOLESTEROL

⚶ How to Hard-Boil an Egg ⚶

The simple hard-cooked egg is a cornerstone of Jewish cooking. Roasted eggs appear on the Passover platter, a symbol of springtime. Hard-cooked eggs enter all manner of appetizers, from the chopped liver on page 15 to the chopped eggs and onions on page 58. At first glance, it might seem as if there's nothing easier than making a hard-boiled egg, but all too often you find an ugly, sulfurous green ring around the yolk. Likewise, unless properly prepared, a hard-boiled egg can be hard to peel. Follow the simple instructions below and you'll have perfect hard-boiled eggs every time. **Note:** *In order to slash the fat and cholesterol, most of the recipes in this book call for only the white part of a hard-cooked egg.*

PREPARATION TIME: 5 MINUTES   COOKING TIME: 11 MINUTES

Fresh eggs

1. Make a tiny hole in the narrow end of the egg with a push pin. Place the eggs in a pot with cold water to cover. Gradually bring to a boil. Reduce the heat slightly and simmer the eggs for exactly 11 minutes.

2. Transfer the eggs to a colander and rinse with cold water. When cool enough to handle, shell the eggs. The prompt cooling and shelling creates an air pocket under the shell, which makes it easier to peel the egg. Cut each egg in half lengthwise and remove and discard the yolk (if desired).

77 CALORIES PER WHOLE EGG; 6.2 G PROTEIN; 5.3 G FAT; 1.6 G SATURATED FAT; .5 G CARBOHYDRATE; 62 MG SODIUM; 212 MG CHOLESTEROL

17 CALORIES PER EGG (WHITE PART ONLY); 3.5 G PROTEIN; 0 G FAT; 0 G SATURATED FAT; .34 G CARBOHYDRATE; 55 MG SODIUM; 0 MG CHOLESTEROL

Index